FREE MARKET
ENVIRONMENTALISM

FREE MARKET ENVIRONMENTALISM

Terry L. Anderson
and Donald R. Leal

Pacific Research Institute for Public Policy / San Francisco
Westview Press / Boulder • San Francisco • Oxford

Funds for the research and writing of this book have been provided by the Earhart Foundation, the Political Economy Research Center (PERC), and the Pacific Research Institute for Public Policy.

Copyright © 1991 by Pacific Research Institute for Public Policy

Published in 1991 in the United States of America by Westview Press, Inc., 5500 Central Avenue, Boulder, Colorado 80301, and in the United Kingdom by Westview Press, 36 Lonsdale Road, Summertown, Oxford OX2 7EW

Library of Congress Cataloging-in-Publication Data
Anderson, Terry Lee, 1946–
    Free market environmentalism / Terry L. Anderson and Donald R. Leal.
        p. cm.
    Includes bibliographical references and index.
    ISBN 0-8133-1101-2.   ISBN 0-936488-33-6 (pbk.).
    1. Environmental policy—United States.   2. Free enterprise—United States.   3. Natural resources—United States—Management.
I. Leal, Donald.   II. Title.
HC110.E5A6665   1991
333.7′0973–dc20   90-48035
                                                                    CIP

Printed and bound in the United States of America

The paper used in this publication meets the requirements of the American National Standard for Permanence of Paper for Printed Library Materials Z39.48-1984.

10   9   8   7   6   5   4

CONTENTS

v

TABLES AND FIGURES

ACKNOWLEDGMENTS

When the Political Economy Research Center (PERC) was established ten years ago, none of us could have foreseen the extent to which free market environmentalism would become commonplace in policy debates. Originally, these ideas were on the fringes of the debate, but today the role of markets in the environment is increasingly accepted as the solution rather than the problem. This acceptance is greatest in the areas where research at PERC has developed the theory and examples of free market environmentalism.

Throughout the writing of this book, several people have been patient enough to provide very useful comments. We are especially indebted to our colleagues, Michael D. Copeland, Jane S. Shaw, and Richard L. Stroup, for their comments and suggestions. The chapters on water and recreation were originally reviewed by people at the Cato Institute and the Reason Foundation and have been revised from papers those two groups supported. Michael Greve was the first person to provide systematic comments on the entire manuscript. He forced us to tighten our arguments and improve our style. Rodney Hide of Lincoln University, New Zealand, provided inspiration and insight while Terry Anderson was a Fulbright Fellow there. In the later stages of production, Brent Haglund, Del Gardner, and Chip Mellor were of considerable help. All will find the manuscript much easier to read and much clearer because of the editorial assistance from Marianne Keddington.

Several people at PERC and the Pacific Research Institute (PRI) deserve credit for bringing this project to fruition. Monica Lane Guenther at PERC did her usual good job of coordinating budgets and conferences relating to the project and providing editorial comments. Dianna Rienhart and Judy Fisher, also at PERC, were responsible for the typing and initial editing. Without these individuals, free market environmentalism as a concept or a book would not have been possible. Linda C. Rosen at PRI coordinated production, putting up with our tardiness. Finally, Chip Mellor, president of the Pacific Research Institute, deserves credit for more than his initiative and support for the project. He has continually provided encouragement and given critiques that have improved our understanding of the "tougher problems" presented in Chapter 11.

Projects like this always require financial support from people and institutions who are willing to take a risk. In addition to funding from PERC and PRI, The Earhart Foundation, The Sarah Scaife Foundation, The Liberty Fund, and The M. J. Murdock Charitable Trust supported the project at various stages of production.

Free market environmentalism is in its infancy compared to centralized approaches to environmental problems. Therefore, we hope this book stimulates environmental entrepreneurs to discover more innovative ways of promoting environmental quality while enhancing economic productivity. With such entrepreneurship, future generations will be left with an improved stock of physical, human, and environmental capital.

Terry L. Anderson and Donald R. Leal
Political Economy Research Center

1

VISIONS OF THE ENVIRONMENT

Many people see free markets and the environment as incompatible; for them, the very notion of free market environmentalism is an oxymoron. Even many "free marketeers" find themselves on opposite sides of the fence when it comes to governmental regulation of the environment. Some will hold fast to the conviction that markets work best to allocate most of the goods and services we enjoy, but they will also argue that the environment is different and is too precious to be allocated on the basis of profits.

The view that markets and the environment do not mix is buttressed by the perception that resource exploitation and environmental degradation are inextricably linked to economic growth. This view, which first emerged with industrialization, builds on fears that we are running out of resources because economic growth based on materialistic values is tempting us to squander our natural endowment. During the Industrial Revolution in England, the Reverend Thomas Malthus articulated this view by hypothesizing that exponential population growth would eventually result in famine and pestilence; productivity simply would not be able to keep up with population. The human propensity to reproduce, according to Malthus, would eventually surpass our ability to feed ourselves.

Modern-day Malthusians have given such dire predictions an aura of credibility by using complex computer models to predict precisely

1

when Malthusian calamities will occur. In early 1974, a group of scientists from the Massachusetts Institute of Technology predicted:

> If the present growth trends in world population, industrialization, pollution, food production, and resource depletion continue unchanged, the limits to growth on this planet will be reached sometime within the next one hundred years. The most probable result will be a rather sudden and uncontrollable decline in both population and industrial capacity.[1]

In a graph generated by its computer model, the scientific team showed that the "uncontrollable decline" would begin shortly after the turn of the century—in 2005, to be exact—with a precipitous decline in industrial output, food supplies, and population.[2]

The Global 2000 Report commissioned by President Jimmy Carter arrived at similar conclusions in its prediction of what the state of the world's population and natural resources would be at the turn of the next century. "If present trends continue," the report claimed, "the world in 2000 will be more crowded, more polluted, less stable ecologically, and more vulnerable to disruption than the world we live in now. Serious stresses involving population, resources, and environment are clearly visible ahead." In every resource category, Global 2000 predicted overuse and declines in quantity and quality.

But there is no indication that these predictions will come to pass, and many of them have already been proven wrong.[3] The problem rests in the acceptance of Malthus's initial premise that demands on resources will be exponential while the supply is finite. All of these forecasts fail to take account of the ability of humans to react to problems of scarcity by reducing consumption, finding substitutes, and improving productivity. As economist Julian Simon observed, the "ultimate resource" is the human mind, which has allowed us to avoid Malthusian cycles.[4]

Neo-Malthusians might agree with Simon about the value of the human mind, but they generally see political controls of resource use as the only way to implement this human ingenuity. If markets that promote resource consumption are the cause of the problem, then government must be the solution. When nineteenth-century timber harvests denuded portions of the upper Midwest, there was a call to nationalize the forests to ensure against predicted timber famines. Although there has been no timber famine and private forests continue to be more productive than public forests, the political response has endured. From land to water to air, governmental control—which means political control—is seen as a necessary check on the environmental ravages of free markets.

This book will challenge this common perception and offer an alternative way of thinking about environmental issues, markets, and political choice. This way of thinking does not always provide solutions; instead, it concentrates on how alternative processes link information about the environment with individual incentives to interact with it. Here, the environment and the market are inextricably connected in a positive rather than a negative way.

At the heart of free market environmentalism is a system of well-specified property rights to natural resources. Whether these rights are held by individuals, corporations, non-profit environmental groups, or communal groups, a discipline is imposed on resource users because the wealth of the owner of the property right is at stake if bad decisions are made. Of course, the further a decision maker is removed from this discipline—as he is when there is political control—the less likely it is that good resource stewardship will result. Moreover, if well-specified property rights are transferable, owners must not only consider their own values, they must also consider what others are willing to pay.

The Nature Conservancy's private land management program offers an excellent example of how free market environmentalism works.[5] When the Conservancy obtains title to a parcel of land, the group's wealth, defined in terms of preserving habitat for a rare or endangered species, depends on good stewardship. When The Wisconsin Nature Conservancy was given title to forty acres of beachfront property on St. Croix, Virgin Islands, some may have thought that the group would protect that pristine beach at all costs. But the Conservancy traded the property (with covenants) for a larger parcel of rocky hillside in northern Wisconsin. The trade allowed the Conservancy to protect an entire watershed containing many endangered plant species. To be sure, trade-offs were made, but through the exchange of well-defined and enforced property rights—that is, markets—The Nature Conservancy's wealth in the form of environmental amenities was enhanced.

Free market environmentalism emphasizes an important role for government in the enforcement of property rights. With clearly specified titles—obtained from land recording systems, strict liability rules, and adjudication of disputed property rights in courts—market processes can encourage good resource stewardship. It is when rights are unclear and not well enforced that over-exploitation occurs.

This way of thinking will be alien to some and acceptable to others largely because of the different "visions" each person brings to the issue. In *A Conflict of Visions*, Thomas Sowell described a vision as

> what we sense or feel *before* we have constructed any systematic reasoning that could be called a theory, much less deduced any specific consequences as hypotheses to be tested against evidence. . . . Visions are the foundations on which theories are built.[6]

The theory of free market environmentalism is founded on certain visions regarding human nature, knowledge, and processes. A consideration of these visions helps explain why some people accept this way of thinking as the only alternative to bureaucratic control and why others reject it as a contradiction in terms.

Human nature. Free market environmentalism views man as self-interested. This self-interest may be enlightened to the extent that people are capable of setting aside their own well-being for close relatives and friends or that they may be conditioned by moral principles. But beyond this, good intentions will not suffice to produce good results. Developing an environmental ethic may be desirable, but it is unlikely to change basic human nature. Instead of intentions, good resource stewardship depends on how well social institutions harness self-interest through individual incentives.

Knowledge. In addition to incentives, good resource stewardship depends on the information available to self-interested individuals. Free market environmentalism views this information or knowledge as diffuse rather than concentrated. Because ecosystems depend on the interaction of many different natural forces, they cannot be "managed" from afar. The information necessary for good management varies significantly from time to time and from place to place, and resource management requires knowledge that can only be obtained "on the ground." Therefore, knowledge cannot be gathered into a single mind or group of minds that can then capably manage all of society's natural resources.

The difference between perceptions of knowledge under centralized, political resource management and free market environmentalism centers on the distribution of knowledge among individuals. In visions of centralized, political control, the distribution has a low mean with a high variance. That is, the common man is not perceived as knowing much about the environment, and what he does know (including knowledge of his own values) is incorrect; the high variance means that experts can manage for the good of the masses. Free market environmentalism sees a much smaller knowledge gap between the experts and the average individual. In this view, individual property owners, who are in a position and have an incentive to obtain time- and place-specific information about their resource endowments, are better suited than centralized bureaucracies to manage resources.

Processes or solutions. These visions of human nature and knowledge combine to make free market environmentalism a study of process rather than a prescription for solutions. If man can rise above self-interest and if knowledge can be concentrated, then the possibility for solutions through political control is more likely. But if there are self-interested individuals with diffuse knowledge, then processes must generate a multitude of solutions conditioned by the checks and balances implicit in the process. By linking wealth to good stewardship through private ownership, the market process generates many individual experiments; and those that are successful will be copied. The question is not whether the right solution has been achieved but whether the relevant trade-offs are being considered in the process.

These three elements of free market environmentalism also characterize the interaction of organisms in ecosystems. Since Charles Darwin's revolutionary study of evolution, most scientific approaches have implicitly assumed that self-interest dominates behavior for higher as well as lower forms of life. Individual members of a species may act in "altruistic" ways and may cooperate with other species, but species survival depends on adjustments to changing parameters in ways that enhance the probability of survival. To assume that man is not self-interested or that he can rise above self-interest because he is part of a political process requires heroic assumptions about homo sapiens vis-à-vis other species.

Ecology also emphasizes the importance of time- and place-specific information in nature. Because the parameters to which species respond vary considerably within ecosystems, each member of a species must respond to time- and place-specific characteristics with the knowledge that each possesses. These parameters can vary widely, so it is imperative for survival that responses utilize the diffuse knowledge. Of course, the higher the level of communication among members of a species, the easier it is to accumulate and concentrate time- and place-specific knowledge. Again, however, it requires a giant leap of faith to assume that man's ability to accumulate and assimilate knowledge is so refined that he can centrally manage the economy or the environment for himself and for all other species. Recent evidence from Eastern Europe underscores the environmental problems that can arise with centralized management.

Ecology is also the study of processes and interaction among species; it is not a scientific prescription for solutions to environmental changes.

Like free market environmentalism, ecology focuses on the information and incentives that reach the members of a species. When a niche in an ecosystem is left open, a species can "profit" from filling that niche and other species can benefit as well. If an elk herd grows, there is additional food for bears and wolves and the number of predators will expand as they take advantage of this "profit" opportunity. Individual elk will suffer at the expense of predators, but elk numbers will be controlled. In the process, plant species will survive and other vertebrates will retain their place in the ecosystem. No central planner knows the best solution for filling niches; it is the individualistic process that rewards the efficient use of time- and place-specific information.

Comparing free market environmentalism with ecosystems serves to emphasize how market processes can be compatible with good resource stewardship and environmental quality. As survival rewards species that successfully fill a niche, increased wealth rewards owners who efficiently manage their resources. Profits link self-interest with good resource management by attracting entrepreneurs to open niches. If bad decisions are being made, then a niche will be open. Whether an entrepreneur sees the opportunity and acts on it will depend on his ability to assess time- and place-specific information and act on his assessment. As with an ecosystem, however, the diffuse nature of this information makes it impossible for a central planner to determine which niches are open and how they should be filled. If the link between self-interest and good resource stewardship is broken because good stewards cannot reap the benefits, do not bear the costs of their decisions, or receive distorted information through political intervention, then the efficacy of free market environmentalism will be impaired in the same way that the efficacy of an ecosystem would be impaired by centralized planning.

Visions of what makes good environmental policy are not easily changed; if they are to change, it will be because we recognize that our visions are not consistent with reality. We must ask ourselves whether well-intentioned individuals armed with sufficient information dominate the political decisions that affect natural resources and the environment. Environmentalist Randal O'Toole answered this question in the context of the U.S. Forest Service:

> While the environmental movement has changed more than the Forest Service, I would modestly guess that I have changed more than most environmental leaders. . . . In 1980, I blamed all the deficiencies in the markets on greed and big business and thought that government should correct these deficiencies with new laws, regulatory agencies, rational plan-

ning, and trade and production restrictions. When that didn't work, I continued to blame the failure on greed and big business.

About 1980, someone suggested to me that maybe government didn't solve environmental or other social problems any better than markets. That idea seemed absurd. After all, this is a democracy, a government of the people, and what the people want they should be able to get. Any suggestion that government doesn't work was incomprehensible.

But then I was immersed in the planning processes of one government agency for ten years (sort of like taking a Berlitz course in bureau-speaking). I learned that the decisions made by government officials often ignored the economic and other analyses done by planners. So much for rational planning. Their decisions also often went counter to important laws and regulations. So much for a democratic government.

Yet I came to realize that the decisions were all predictable, based mainly on their effects on forest budgets. . . .

I gradually developed a new view of the world that recognized the flaws of government as well as the flaws in markets. Reforms should solve problems by creating a system of checks and balances on both processes. . . . The key is to give decision makers the incentives to manage resources properly.[7]

This book provides a "Berlitz course in free market environmentalism." It also challenges entrenched visions. The development of free market environmentalism has progressed from an examination of the relatively easy problems of land and energy development to the tougher problems of water quality and quantity. The evolution of land and water rights on America's frontier illustrates how the creation of property rights responds to scarcity. Massive reservations of land as public domain halted this privatization movement and often subsidized environmental destruction. There is good evidence that political land management has ignored important recreational and amenity values and that there is a potential for providing them through markets in ways that promote harmony between development and ecology. Free market environmentalism has caught on in the area of water policy, and it holds the promise of a more efficient and environmentally acceptable allocation of that scarce resource. If land use constitutes an "easy" problem for free market environmentalism, pollution problems challenge the paradigm. But there is a clear advantage to using the paradigm of free market environmentalism to examine air pollution problems ranging from acid rain to global warming.

By confronting our entrenched visions, we can move beyond the status quo of political control of the environment and unleash environmental entrepreneurs on the tougher problems we face. The popularity of Earth Day 1990 illustrated the heightened environmental consciousness of people around the world. Most of the proposed solutions to perceived environmental problems, however, call for centralized approaches that are not consistent with the science of ecology. Moreover, these solutions pit winners against losers in a zero-sum game that tears at the social fabric. Free market environmentalism depends on a voluntary exchange of property rights between consenting owners and promotes cooperation and compromise. In short, it offers an alternative that channels the heightened environmental consciousness into win-win solutions that can sustain economic growth, enhance environmental quality, and promote harmony.

NOTES

1. Donnella H. Meadows, Dennis L. Meadows, Jorgen Randers, William W. Behrens III, *The Limits to Growth: A Report for the Club of Rome's Project on the Predicament of Mankind.* (New York: A Potomac Associates Book, New American Library, 1974), ix–x.

2. For a discussion of additional apocalyptic predictions, see Edith Efron, *The Apocalyptics* (New York: Simon and Schuster, 1984), chap. 1.

3. *Global 2000 Report to the President* (Washington, D.C.: Government Printing Office, 1980), 1. For a critique of the *Global 2000* findings and for data refuting the predictions, see Julian Simon and Herman Kahn, *The Resourceful Earth: A Response to Global 2000* (Oxford, England: Basil Blackwell, 1984).

4. Julian Simon, *The Ultimate Resource* (Princeton, N.J.: Princeton University Press, 1981).

5. The Nature Conservancy controls thousands of acres of private land that fit the free market environmentalism model. But the Conservancy also turns many of its lands over to public agencies, thereby perpetuating political control of resources.

6. Thomas Sowell, *A Conflict of Visions* (New York: William Morrow and Company, 1987), 14.

7. Randal O'Toole, "Learning the Lessons of the 1980s," *Forest Watch* 10 (January–February 1990): 6.

2

RETHINKING THE WAY
WE THINK

Most natural resource and environmental policy has been premised on the assumption that markets are responsible for resource misallocation and environmental degradation and that centralized, political processes can correct these problems. In general, the failure of markets is attributed to private decision makers who do not take into account all costs and benefits, to the unequal availability of information to all buyers and sellers, or to monopolies distorting prices and outputs.[1] In essence, market failure is blamed on the lack of information, inappropriate incentives, or both. To counter market failures, centralized planning is seen as a way of aggregating information about social costs and social benefits in order to maximize the value of natural resources. Decisions based on this aggregated information are to be made by disinterested resource managers whose goal is to maximize social welfare.

Economic analysis in general and natural resource economics in particular have approached resource policy as if there is a "socially efficient" allocation of resources that will be reached when scientific managers understand the relevant trade-offs and act to achieve the efficient solution. For example, forest resources are supposed to be managed to achieve the "greatest good for the greatest number" through "multiple use management" undertaken by an "elite corps of professionals." When problems with management are recognized, they are attributed to "bad people in government" and the solution is to replace them with better trained, better financed managers.

But there is a more realistic way of thinking about natural resource and environmental policy. This alternative recognizes and emphasizes the costs of coordinating human actions. There is no assumption that costs of engaging in a transaction are zero or that there is perfect competition. To the contrary, understanding alternative policies requires that we specify coordination costs and discover why and where competitive forces may not be working.[2]

This analytical framework applies equally to markets and politics. If all people lived alone on remote islands, there would be no costs of coordination; but in a complex society where people gain from trade, interacting individuals must measure and monitor the actions of one another. In the marketplace, consumers must signal to suppliers what quantity and quality of products they demand at what prices; suppliers must determine which products to produce and which input combinations to use. Both demanders and suppliers must monitor one another to ensure that products are delivered and paid for. To the extent that actions can be effectively measured and monitored, demanders and suppliers will internalize costs and benefits, profits will be made, and efficient resource allocation will be a by-product.

Similarly, citizens who demand goods and services from government must monitor the politicians and bureaucrats who supply them. Like a consumer displeased with food purchased from the supermarket, a citizen who is unhappy with the actions of his political representative has experienced the cost of measuring and monitoring supplier performance. Outcomes do not always reflect citizens' desires; the political process may supply too many of goods like nuclear arms or too little of goods like quality education. As with market analysis, policy analysis must focus on how well the political process internalizes costs and benefits to citizens and their political agents so that resources will not be squandered.

In rethinking natural resource and environmental policy, two facts must be recognized. First, *incentives matter to all human behavior.* No matter how well intended professional resources managers are, incentives affect their behavior. Like it or not, individuals will undertake more of an activity if the costs of that activity are reduced; this holds as much for bureaucrats as it does for profit-maximizing owners of firms. Everyone accepts that managers in the private sector would dump production wastes into a nearby stream if they did not have to pay for the cost of their action. Too often, however, we fail to recognize the same elements at work in the political arena. If a politician is not personally accountable for allowing oil development on federal lands or for permitting an agency to dump hazardous wastes into the environment, then we can expect too much development or too much dumping. Moreover, when the beneficiaries of these policies do not have to pay the full cost, they will demand more of each from political representatives.

Second, *information costs are positive in both the private and political sectors.* In a world of scarcity, both private and political resource managers must obtain information about the relative values of alternative uses. When one resource use rivals another, trade-offs must be made. Resource managers can only make these trade-offs based on the information coming to them or on their own values. If they believe lumber is more valuable than wildlife habitat, trees will be cut. Timber managers may know how fast trees grow under certain conditions, but they cannot know what the value of the growth is without incurring some cost in obtaining that information. The lumber market provides information on timber value as a commodity, but information about the value of wildlife habitat and environmental amenities is more costly because those markets are less developed. Private timber managers for International Paper, for example, are being forced to consider wildlife habitat in their timber production decisions because prices tell them that consumers are willing to pay increasingly more for hunting, camping, and recreation. Political managers who "give away" recreational services from political lands lack this price information and have less incentive to react to changing values.

When incentives matter and information is costly, resource management is complicated so that it is not sufficient to rely on good intentions. Even if the superintendent of national parks believes that grizzly bear habitat is more valuable than more campsites, his good intentions will not necessarily yield more grizzly bear habitat. In a political setting where camping interests have more influence over a bureaucrat's budget, his peace and quiet, or his future promotion, intentions will have to override incentives if grizzly bear habitat is to prevail. But if a private resource owner believes that grizzly bear habitat is more valuable and can capitalize on that value, then politics will not matter. Moreover, if those who demand grizzly habitat are willing to pay more than those who demand campsites, then incentives and information reinforce one another. Management simply cannot be adequately analyzed without careful attention to the information and incentives that actors face under alternative institutional arrangements.

SCIENTIFIC MANAGEMENT
OR ECONOMICS WITHOUT PRICES

For years economists have tried to use computer modeling techniques to simulate the market allocation of natural resources. The U.S. Forest Service, for example, developed FORPLAN, a forest simulation model, to specify the necessary conditions for efficient national forest use. The rationale of such models is simply that if the additional or marginal value of one resource use is greater than another, then allocation will be improved if the resource is reallocated from the latter to the former. This form of analysis teaches us that there are many margins for adjustment and that few decisions have all-or-nothing consequences. When water is allocated for fish or irrigation, trade-offs must be made; it is not an either-or decision. Put simply, neither demand nor supply is unresponsive to price changes. If prices rise, then demanders will make marginal adjustments by shifting consumption to the nearest substitutes; suppliers will adjust by substituting among resources and technologies.

The logic of this analysis combined with models and computers that can simulate resource use can lure policy analysts into believing that the maximization of resource value is a simple matter. Unfortunately, in this case logic and simplicity are not good guides because they mask the information costs and incentives. Consider the case of multiple use management of the national forests, where the scientific manager is supposed to trade off timber production, wildlife habitat, aesthetic values, water quality, recreation, and other uses to maximize the value of the forest. Because the managers are not supposed to be motivated by profit or self-interest, it is assumed that they will impartially apply economic theory and quantitative methods to accomplish efficient resource allocation. The scientific manager, armed with the economic concepts of marginal analysis, is supposed to be "always analytical. . . . Always, the economist's reasoning, his analytical framework . . . , and his conclusions are exposed forthrightly to the examination and criticism of others. In these ways, *scientific objectivity* is actively sought."[3]

To apply marginal analysis to multiple use, decision makers must attach values to the relevant margins. Scientific management assumes that these values are known and, therefore, that there is an efficient solution. The decision maker must only acquire the "correct" information about resource values in alternative uses and reallocate those resources until marginal equalities hold. Management is simply the process of finding the socially optimal allocation. Thomas Sowell has captured the traditional resource economics perspective on information:

Given that explicitly articulated knowledge is special and concentrated . . . the best conduct of social activities depends upon the special knowledge of the few being used to guide the actions of the many. . . . Along with this has often gone a vision of intellectuals as disinterested advisors. . . .[4]

If knowledge of values that must be traded off against one another were "special and concentrated," then scientific management might be possible. But as F. A. Hayek has pointed out,

the economic problem of society is . . . not merely a problem of how to allocate "given resources"—if "given" is taken to mean given to a single mind which deliberately solves the problem set by these "data." It is rather a problem of how to secure the best use of resources known to any of the members of society, for ends whose relative importance only these individuals know. Or, to put it briefly, it is a problem of utilization of knowledge not given to anyone in its totality.[5]

The very information and knowledge necessary for trade-offs made using scientific management are subjective and are only revealed through human action.

As analytical tools, economic models focus on the importance of marginal adjustments, but they cannot instruct managers in which trade-offs to make or which values to place on a resource. In the absence of subjective individual evaluations, the marginal solutions derived by sophisticated efficiency maximization models are unachievable ideals. Unfortunately, these models have been used as guides to tell resource managers how to achieve efficient allocation; in fact, they can only provide a way of thinking about trade-offs. Managers argue that these models have added sophistication and authority to political management efforts, allowing shadow prices (that is, prices that are not real but images of what would exist if there was a market) to be derived and used in lieu of actual market processes. The Forest Service and the Bureau of Land Management, enamored with these models, assume that with sufficient data and large enough computers it is possible to produce wise and efficient management plans. Forest economist Richard Behan stated that the planning acts that guide the Forest Service mandate "with the force of law that forest plans can be rational, comprehensive, and essentially perfect."[6] But no matter how rational or comprehensive they may be, models built on marginal analysis will always be constrained by information requirements.

The market process generates information on the subjective values that humans place on alternative resource use as individuals engage in voluntary trades. The decentralized decisions made in markets are crucial, because "practically every individual has some advantage over all others in that he possesses unique information of which beneficial use might be made, but of which use can be made only if the decisions depending on it are left to him or are made with his active cooperation." Once we understand that most knowledge is fragmented and dispersed, then "systemic coordination among the many supersedes the special wisdom of the few." Traditional economic analysis has failed to recognize this fundamental point. The information necessary for "efficient" resource allocation depends on the knowledge of the special circumstance of time and place.[7]

The idea of scientific management has also misguided public policy because it ignores the incentives of decision makers in the political sector. The economic analysis of markets focuses on incentives in the form of prices that determine the benefits and costs that decision makers face. Market failure is said to result when any benefits are not captured or costs are not borne by decision makers. The existence of these externalities or third-party effects means that either too little of a good is produced in the case of uncaptured benefits or too much in the case of unborne costs. A system of private water allocation, for example, may not provide a sufficient supply of instream flows for wildlife habitat and environmental quality because owners of water cannot easily charge recreationalists and environmentalists who benefit from free-flowing water. And too much pollution exists because firms do not have to pay the full cost of waste disposal, so they "overuse" the air or water as a garbage dump. Such under- or over-production is often taken as a sufficient condition for taking political control of resource allocation.

There is, however, an asymmetry in the analysis of market and political processes because of a failure to recognize that the *political sector operates by externalizing costs.* Consider the reasoning that political agents apply to scientific management. When land is diverted from timber production to wilderness, there is an opportunity cost associated with the reallocation. Private landowners interested in maximizing the value of the resource must take this cost into account in the "price" of wilderness. The bureaucratic manager or politician who does not own the land, however, does not face all the opportunity costs of his decisions. He will take the values forgone into account only if the political process makes him do so. If we assume that the political process worked perfectly (which is the equivalent of *assuming* that markets work perfectly), then the countervailing powers of the opposing sides would internalize the benefits and costs for the decision maker.

But there is little reason to believe that the political process works perfectly or even tolerably well. Because politicians and bureaucrats are rewarded for responding to political pressure groups, there is no guarantee that the values of unorganized interests will be taken into account *even if* they constitute a majority of the population. For example, most Americans will pay marginally higher prices for petroleum products if oil production is not allowed in the Arctic National Wildlife Refuge. Because this cost to each individual is low and the costs of information and action are high relative to the benefits, each person will remain rationally ignorant; that is, he will not become informed on the issue. But organized groups that favor preserving wildlife habitat in the pristine tundra can gain by stopping drilling in the refuge. To the extent that those who benefit from wildlife preservation do not have to pay the opportunity costs of forgone energy production, they will demand "too much" wildlife habitat. In the absence of a perfect political process, we must depend on good intentions to overpower the special interest incentives built into the imperfect system. This takes a giant leap of faith.

Traditional thinking about natural resource and environmental policy ignores the most basic economic tenet: *incentives matter*. Markets with positive costs of eliminating third-party effects have been compared with a political process where those costs are ignored or assumed to be zero. Consider the approach taken in a leading natural resource economic textbook:

> . . . "the government" is a separate agent acting in the social interest when activity by individuals fails to bring about the social optimum. . . . we discuss some limits of this approach, but it permits us to abstract from the details of the political process.[8]

When we abstract from the details of the political process, we ignore incentives inherent in that process. Daniel Bromley claimed that government agencies are

> politically responsible to the citizenry through the system of . . . elections and ministerial direction. However imperfect this may work, the *presumption* must be that the wishes of the full citizenry are more properly catered to than would be the case if all environmental protection were left to the ability to pay by a few members of society given to philanthropy.[9]

But why must we "presume" that the "wishes of the full citizenry are more properly catered to"? And what does "full citizenry" mean? Is there unanimous consent? Does a majority constitute the "full citizenry" when voting turnout is traditionally low? Bromley also charged that "claims for volitional exchange are supported by appeal to a body of economic theory that is not made explicit," but there is little made explicit when we "abstract from the details of the political process" by presuming "that the wishes of the full citizenry are more properly catered to" in the political process.[10]

Because traditional thinking about resource and environmental policy pays little attention to the institutions that structure and provide information and incentives in the political sector, practitioners often seem surprised and puzzled that efficiency implications from their models are ignored in the policy arena. In the private sector, efficiency matters because it influences profits; in the political sector, prices and incentives are often very different. Political resource managers make trade-offs in terms of political currencies measured in terms of special interest support; at best, this unit of account provides imprecise measures of the subjective values of citizens.

The incentive structure in the political sector is complicated because the bottom line depends on the electoral process where votes matter, not efficiency. Because voters are rationally ignorant, because benefits can be concentrated and costs diffused, and because individual voters seldom (and probably never) influence the outcome of elections, there is little reason to expect that elections will link political decisions to efficiency in the same way that private ownership does in the market process.[11]

Under private ownership, profits and losses are the measure of how well decision makers are managing. Even where shareholders in a large company have little effect on actual decisions, they can observe stock prices and annual reports as a measure of management's performance. In other words, private ownership gives owners both the information and the incentive to measure performance. In the political sector, however, both information and incentives are lacking. Annual budget figures offer information about overall expenditures and outlays, but it is not clear who is responsible and whether larger budgets are good or bad. Even when responsibility can be determined, there is no easy way for a citizen to "buy and sell shares" in the government. Therefore, citizens remain rationally ignorant about most aspects of political resource allocation and rationally informed about issues that directly affect them. The rewards for political resource managers depend not on maximizing net resource values but on providing politically active constituents with what they want with little regard for cost. Although it may not be possible to state precisely what is maximized by politicians and bureaucrats, it is clear that efficiency is not the main goal. If political resource managers were to follow the tenets of traditional natural resource economics, it would have to be because there were honest, sincere people (professional managers) pursuing the public interest.

Anthony Fisher has provided perhaps the best summary of the problem:

> We have already abandoned the assumption of a complete set of competitive markets. . . . But if we now similarly abandon the notion of a perfect planner, it is not clear, in my judgment, that the government will do any better. Apart from the question of the planner's motivation to behave in the way assumed in our models, to allocate resources efficiently, there is the question of his ability to do so.[12]

Without information and incentives, scientific management becomes economics without prices.

GETTING THE INCENTIVES RIGHT

The constraint on the gains from trade in market processes is that each party to a transaction must measure and monitor the activities of the other. If individuals were self-sufficient, these costs disappear, but they would also forgo the gains from specialization and trade. Hence, the problem we all face is to trade off the gains from specialization against the costs of measuring and monitoring the performance of those with whom we interact.

This framework is useful for examining relationships in the political sector where citizens "hire" politicians or bureaucrats to produce certain goods and services. At a minimum, this relationship grants to the government a monopoly on the use of coercion, which enables it to enforce voluntary contracts between individuals. In addition, citizens may assign to the state the role of producing goods for which coercion is necessary because the costs of measuring and monitoring voluntary transactions are prohibitive. For example, if the costs of excluding fishermen from a free-flowing stream are high, then there will be little incentive for the private sector to provide this amenity; market failure is said to result in the underproduction of these "public goods." By using the coercive power of government to charge all citizens (or at least all fishermen), this problem can be overcome. Unfortunately, this solution raises another problem: How can the citizens be certain that the state is producing the desired bundle of public goods? Indeed, the fundamental dilemma of political economy is: Once the state has the coercive power to do what voluntary (market) action cannot do, how can that power be constrained from being usurped by special interests?

At least two variables are important in determining the resolution of this dilemma. First, the complexity of the good in question will have a direct bearing on the ability of a consumer or citizen to measure the performance of suppliers. If lands managed by the political sector produce timber, measuring the board feet of production may be simple; but if those same lands are for "multiple use," then it is much more costly to determine how closely actual results approximate the results desired. Goods such as environmental quality, risk management, soil conservation, national heritage, and wilderness values are all costly to measure.

The second determinant will be the costs of monitoring political agents who provide public goods, and these costs will be directly related to the proximity, both in time and space, of the agent to the citizen. Monitoring the behavior of a local zoning board is less costly than monitoring the behavior of the director of the National Park Service. Furthermore, before we had telephones and computers, monitoring agent behavior was more costly because of the time required for communication. A free press and free access to governmental information reduced these costs. At the same time, however, the multitude of decisions made at various levels of government and the large number of constituents represented by each political agent raised the cost of monitoring.

Because the same kinds of costs exist with market transactions, we must complete the analysis by comparing the measurement and monitoring costs of the political sector with those of the private sector. For all market transactions, both buyers and sellers must incur measurement and monitoring costs. The buyer must consider a product's value in quantity and quality terms and weigh that value against alternative goods. The seller must monitor production and discover mechanisms for making sure buyers cannot enjoy the benefits of the good without paying. For example, a hunter purchasing hunting rights must consider the value of the hunting experience relative to other opportunities. The seller must determine whether it is worth enhancing hunting opportunities and whether nonpaying hunters can avoid paying the fee (that is, trespassing) while still reaping the benefits. If the costs for either buyer or seller are sufficiently high, the potential net gains from trade will be reduced and trades may not take place.

There are three important characteristics of private sector transactions, however, that tend to mitigate these costs. First, measurement costs are greatly reduced in market transactions by prices. Prices convey valuable, condensed information that allows consumers to compare and aggregate inputs and outputs. In the absence of price information that transforms subjective values into an objective measure, comparing values of alternative resource uses is difficult. Because many governmental goods and services are not priced, transaction costs are higher in the political sector.

Prices also allow a measure of efficiency through profits and losses. If a shareholder wants to know how well the management of his firm is performing, he can at least consult the profit-and-loss statement. This is not a perfect measure of performance, but continual losses suggest that actual results differ from those that are desired. This can tell the shareholder that he should consider alternative managers who can produce the product at a lower cost or he should reconsider the market for the product. Compared to the political sector where the output of government is not priced and where agency performance is not measured by the bottom line, profits and losses in the private sector provide concise information with which owners can measure the performance of their agents.

Second, the political and private sectors differ in the degree to which measurement and monitoring costs are borne by those who demand the goods. In the political process, voters ultimately decide who the suppliers will be. In order to make good decisions, voters must gather information about alternative candidates or referenda issues and vote on the basis of that information. If an individual invests a great deal of effort into becoming informed and votes on what is best for society, he does a service for his fellow citizens. If the voter is not well informed and votes for things that will harm the society, then this cost is spread among all voters. In other words, well-informed voters produce a classic public good, and, as with any public good, we can expect voters to under-invest in becoming informed, thus remaining "rationally ignorant." In contrast, consumers in the private sector bear the costs of being informed, but they also reap the benefits of good choices and bear the costs of bad ones. When a landowner hires a forest manager, he will seek information on the manager's ability and he will monitor his performance. If the landowner assumes none of the these costs and gets a bad manager, then the owner will bear the costs directly; if he pays the costs and management quality is improved, then the benefits are internalized to the landowner in the form of higher profits. It is the clear assignment of these profits and losses that distinguishes the private from the political sector.

Third, private sector relationships differ from those in the political sector in terms of the cost of choosing alternative suppliers. In the political sector, if a citizen does not believe he is getting from government the goods and services he desires, then he can attempt to sway a majority of the voters and elect new suppliers or he can physically move from one location to another. In either case, the costs of changing suppliers is much higher than in the private sector, where there is greater competition among potential agents. For example, if a local supermarket does not sell what a customer desires, then he has many alternative producers from whom to choose. Even in the more complex case of corporate managers, a stockholder can easily change agents by selling shares in one company and purchasing shares in another. In short, because changing suppliers in the private sector does not require agreement from a majority of the other consumers, change is less costly. This condition imposes a strong competitive discipline. In general, information through prices, internalization of costs and benefits from monitoring by individuals, and agent discipline imposed by competition reduce measurement and monitoring costs.

Where market transactions fail to occur for natural resources and environmental amenities, it is usually because the costs of measuring and monitoring resource use are high. For example, suppose a land-owner is deciding whether to forgo one type of production to enhance an aesthetic quality. If the aesthetic quality is a beautiful flower garden, a high fence may be sufficient to exclude free riders and capture the full benefits from the product. If the trade-off is between cutting trees and preserving a beautiful mountainside, however, excluding casual sightseers may be far too costly.

The key, therefore, to effective markets in general and free market environmentalism in particular is the establishment of well-specified and transferable property rights. When a conservation group purchases a conservation easement on a parcel of land, the exchange requires that property rights be well defined, enforced, and transferable. The physical attributes of the resources must be specified in a clear and concise manner; they must be measurable. For example, the rectangular survey system allows us to define ownership rights over land and clarifies disputes over ownership. The system may also help us define ownership to the airspace over land, but more questions arise here because of the fluidity of air and the infinite vertical third dimension above the ground. If property rights to resources cannot be defined, then they obviously cannot be exchanged for other property rights.

Property rights also must be defendable. A rectangular survey may define surface rights to land, but conflicts are inevitable if there is no way to defend the boundaries and prevent other incompatible uses. Barbed wire provided an inexpensive way to defend property rights on the western frontier; locks and chains do the same for parked bicycles. But enforcing one's rights to peace and quiet by "fencing out" sound waves may be much more difficult, as will keeping other people's hazardous wastes out of a groundwater supply. Whenever the use of property cannot be monitored or enforced, conflicts are inevitable and trades are impossible.

Finally, property rights must be transferable. In contrast to the costs of measuring and monitoring resource uses, which are mainly determined by the physical nature of the property and technology, the ability to exchange is determined largely by the legal environment. Although well-defined and enforced rights allow the owner to enjoy the benefits of using his property, legal restrictions on the sale of that property preclude the potential for gains from trade. Suppose that a group of fishermen values water for fish habitat more highly than farmers value the same water for irrigation. If the fishermen are prohibited from renting or purchasing the water from the farmers, then gains from trade will not be realized and potential wealth will not be created. Moreover, the farmer will have less incentive to leave the water in the stream.

In sum, free market environmentalism presupposes well-specified rights to take actions with respect to specific resources. If those rights cannot be measured, monitored, and marketed, then there is little possibility for exchange. Garbage disposal through the air, for example, is more of a problem than solid waste disposal in the ground because property rights to the Earth's surface are better defined than property rights to the atmosphere. Private ownership of land works quite well for producing timber, but measuring, monitoring, and marketing the land for endangered species habitat requires entrepreneurial imagination.

Imagination is crucial to free market environmentalism, because it is in the areas where property rights are evolving that resource allocation problems occur. Where environmental entrepreneurs can devise ways of marketing environmental values, market incentives can have dramatic results. It is important to recognize that any case of external benefits or costs provides fertile ground for an entrepreneur who can define and enforce property rights. A stream owner who can devise ways of charging fishermen can internalize the benefits and costs and gain an incentive to maintain or improve the quality of his resource. The subdivider who puts covenants on deeds that preserve open space, improve views, and generally harmonize development with the environment establishes property rights to these values and captures the value in higher asset prices.

The property rights approach to natural resources recognizes that property rights evolve depending on the benefits and costs associated with defining and enforcing rights. This calculus will depend on such variables as the expected value of the resource in question, the technology for measuring and monitoring property rights, and the legal and moral rules that condition the behavior of the interacting parties. At any given time, property rights will reflect the perceived benefits and costs of definition and enforcement. To observe actions that are not accounted for in market transactions—that is, for which property rights have not been specified—and call them externalities or market failure ignores the evolutionary nature of property rights.[13] As the perceived costs and benefits of defining and enforcing property rights change, property rights will evolve.

This does not mean that there is no role for government in the definition and enforcement process or that property rights will always take all costs and benefits into account. The costs of establishing property rights are positive and *potentially* can be reduced through governmental institutions, such as courts. Furthermore, because transaction costs are positive, contracts that take costs into account will not always be forthcoming. In the case of water pollution from sources that cannot be identified (with current technology) at low costs, for example, the definition and enforcement of property rights governing water use may be impossible. And excluding non-payers from enjoying a scenic view may be costly enough that a market cannot evolve under current technologies and institutions. In these cases, there is a utilitarian argument for considering government intervention. But there is still no guarantee that the results from political allocation will work very well. If markets produce "too little" clean water because dischargers do not have to pay for its use, then political solutions are equally likely to produce "too much" clean water because those who enjoy the benefits do not pay the cost.

CONCLUSION

Traditional economic analysis stresses the potential for market failure in the natural resource and environmental arena on the grounds that externalities are pervasive. Free market environmentalism explicitly recognizes that this problem arises because it is costly to define and enforce rights in both the private and political sectors. In fact, the symmetry of the externality argument requires that specific attention be paid to politics as the art of diffusing costs and concentrating benefits. Assuming that externality problems in the environment can be solved by turning to the political sector ignores the likelihood that government will externalize costs. Just as pollution externalities can generate too much dirty air, political externalities can generate too much water storage, clear-cutting, wilderness, or water quality.

Free market environmentalism emphasizes the importance of market processes in determining optimal amounts of resource use. Only when rights are well-defined, enforced, and transferable will self-interested individuals confront the trade-offs inherent in a world of scarcity. As entrepreneurs move to fill profit niches, prices will reflect the values we place on resources and the environment. Mistakes will be made, but in the process a niche will be opened and profit opportunities will attract resource managers with a better idea. Remember that even externalities offer profit niches to the environmental entrepreneur who can define and enforce property rights to the unowned resource and charge the free-riding user. In cases where definition and enforcement costs are insurmountable, political solutions may be called for. Unfortunately, however, those kinds of solutions often become entrenched and stand in the way of innovative market processes that promote fiscal responsibility, efficient resource use, and individual freedom.

NOTES

1. For a summary of the standard criticisms of natural resource markets, see Charles Howe, *Natural Resource Economics* (New York: John Wiley and Sons, 1979), 103.

2. This framework for thinking about the environment has been called the New Resource Economics and was first formally discussed in Terry L. Anderson, "New Resource Economics: Old Ideas and New Applications," *American Journal of Agricultural Economics* 64 (December 1982): 928–34.

3. Alan Randall, *Resource Economics* (Columbus, Ohio: Grid Publishing Company, 1981), 36.

4. Thomas Sowell, *A Conflict of Visions* (New York: William Morrow and Company, 1987), 46.

5. F. A. Hayek, "The Use of Knowledge in Society," *The American Economic Review* 35 (September 1945): 519–20.

6. Richard W. Behan, "RPA/NFMA—Time to Punt," *Journal of Forestry* 79 (1981): 802.

7. Hayek, "The Use of Knowledge," 80; Sowell, *A Conflict of Visions*, 48.

8. John M. Hartwick and Nancy D. Olewiler, *The Economics of Natural Resource Use* (New York: Harper and Row, 1986), 18.

9. Daniel W. Bromley, *Property Rights and the Environment: Natural Resource Policy in Transition* (Wellington, New Zealand: Ministry for the Environment, 1987), 55.

10. Ibid., 54.

11. For a more detailed discussion, see James Gwartney and Richard Stroup, *Economics: Private and Public Choice*, 4th ed. (New York: Harcourt Brace & Jovanovich, 1987), 687–99.

12. Anthony C. Fisher, *Resource and Environmental Economics* (Cambridge, England: Cambridge University Press, 1981), 54.

13. See Terry L. Anderson and P. J. Hill, "The Evolution of Property Rights: A Study of the American West," *Journal of Law and Economics* 12 (October 1975): 163–79.

3

FROM FREE GRASS TO FENCES

Roaming across the northern and western borders of Yellowstone National Park into Montana, the bison that summer in the park enter private lands in search of winter grazing.[1] Montana ranchers object to the migration, because many of the bison carry the brucellosis virus, a disease that can infect cows and cause them to abort their calves. These stockgrowers certify to buyers that their cattle herds are free from brucellosis, which allows them to ship their animals all over the world. If the cattle were to be infected with the virus, then the demand for them would decline and ranchers would suffer a loss.

The migration of the Yellowstone bison is a classic case of an externality that can result from ill-defined property rights, and the consequences of that externality dramatize the importance of opening the door for innovative solutions. Yellowstone Park officials do not own the wildlife in the park and cannot be sued for any harm the animals might cause, so they have no personal responsibility for damages if cattle contract brucellosis from the trespassing bison. The park officials are simply caretakers with concerns that are not like those of a dog owner, for example, whose pet wanders into a neighbor's yard and digs

This chapter adapted from *Managing the Commons,* edited by Garrett Hardin and John Baden, copyright © by W. H. Freeman and Company, is reprinted with permission.

up a flower bed. The dog owner is liable for any damage the animal does; the park official has no such liability.

The externalities produced by the roaming bison have important similarities with other forms of pollution. Migrating bison cause harm when they cross into the physical space of others, just as fluid from a hazardous waste site leaves the confines of the dump and pollutes groundwater. With bison and with pollution, making the owner of the "pollutant" pay for the damage caused would reduce the level of "emissions." We should not expect a zero risk of brucellosis or zero amounts of pollution under a system of accountability, unless the owner's cost of controlling the source of the damage was low relative to the expected liability of the harm. It is interesting, however, that on the one hand environmentalists will argue that all precautions, regardless of cost, should be taken to control discharge from hazardous waste sites, while industrial producers argue that the costs and benefits of control must be considered; on the other hand, it is the cattle producers in the bison case who call for no "discharge" and environmentalists who claim that a little "pollution" will not matter.

In the context of free market environmentalism, both migrating bison and pollution problems can be solved by establishing property rights. Making those who own a hazardous waste site liable for the ooze that may damage the groundwater gives the owners an incentive to take precautions to prevent damages from "migrating waste." When Hooker Chemical, for example, disposed of its wastes at the now infamous Love Canal, it took great pains to seal the canal to prevent the wastes from leaking into surrounding land and groundwater. But after the local school board purchased the land for one dollar, under threat of condemnation, safety at the disposal site was compromised by political decision makers who allowed the site to be developed against Hooker's warnings. The school board could act irresponsibly because it was not clearly liable for its actions.[2] The same is true in the case of the Yellowstone bison.

Because Yellowstone National Park officials are not liable for the potential damages from brucellosis carried by the bison, the responsibility falls on someone else's shoulders. In this case, the owner has never been identified. The Montana legislature instituted a hunting season on bison who wandered from the park into Montana. Once the animals cross the park boundary, they become fair game for hunters who carry bison permits. But it is still unclear who owns the bison. If the Park Service owned the bison, then it would be responsible for trespassing animals and it would have an incentive to find innovative ways of controlling their movement or eliminating the virus they carry. If the state owned the bison, then it would have the authority to manage the herd size both inside and outside the park and would be responsible for any damage the animals might cause. But neither situation holds. The only time that property rights to the bison are clearly established is at the point of kill when the hunter claims his prize.

Non-hunters and animal rights supporters have expressed their opposition to the hunting of park bison, but in general they have also been unwilling to take responsibility for the bison. Only the Fund for Wildlife has tried to construct a fence along part of the migration route to keep the bison in the park, and for a time the Fund paid the owners of a ranch that borders the park to close their property to hunting. Admittedly, it is difficult to imagine a mechanism for establishing clear property rights to the bison, and fencing the perimeter of a 2.2 million-acre national park seems impossible. Until property rights can be established and owners made accountable, however, conflicts resulting from the "pollution" will be inevitable.

Our purpose is not to propose a definitive solution to the bison problem but to explain why the door to property rights should always be kept open for addressing such problems. Our collective imagination is often constrained by the technology and the economics of a particular time and place. By examining the evolution of property rights in the American West, however, we can see that changing economic and technological conditions do generate innovative property rights solutions.

THE COWBOY FRONTIER

Imagine yourself in 1840, riding to the top of a divide in what would one day become the state of Montana and gazing on an endless sea of grass. Knowing that eastern markets are hungry for beef, you decide that there is profit potential in grazing cattle on the prairie grass and driving them to eastern railheads. Competition for the grass seems unlikely, since there are similar valleys over almost every divide. But as time passes and as more cattlemen take advantage of the profit opportunities from grazing the prairies, land, grass, and water become more scarce and an additional cow in your valley reduces the land's grazing potential. Your breeding program has produced a hearty stock that can gain weight on the prairie grass and endure harsh winters, and you do not want other cattle mixing with yours. It is also becoming clear that water will soon become a constraint; if someone else uses the water for irrigation or mining, it will not be available to you.

Common law, as applied in the East, presupposed that cattle would be fenced, making cattle owners responsible for any damages their animals caused. Common law also allocated water to riparian owners in co-equal amounts, making no provision for diversion because abundant precipitation made irrigation unnecessary. To western cattlemen, however, establishing property rights according to eastern common law appeared to be as impossible as fencing in the bison at Yellowstone. Stone and timber were not available for fencing, and water was always in short supply and not always available where it was needed. Eastern institutions and ideas simply were not appropriate for the Great Plains. Historian Walter Prescott Webb captured the essence of the problem:

> The Easterner, with his background of forest and farm, could not always understand the man of the cattle kingdom. One went on foot, the other went on horseback; one carried his law in books, the other carried it strapped round his waist. One represented tradition, the other represented innovation; one responded to convention, the other responded to necessity and evolved his own conventions. Yet the man of the timber and the town made the law for the man of the plain; the plainsman, finding this law unsuited to his needs, broke it and was called lawless.[3]

The problems on the American frontier centered on who owned the land, the cattle, and the water. Out of these problems frontier entrepreneurs developed new property institutions to define and enforce rights that improved resource allocation. Those institutions were not perfect, but they demonstrate the potential for innovative solutions to resource ownership problems.

LAND

Land on the Great Plains had several characteristics that affected its productive use. The mean average rainfall over much of the region does not exceed fifteen inches a year, precluding the use of land for farming as it was traditionally practiced in the East.[4] The forage on the plains was mainly shortgrass, necessitating large quantities of land for each cow. And the lack of trees meant that it was difficult to fence with natural materials. There was little precedent for the type of agriculture that would be used on the Great Plains, so farmers were forced to drastically alter the productive process.

These same characteristics of the land provided the impetus for changing the methods of defining and enforcing property rights. Initially, land on the Great Plains was not a scarce resource and little attention was paid to the establishment of property rights. "There was room enough for all," historian Ernest Osgood wrote, "and when a cattleman rode up some likely valley or across some well-grazed divide and found cattle thereon, he looked elsewhere for range."[5] For much of the 1860s and 1870s, "squatter sovereignty" was sufficient for settling questions of who owned the land. But the growing demand for land by cattlemen, sheepherders, and farmers eventually increased its value and, therefore, the benefits from engaging in activities to define and enforce property rights.[6]

Initially, settlers attempted to establish some extra-legal claims to property, but as Webb described it: ". . . no rancher owned land or grass; he merely owned cattle and the camps. He did possess what was recognized by his neighbors (but not by law) as range rights."[7] Range rights provided some exclusivity over the use of land; but as the population increased, settlement became more dense and land values rose even more. Individuals and groups began devoting more resources toward defining and enforcing private property rights, and early laws provided ways to punish those who drove their stock from the accustomed range. The idea of accustomed right on the basis of priority rights was also reflected in the claim advertisements that appeared in local newspapers. At the time, it was easy for cattlemen to define their "range rights":

> I, the undersigned, do hereby notify the public that I claim the valley, branching off the Glendive Creek, four miles east of the Allard, and extending to its source on the South side of the Northern Pacific Railroad as a stock range.—Chas. S. Johnson[8]

Such activities could not be enforced in any court of law, but they were inexpensive and they put others on notice that claims existed.

As the value of grazing land rose, so did the rate of return on defining and enforcing property rights. To capture these returns, cattlemen organized in groups and used the coercive authority of government to protect their property. By banding together in stockgrowers' associations, cowmen attempted to restrict entry onto the range by controlling access to limited water supplies. These groups also put pressure on state and territorial governments to pass laws that would punish those who drove stock from their "accustomed range." In 1866, the Montana territorial legislature passed a law controlling grazing on public land, and in 1884 a group of cattlemen in St. Louis suggested that the federal government allow the leasing of unclaimed land.[9] Gradually, the West moved toward private property by restricting entry onto land that was once held in common.

The influence of cattlemen's and other land associations remained strong until the winter of 1886–1887, the severest one the new businesses of the northern plains had yet encountered, with snow, ice, wind and below-zero temperatures gripping the area from November to April, in a succession of storms that sent the herds drifting helplessly, unable to find food or water.[10]

Thousands of cattle died that winter, and many ranchers went broke and left Montana and Wyoming to make a living elsewhere. Land values declined, reducing the need to expend resources on enforcing property rights. From 1886 to 1889, membership in the Wyoming Stock Growers Association dropped from 416 to 183.[11] A similar decline was evident in the Montana Stock Growers Association. In his 1887 presidential address, attended by only one-third of the Montana members, Joseph Scott concluded that "had the winter continued twenty days longer, we would not have had much necessity of an Association; we would not have had much left to try to do."[12]

Although the laws and restrictions on land use took ranchers a step toward exclusive ownership, they still did not stop livestock from crossing range boundaries. Only physical barriers could accomplish that, but fences of smooth wire did not hold stock well and hedges were difficult to grow and maintain. The cost in money and time was simply too high. But when barbed wire was introduced in the West in the 1870s, the cost of enclosing land was dramatically reduced. To homesteaders whose land was invaded by cowboys and herds that trampled crops, barbed wire "defined the prairie farmer's private property."[13]

Some stockmen ridiculed the new fencing material, but others saw the advantage of controlling their own pastures. In Texas, for example, "they began buying land with good grass and water and fencing it. In 1882, the Frying Pan Ranch, in the Panhandle, spent $39,000 erecting a four-wire fence around a pasture of 250,000 acres."[14] Other cattlemen enclosed their "accustomed range" with the inexpensive and easy to use barbed wire. But a federal law passed in 1885 forbade the fences and provided for the "prosecution of those who stretched fences out upon the public domain."[15] Then, the inevitable conflicts over ownership were settled through both range wars and legal institutions.

Between 1860 and 1900, changing land values and costs of fencing caused individuals and groups to devote more effort to definition and enforcement activity. As a result, the institutions governing landownership on the Great Plains moved toward exclusivity. Measures were enacted that attempted to control grazing on the public domain, and efforts were made to lease unclaimed public lands from the government. During the 1870s and 1880s, many acres of land were privately claimed under the homestead, preemption, and desert land laws. Finally, land was granted outright to the transcontinental railroads, which transferred much of it to private hands.[16]

LIVESTOCK

As with land, new institutions were also needed in the West for defining and enforcing property rights in livestock. In the East, where farms and herds were much smaller, it was easy for an owner to watch his animals and to know when they strayed from his property. Identifying animals by their natural markings was also feasible on farms that had only a few head of livestock. Furthermore, the lack of common property in the East and the availability of stone and rails for fencing made enforcement of property rights less costly. But a western livestock producer not only had to run his cattle over a large acreage, he also had to pasture them on lands over which he did not always have exclusive control. These factors, combined with the difficulty of fencing large areas where wood was scarce, made eastern methods of enforcing property rights to livestock costly on the plains.

The settlers had to search for alternatives. During the 1860s, sheepmen turned to herding, while "property rights in unbranded cattle were established by the fact that they ran on a certain range. . . ." As long as individuals agreed on who owned the animals, there was little need to devote valuable resources to definition and enforcement questions. Increasing human and cattle populations in the West, however, created more disagreement and incentives changed. As Osgood described it: "The questions arising over the ownership of cattle and the rights of grazing were intensified as the number and value of the herds increased."[17]

Cattlemen responded by increasing their property rights activities. Although cattlemen had used branding to identify their stock since they had first come to the region, the laws governing branding activity changed.

> There was a time when brands were relatively few and a man could easily remember who owned the different ones, but as they grew more numerous it became necessary to record them in books that the ranchers could carry in their pockets. Among the first laws enacted by territorial legislatures were those requiring the registration of brands, first in counties and later with state livestock boards.[18]

Laws passed in Wyoming and Montana provided for the central registration of distinctive brands, but more laws were needed as the population increased.[19] Osgood captured the effect of this shift on enforcement activity in cattle raising:

> . . . additional laws were passed to further define and enforce rights to cattle. Legislatures passed laws requiring that cattle driven through a territory had to have their brands inspected. Brands were made transferable, and penalties were imposed on those who failed to obtain a bill of sale with a list of brands on the animals purchased. As the complexity and number of brands increased, the resolution of conflicts was turned over from the county clerk to a larger committee including resident stock growers. Laws regulating illegal branding were strengthened by making offenses a felony.[20]

Individual efforts to define and enforce property rights in livestock were complemented by voluntary collective action that gave cattlemen the opportunity to capture gains from economies of scale. Originally, each rancher gathered and branded his own cattle. On the open range, this meant that herds were rounded up as many times as there were individual operators. As the number of operators increased, however, the cost of handling the cattle in this fashion increased proportionately and cooperation became profitable.

The cattlemen on the plains also used "human fences," or line camps, to enforce their rights to cattle and land. The movie scene of cowboys sitting around a campfire singing songs comes from the camps that were established on the perimeters of range areas. Cowboys spent their days—and nights—making certain that cattle did not wander from their designated range. The line camps also helped enforce property rights by guarding against rustling. But human fences, while effective, were expensive.

Technology provided the alternative that dramatically changed the face of the American West. In the 1870s, homesteaders and ranchers began using barbed wire to define and enforce their rights to land. By confining cattle to a certain range, cattlemen could reduce both their losses from strays and the costs of rounding up the cattle for branding and shipping. Furthermore, once their cattle were separated from other herds on the range, ranchers could practice controlled management and breeding. In 1874, 10,000 pounds of barbed wire were sold; by 1880, just six years later, over 8.5 million pounds had been sold and the fencing was being used throughout the West.[21]

Most of the changes in defining and enforcing property rights were toward greater exclusivity, but we would expect to find a movement in the opposite direction if asset values declined. An example of this occurred in the 1920s in eastern Montana. From 1918 until 1926, the prices of horses in Montana dropped dramatically, from $98 to $29 per head.[22] Prices were depressed as farmers replaced their horses with machines and the U.S. Cavalry stopped buying horses. With the incentive to maintain ownership reduced, many horse owners found it unprofitable to define and enforce property rights to the animals and, therefore, allowed their animals to run the open range. As a result, wild horse herds increased so rapidly that community roundups were held to clear the range of the unclaimed property. Many of the wild horses that cause grazing problems on public lands today are descended from the horses abandoned during the 1920s.

WATER

Water presented special ownership problems in the West.[23] Like livestock, water moves freely across many pieces of real estate, but unlike livestock, it is nearly impossible to "corral" except in reservoirs. Complicating the matter further, the quantity of water can vary from season to season and even from day to day. This is especially true on the Great Plains, where average rainfall ranges from between 15 and 20 inches a year. The ever-changing physical nature of the resource makes definition and enforcement of rights to water most difficult. Sir William Blackstone, an eighteenth-century jurist, described it this way: "For water is a moving, wandering thing, and must of necessity continue common by the law of nature; so that I can only have a temporary, transient, usufructuary property therein."[24]

To frontiersmen and settlers on the plains, having access to water was essential. As a result, initial settlement patterns in the region can be traced to river and stream bottoms. During the early years of white settlement, if an individual found a stream location occupied, he simply moved on to another site where there was a supply of water. As long as there was unoccupied land adjacent to streams and as long as the primary use of water was domestic and livestock consumption, westerners found it sufficient to enforce water rights using riparian doctrine from common law, which gave all riparian owners co-equal rights to undiminished flows.[25]

As settlement pressure increased, however, and as water was used to irrigate nonriparian land, pressures for changing water institutions grew. Especially in the arid states on the western plains, where water was essential for raising crops or livestock, land with available water became increasingly scarce and the value of water rights rose. In gold-mining areas, water was required at the mine site, which was often far from the nearest stream. These conditions induced individuals to devote more resources to redefining property rights in water. In the mining regions, for example, there was no established custom of mining and no recognized law, so miners set up mining districts, formed miners' associations, and established mining courts that provided laws.

> These miner's rules and regulations . . . were very simple and as far as property rights were concerned related to the acquisition, working, and retention of their mining claims, and to the appropriation and diversion of water to be used in working them. . . . There was one principle embodied in them all, and on which rests the "Arid Region Doctrine" of the ownership and use of waters, and that was the recognition of discover, followed by prior appropriation, as the inception of the possessor's title, and development by working the claim as the condition of its retention.[26]

Miners recognized the need for an alternative system of water law in the West and worked hard to have California and United States courts recognize their customs and regulations regarding water.[27]

Although precedent established in California in 1850 lowered the cost of establishing property rights in water, the growing scarcity of water on the Great Plains increased the benefits to definition and enforcement activity. Settlers moved toward a system of water laws that (1) granted to the first appropriator an exclusive right to the water and granted to later appropriators rights conditioned on the prior rights of those who had gone before; (2) permitted the diversion of water from streams for use on nonriparian lands; (3) forced water appropriators to forfeit their rights if the water was not used, and (4) allowed for the transfer and exchange of water rights between individuals.[28]

The activities designed to establish and enforce exclusivity were strongest in areas where water was the scarcest. In Montana, Wyoming, Colorado, and New Mexico, where rainfall averages fifteen inches per year, the common law of riparian ownership was completely abandoned; where rainfall was greater, in North Dakota, South Dakota, Nebraska, Kansas, Oklahoma, and Texas, states only modified the doctrine.[29] The evolution of water law on the Great Plains was a response to the benefits and costs of defining and enforcing the rights to that valuable resource.

CONCLUSION

Property rights are not static; the social arrangements, laws, and customs that govern asset ownership and allocation are continually evolving. As long as the benefits of establishing ownership claims are low relative to the costs, there is little incentive for individuals to define and enforce private property rights. In this case, any "tragedy of the commons" will be small. As the ratio of perceived benefits and costs changes, however, so will the level of definition and enforcement activity. The higher the value of an asset and the higher the probability of losing the right to use that asset, the greater the incentive will be for "institutional entrepreneurs" to devise innovative mechanisms for establishing property rights. Technological advances or lower resource prices, which reduce the opportunity costs of definition and enforcement, will increase property rights activity. As open access created conflicts in the American West, individual efforts were channeled toward solving the problems of ownership to land, livestock, and water.

These examples teach us that we should not be too quick to conclude that market-based, property rights solutions will not work for natural resources. Before the invention of barbed wire, fencing vast tracts of land on the Great Plains seemed impossible. Given current technology, fencing bison, whales, or grizzly bears seems equally impossible. But as asset values change, so do incentives.

Some environmental groups have proposed that wolves be re-introduced into Yellowstone National Park, but ranchers oppose the plan because they fear that the wolves will leave the park and prey on livestock. Could the wolves be fenced? Technology is currently available for "fencing" dogs by burying a cable that emits a radio signal on the perimeter of a piece of land; the signal, received in the dog's collar, shocks the animal, which then retreats from the perimeter. Could the same technology be applied to wolves? When red wolves were re-introduced into South Carolina wildlands, they were equipped with radio collars that allow the animals to be tracked. If a wolf wanders too far afield, a radio-activated collar injects the animal with a tranquilizing drug so that it can be returned to its designated habitat. Whales also can be "branded" by genetic prints and tracked by satellites, providing another way to define property rights.

Lessons from the American West teach us not to underestimate the potential for innovative entrepreneurs solving problems by establishing property rights on the environmental frontier. If environmental entrepreneurs want to take responsibility for migrating bison or wolves, they should be allowed to do so. For free market environmentalism to be effective, the legal barriers to these innovative solutions must be minimized.

NOTES

1. This chapter is adapted from Terry L. Anderson and Peter J. Hill, "From Free Grass to Fences: Transforming the Commons of the American West," in *Managing the Commons*, ed. Garrett Hardin and John Baden (San Francisco: W. H. Freeman, 1977), 200–16.

2. Eric Zuesse, "Love Canal: The Truth Seeps Out," *Reason* 12 (February 1981): 16–33.

3. Walter Prescott Webb, *The Great Plains* (New York: Grosset & Dunlop, 1931), 206.

4. Ibid., 17.

5. Ernest Staples Osgood, *The Day of the Cattleman* (Minneapolis: University of Minnesota Press, 1929), 182.

6. For a discussion of crowding on the open range, see ibid., 181–3.

7. Webb, *The Great Plains*, 229.

8. Quoted in Osgood, *Day of the Cattleman*, 183.

9. Ibid., 21, 201.

10. Maurice Frink, W. Turrentine Jackson, and Agnes Wright Spring, *When Grass Was King* (Boulder: University of Colorado Press, 1956), 98–99.

11. The stockgrowers' lobbying power declined dramatically because of that disastrous winter, and the 1889 territorial legislature repealed many stock laws. See W. Turrentine Jackson, "The Wyoming Stock Growers Association, Its Years of Temporary Decline, 1886–1890," *Agricultural History* 22 (October 1948): 265, 269.

12. Minutes of the Montana Stock Growers Association, 1885–1889, quoted by Ray H. Mattison, "The Hard Winter and the Range Cattle Business," *The Montana Magazine of History* 1 (October 1951): 18.

13. Alistair Cooke, *Alistair Cooke's America* (New York: Knopf, 1973), 237.

14. Jay Monaghan, ed., *The Book of the American West* (New York: Bonanza, 1963), 292.

15. Osgood, *Day of the Cattleman*, 193.

16. For a more complete description of the effort to claim public land, see Gary D. Libecap, *Locking Up the Range: Federal Land Control and Grazing* (San Francisco: Pacific Institute for Public Policy Research, 1981).

17. Osgood, *Day of the Cattleman*, 33, 114.

18. Frink et al., *When Grass Was King*, 12.

19. *Laws of the Montana Territory, 1864–1865*, sess. I, 401; *Laws of Wyoming Territory, 1869*, sess. 1, chap. 62, 426–7.

20. See Osgood, *Day of the Cattleman*, 124–6.

21. For a complete account of the use of barbed wire, see Webb, *The Great Plains*, 309.

22. U.S. Department of Agriculture, Bureau of Agricultural Economics, *Livestock on Farms, January 1, 1867–1935* (Washington, D.C.: Government Printing Office, 1938), 117.

23. For a more complete discussion of water rights, see Terry L. Anderson, *Water Crisis: Ending the Policy Drought* (Washington, D.C.: Cato Institute, 1983).

24. Quoted in Webb, *The Great Plains*, 434.

25. See ibid., 433, 447.

26. Clesson S. Kinney, *Law of Irrigation and Water Rights and the Arid Region Doctrine of Appropriation of Waters*, vol. 1 (San Francisco: Bender-Moss, 1912), sec. 598.

27. See Webb, *The Great Plains*, 444–8.

28. See Wells A. Hutchins, *Water Rights Laws in the Nineteen Western States*, Miscellaneous Publication no. 1206, vol. 1 (Washington, D.C.: Natural Resources Economics Division, U.S. Department of Agriculture, 1971), 442–54.

29. See Webb, *The Great Plains*, 446.

4

FROM BARBED WIRE TO RED TAPE

with Timothy Iijima

If the nineteenth century was an era of acquisition and privatization of the public domain, the twentieth century has been one of massive public reservation. During the first half of the nineteenth century, the federal estate expanded rapidly as states ceded their claims west of the Appalachians and vast tracts were added through purchase or conquest.[1] With the Ordinance of 1785 and the Ordinance of 1787, the original colonies ceded their western lands to the federal government, and the Louisiana Purchase of 1803 enlarged the federal estate by well over 750 millions acres—twice the area of Alaska. Because there was no support for leaving the land in the public domain, the government was faced with how to dispose of it. During its early stages, this movement pitted Alexander Hamilton, who favored selling the public lands to enhance the U.S. Treasury and pay off debts incurred during the Revolutionary War, against Thomas Jefferson, who wanted to promote an agrarian ethic by giving the land to those who were willing to settle and cultivate the western frontier. Neither side in the debate questioned the wisdom of privatization. As a result, the "first privatization movement," from 1790 to 1920, put more than a billion acres of public land into private ownership.

Although most privatization of federal lands occurred between the Civil War and World War II, new land policies were set in motion that eventually created a federal estate totaling one-third of the nation's land and a public domain totaling more than 40 percent. Part of this dramatic transformation occurred because politically influential conservationists, such as Gifford Pinchot and Theodore Roosevelt, had been convinced that private ownership was promoting the rape and ruin of timberlands and, ultimately, a timber famine. Roosevelt warned that "if the present rate of forest destruction is allowed to continue, with nothing to offset it, a timber famine in the future is inevitable."[2] Gifford Pinchot, the first director of the Forest Service, agreed: "We have timber for less than thirty years at the present rate of cutting. . . ."[3]

While the dire predictions never came to pass, the idea that only professional management by public employees could promote good resource stewardship came to dominate the policy debate in the late nineteenth century. The political question was no longer how to dispose of the federal estate, but how to manage it. The answer came in the creation of federal bureaucracies, such as the National Park Service, the Forest Service, and the Bureau of Land Management. Huge quantities of land, timber, minerals, and water became the domain of "an elite corps of professionals."

The cutting of large amounts of timber in the Great Lakes region near the end of the nineteenth century is used as evidence that political control of land is necessary to prevent the "rape and pillage" by private enterprise. Even though timber famines are not of major concern today, conservationists point to this episode as one of the worst environmental disasters of the period and argue that only public ownership could prevent this from happening again. This era encapsulates the view among many conservationists that private interests are driven by short-term profit motives to destroy valuable natural resources. Is this the lesson for the Great Lakes experience? Was private ownership the problem or the solution?

ALLEGATIONS OF WASTE

Immigrants to North America before the turn of the nineteenth century found an abundance of natural resources. Raw land was almost free for the taking, and timber was more of a nuisance than an asset. Except for New England, where naval stores (including masts and turpentine) were valuable, native forests were cleared as soon as possible for growing crops. The trunks of trees were girdled to kill them, and large tracts of forests were burned. When the wood was used to build homes, furniture, and tools, the technology for using wood appeared to be quite wasteful to Europeans who had long found it necessary to conserve wood. The process of hewing a nation from the forest continued until the frontier reached the Great Plains, where settlers confronted fertile but treeless prairies.

Until the settlers reached the Pacific Northwest, the last old-growth forests available to meet timber demands were in the Great Lakes states. During the 1850s, entrepreneurs responded rapidly to price signals from timber markets, and the growth of the Great Lakes timber industry typifies nineteenth-century timber exploitation. Within a few decades, small, local mills had grown into an intensely capitalized, highly integrated industry. Within a few more decades, production peaked, and timber production moved to the Northwest, leaving behind a trail of denuded forests and abandoned mills. By 1910, the rise and decline of the industry was almost complete.[4]

Critics of the nation's logging industry contend that nineteenth-century timber practices were wasteful. With forests in the United States reduced from an estimated 820 million acres at the beginning of the nineteenth century to 495 million acres in 1932, critics like Gifford Pinchot—who was trained in Germany, where timber endowments were very different—saw the extensive use of virgin forests as wasteful and unscientific.[5] These critics referred to the logging practices around the Great Lakes as the "Great Lakes Tragedy." Andrew Rodgers, a historian of American forestry and plant sciences, wrote: "It was assumed that the continent's forest resources were inexhaustible."[6] In his economic history of Wisconsin, Robert Fries warned: "one must not let hindsight obscure the fact that the very immensity of the forest led most people to take them for granted, much as they did the sunshine and the air about them."[7] Bernhard Fernow, the first chief of the United States Division of Forestry, wrote in 1902:

> The natural resources of the Earth have in all ages and in all countries, for a time at least, been squandered by man with a wanton disregard of the future, and are still being squandered wherever absolute necessity has not yet forced a more careful utilization.
>
> This is natural, as long as the exploitation of these resources is left unrestricted in private hands; for private enterprise, private interest, knows only the immediate future—has only one aim in the use of these resources, namely, to obtain from them the greatest possible personal and present gain.[8]

These charges suggest that greed clouded timber managers' perception of resource endowments and led to an unwise or inefficient rate of exploitation.

Some critics charged that additional waste came from logging operations and timber processing. Merk, for example, observed that "it has been estimated that not more than 40 per cent of the magnificent forest . . . ever reached the sawmill." Fries claimed that "a billion more board feet could have been produced in the years 1872–1905 had band saws been used to the exclusion of muley and circular saws." Conservationists who desired public reservations also alleged that the timber industry thrived because it was allowed to trespass on public timberlands. "By 1850 trespassing had become an accepted practice in the Great Lakes pinery. . . . To take trees from the public domain was no more immoral than it was to float a canoe on a public river." One source estimated that between 1844 and 1854 nearly 90 percent of the 500 million board feet shipped from eastern Wisconsin and northern Michigan had been stolen from the public domain.[9]

EVIDENCE TO THE CONTRARY

An economic examination of the charges of widespread waste of timber resources necessitates a careful consideration of what constitutes waste. There is no question that nineteenth-century loggers used techniques that would be considered wasteful today. If wasteful means that loggers threw away wood that could have been processed and used, then they were certainly guilty. But if wasteful means that loggers used economically inefficient practices or that the value of the wood that was thrown away was greater than the cost of conserving it, then the extent of waste is much less clear.

Conservationists' objections to private ownership are buttressed by examples like one from the 1880s in which a logging firm allegedly stole approximately 1.25 million board feet of timber from someone else's land, over a million board feet of which was cut simply to get it out of the way so the best trees could be harvested.[10] If the timber was stolen, of course, there is no guarantee that efficient forestry practices would take place. Therefore, this incident should not draw criticism of private ownership but criticism of the way property rights were enforced, which is the domain of government. Furthermore, even if the timber was not stolen, we cannot be certain that its management was wasteful in the context of the relative scarcities of nineteenth-century labor. Labor was scarce and expensive and resources were abundant and inexpensive.[11] This was particularly true in the lumber industry. Merk wrote: "The remoteness of the lumber camps from settlements, the rough and temporary nature of the work, and the unsatisfactory terms of employment were sufficient . . . to render the labor problem in the pineries a troublesome one."[12] Because of the scarcity of labor, if conserving trees came at the expense of using more labor, then conservation would have been wasteful. "It is to be noted as a characteristic of all sawmill innovations of this day that they were calculated solely to secure an increased output or a saving of labor. Little effort was made toward effecting a saving of lumber since timber was still cheap and abundant."[13] In short, waste and efficiency are not absolute concepts measured by energy input and output; they must be considered in the context of the relative economic scarcity at the time when decisions were made.

The allegation that firms operated under a delusion that timber stands were inexhaustible requires a consideration of the information and the incentives timberland owners and managers had about present and future supplies and demands. Those firms that understood how increasing scarcity resulted from decreasing supplies and increasing demand stood to profit from that knowledge. Moreover, allegations that firms failed to adequately conserve timber for the future fail to consider the economics of resource allocation over time.[14]

In the long run, a firm can remain profitable only if it accounts for both present and future demand. Firms that recklessly exploit a resource for the quickest possible financial gain, whether because of ignorance or carelessness, only make it more profitable for informed firms to purchase and hold large amounts of the resource off the market for an extended period of time. An informed owner of resources who notices that much of the supply is being squandered and sold for immediate gain will anticipate an increase in prices. In this way, the nation's future demands for timber would be efficiently accounted for if only a few firms foresaw a "timber famine."

In the case of timberlands, prudent investors would only forgo cutting if they expected its value as standing timber to increase faster than the return on alternative investments. Typically, forestland was inspected, appraised, purchased, and sold to lumber mills, activities that depended on current and future prices. The decision for an owner was whether and for how long to hold timber and at what rate to harvest it. If he expected to earn a higher rate of return by placing his assets in some alternative form of investment, then holding onto timber was a losing proposition. In this case, the economic decision would have been to sell the timber (presumably to be cut and processed) and put the proceeds into stocks, bonds, or other investments. Alternately, a timber owner would have been foolish to sell trees that he expected to increase in value at a rate higher than the prevailing return on other investments. Through this process, the long-run prevailing interest rate serves as a guide for determining the rate at which timber resources would be harvested. In other words, if timber owners believed the predictions of a timber famine, they surely would have expected future timber prices to be significantly higher and would have had an incentive to profit by efficient management. Their behavior, however, suggests that they did not believe the predictions.

This reasoning implies that under efficient management, timber prices should have been steadily increasing at the prevailing interest rate.[15] If timber prices were not rising at the prevailing interest rate, it would have been more efficient and profitable to liquidate the trees at a faster pace, investing the proceeds in other assets. Conversely, if timber prices were rising faster than the return on other assets, it would have made sense for private owners to reduce their harvest rate, thereby retaining an investment in growing timber. The early conservationists' allegation that timber was being harvested "too fast" suggests that current prices were being suppressed and that once the timber famine was realized there would be a price shock similar to the one that occurred during the energy crisis in the 1970s.

Any price shock caused by an expected timber famine would have been exacerbated if the timber companies had been stealing trees from government lands rather than legitimately cutting from their own property. There is certainly evidence that timber was commonly taken from government lands during the early part of the nineteenth century. If this were pervasive, however, the market would have reacted violently when the supplies available from government lands were depleted. With theft, it is reasonable to expect rapid harvesting to keep the price of lumber low until the free trees were depleted, at which time the price would jump to reflect the price that lumber mills would be forced to pay for private, scarce timber. Evidence that Midwest timber prices steadily increased and was free of price shocks suggests that timber theft did not interfere significantly with efficient timber allocation.

Economists Ronald Johnson and Gary Libecap have examined the time-path of timber prices and found no such discontinuity. To the contrary, they found a steady and smooth rise in nineteenth-century timber prices. Johnson and Libecap examined stumpage prices (the price of standing timber) and reported that rates of return were relatively constant through 1900, with the rate of change in stumpage prices hovering at around 6 percent. This is within approximately one percentage point of the prevailing yield on railroad bonds over the same period of time.[16]

Consideration of lumber prices (the price of processed wood) generated a similar conclusion. Warren and Pearson reported "a steady increase in the purchasing power in the price of lumber from 1789 to the present time. From 1798 to 1914, the purchasing power of lumber increased at the compound rate of 1.54 per cent per year."[17] The rise in price was steady and absent of price shocks. Neither the legend of inexhaustibility nor timber theft was significant enough to affect the market price of timber.

Lumbermen, in fact, made attempts to artificially raise the prices of processed wood through cartels. They formed organizations, issued price lists, and agreed on restricted production levels. In spite of these efforts, they failed to have any measurable long-run effect on the price of processed lumber. Curiously, monopoly is commonly cited among the irresponsible excesses practiced by the timber industry. The steady rise in the prices of either stumpage or lumber suggests that these allegations are false. This indicates that trees were held, sold to mills, processed, and sold as lumber in a well-functioning market in which property rights were secure and increasing scarcity was accounted for.

There are several important consequences that result from this efficient market. As the price gradually works its way up, firms gain an economic incentive to search out new and less expensive alternative resources. Firms that find less expensive alternatives to higher-priced timber will profit as the consuming public switches to the alternatives; firms that do not seek those alternatives risk losing a significant share of business to those that do. This explains why firms began developing production in the timber stands on the West Coast and in the South, where tremendous amounts of standing timber were available.[18] Furthermore, because the price of timber will rise gradually, transition to a different source is likely to be phased in gradually. In these ways, a stable supply of resources is assured for the economy.

As these effects on the supply are taking place, the economy's demand for the diminishing resource is scaled back as consumers find it financially important to conserve, to develop more efficient ways of using the resource, and to substitute other materials. During the late nineteenth century, for example, the railroads foresaw increasing scarcity, and they invested in research on ways to protect wooden bridges and ties against decay, on the possibility of using steel to make ties and bridges, and on the science of efficient bridge architecture.[19] The switch from wood to coal as a source of power provides another example.

Additional evidence that private timber owners were managing their resources for the long haul is found in the lag between the establishment of property rights and the beginning of logging operations. In fact, many historical accounts of nineteenth-century land policy lament the way speculation held land off the market and delayed development. In the case of timber, however, such a delay is consistent with good resource stewardship.[20]

Beginning in the 1850s, speculating on timberland in the Great Lakes region quickly became big business. When tracts were opened for bidding, speculators assessed the timber potential in order to make informed bids. They also made an effort to gather information on the general conditions of resource scarcity, so that they could estimate the future value of the trees they were purchasing. During the years when federal lands were being sold in the Great Lakes region, annual land claims rose proportionally to annual lumber production, and private ownership was secured well before major harvesting began in an area.[21]

Philetus Sawyer, a lumber tycoon and United States senator, attributed his fortune to early, well-placed purchases of forestlands, some of which he kept off the market for as much as a quarter-century. Sawyers profited because he went to the expense of investigating the quality of forestland, about which little was known, and invested capital in trees whose value would not be realized for some time.[22]

Historian Paul W. Gates has described one of the most successful land speculation projects in American history. As a land grant college, Cornell University obtained rights to nearly a million acres from the federal government in the 1860s. It claimed approximately one-half million acres in Wisconsin, managed the lands, and gradually sold them. Most of the land was sold by 1890, although final sales were not completed until 1925. Cornell hired a talented and well-placed land agent who meticulously chose stands and skillfully negotiated the timber's sale to lumber mills. By carefully controlling the timing of when it sold its lands for timber development, Cornell sold lands that were initially worth five dollars an acre for twenty dollars; the richest tract brought eighty-two dollars an acre. Gross revenues minus gross expenses from Cornell's land sales amounted to approximately $5 million.[23]

In the context of economic theory and in light of historical data, the allegations of waste and inefficiency have little credibility. The conservationists' warnings were based on insufficient information and wrong assumptions. As economist Sherry Olson put it, "we succeeded in avoiding the 'inevitable.' Yet we did not do it by following the doctor's advice."[24]

Timber theft did occur before 1860, but only because by that time the government had just begun making the public domain available for private ownership. When the majority of good forestlands were publicly owned and few forestlands were open to private ownership, the industry had no choice but to take public resources.[25] It is to the government's credit that little time was wasted in selling off land in the Great Lakes region; in doing so, it allowed the market to allocate the resources according to scarcity rather than on the first-come, first-served basis of theft.[26]

The lumbermen themselves expressed the final word on timber theft from the public domain in 1879, when Congress considered legislation that was perceived as reducing the punishment for the crime. Lumbermen with privately owned lands, who had strongly opposed penalties for timber theft in the 1850s, now strongly opposed the "bill to license timber thieves." The simple fact was that these lumbermen had no desire to compete with producers who had a source of cheap, stolen trees.[27]

COMMODITY EFFICIENCY OR AESTHETICS?

Most of the early conservationists' arguments were concerned with timber production and timber famine and not wilderness or aesthetic values common in today's policy debates. No one would deny that most of the old growth timber was harvested in the Great Lakes region, but wilderness was not a scarce commodity at the time. Furthermore, except for a few isolated areas where poor soil quality has retarded reforestation, most of the denuded lands have recovered to become productive timber or agricultural lands.

This leaves the question of whether the Great Lakes timberlands were wasted in terms of aesthetic or environmental values that are not included in commodity considerations. We must keep in mind that decisions, whether in the private or political sector, are always made in the context of contemporary values. In 1900, per capita income was one-tenth of what it is today, and most of the population was not wealthy enough to demand aesthetic values. Backpacking, canoeing, fishing, and hunting were not leisure activities; they were a means of transportation and food production. The untamed wilderness—where today we look for peace and quiet—was a nuisance and a source of danger. One writer observed in 1857:

> The lumbermen on the Upper Wisconsin, are not only men of means to prosecute their business with eminent success, but they have the further qualifications of intelligence, energy, and perseverance . . . the proof is in the reduction by them, in a few short years, of those wild wastes, into a land of productive industry, equalled by no other in the state—scarcely in the west.[28]

Only with economic growth, which was built in part on resource use, have we become able to afford aesthetic values.

Although the conservation movement was gaining strength as logging activity progressed through the old-growth forest of the Great Lakes region, there is significant evidence that these logging activities were widely viewed as beneficial. For example, "the idea of conservation seems not to have taken hold of the people of Minnesota during the years when these natural resources were being harvested so rapidly."[29] Merk concluded that "the swift forest destruction that accompanied the expansion of the lumber industry gave concern only to a few obscure idealists."[30]

Conservation legislation moved forward only in small steps and against strong opposition. In 1910, Edward Griffith, Wisconsin's first state forester, urged that counties be empowered to acquire forests in cooperation with the State Board of Forestry. The public responded with open hostility. The county board of Oneida County referred to it as "Mr. Griffith's pet scheme to gobble up our best agricultural lands." Rosholt wrote:

> In short, it was still the will of the people, even though most of the pine timber was already gone, to do nothing towards reforestation or towards calling a halt to indiscriminate timber cutting, while encouraging cultivation of land no matter how sandy, stony, swampy, or unsuited to farming it was.[31]

The economics of nineteenth-century timber harvesting, however, did not always work against the environment. In fact, the remaining virgin stands in the Great Lakes area have been saved largely by market forces. Where timber stands are largely inaccessible, difficult to log, or sparse, the timber was left generally untouched throughout the nineteenth century because logging those areas would not have been profitable. In northern Michigan and parts of Canada, thousands of acres were spared because the cost of logging them was simply not worth the value of the timber. Examples of such land include several thousand acres at the core of Porcupine Mountains Wilderness State Park in northern Michigan, smaller portions of the Boundary Waters Canoe Area in northern Minnesota, and numerous other scattered old-growth stands in the northern Midwest.[32] Thus, economic realities aided in preserving many trees.

As people became more interested in leisure, recreation, and the environment, private individuals purchased and preserved several timber stands, such as the Huron Mountain Club near Big Bay, Michigan; the 17,000-acre "McCormick Tract," just south of the Huron Mountain Club; and the 21,000-acre "Sylvania Tract" of the Ottawa National Forest. The Sylvania Tract, originally owned by Fisher Body Company, and the McCormick Tract, which was the private retreat of Cyrus McCormick, have been donated to the Forest Service. The Huron Mountain Club continues to privately care for thousands of acres of old-growth forest.[33]

This does not mean that private entrepreneurs made no mistakes. The Kingston Plains offers a pointed example. Unlike most land in the Great Lakes area, which is now productive farmland, timberland, or recreational land for fishermen, hunters, and hikers, the Kingston Plains has never recovered from logging done a hundred years ago. Efforts have been made to replant the area, but the soil is too infertile and sandy. It took hundreds of years for the original forest to grow, and it will take hundreds of years for the area to recover.[34] This does not imply, however, that cutting the trees was a bad decision. When the trees were cut, good timber stands in the Great Lakes area were selling for around $20 per acre.[35] In order to determine whether it would have made more sense to invest in trees by foregoing the harvest, we must consider the return on other investments. Had the income from selling these trees been invested in bonds or some other form of savings at the time, it would now be worth approximately $110,000 per acre, or $2.8 billion for the forty square miles.[36] If the trees at Kingston Plains had been left standing, would the benefits derived over the past one hundred years from preserving land for wildlife habitat, hiking, and other environmental amenities have been worth forgoing the benefits society received from logging? The answer is highly subjective, but the tremendous benefits from exploiting the Kingston Plains cannot be ignored. Because the land in this area is not worth anything close to this, we must infer that harvesting the trees was the correct choice.

CONCLUSION

The evidence on Great Lakes timber production during the late nineteenth century presents no justification for the political management of lumber-producing lands. When judged against prudent investment criteria, nineteenth-century timber markets were efficient. Even if non-market, non-commodity values are included in the calculations, it is not clear that markets incorrectly accounted for these values. And considering the contemporary values of nineteenth-century citizens, it is difficult to argue that even the most omniscient decision maker would have behaved differently. It is not clear that transferring management of the Great Lakes timberlands to the political arena *would have* or *should have* done anything to alter resource allocation.

Nevertheless, the conservationists won the battle in the political arena. From policies of disposal of the federal estate, we moved to policies of reservation and political management. The establishment of Yellowstone National Park in 1872 and the extensive national forest reserves in 1891 marked a significant change in the view of the federal government in resource management. With over one-third of the nation's land (in the lower forty-eight states) now under control of the federal government and another 7 percent under control of the states, it is vital that we critically examine the results of political control.

NOTES

1. See Douglass C. North, Terry L. Anderson, and Peter J. Hill, *Growth and Welfare in the American Past: A New Economic History* (Englewood Cliffs, N.J.: Prentice-Hall, 1983), 111–21.

2. Theodore Roosevelt, in *Proceedings of the American Forest Congress* (Washington, D.C.: American Forestry Association, 1905), 9.

3. Gifford Pinchot, *The Fight for Conservation* (New York: Doubleday and Page, 1910), 123–4.

4. See Robert F. Fries, *Empire in Pine: The Story of Lumber in Wisconsin* (Madison: State Historical Society of Wisconsin, 1951), 8–23, 250–1; Ronald N. Johnson and Gary D. Libecap, *Explorations in Economic History* 17 (1980): 376–7; Agnes M. Larson, *History of the White Pine Industry in Minnesota* (Minneapolis: University of Minnesota Press, 1949), 11, 29–28, 220–1, 404; Frederick Merk, *Economic History of Wisconsin During the Civil War Decade* (Madison: State Historical Society of Wisconsin, 1916), 60–73.

5. See Sherry H. Olson, *The Depletion Myth: A History of Railroad Use of Timber* (Cambridge, Mass.: Harvard University Press, 1971).

6. Andrew D. Rodgers III, *Bernhard Edward Fernow: A Story of North American Forestry* (Princeton, N.J.: Princeton University Press, 1951), 1.

7. Fries, *Empire in Pine*, 15.

8. Bernhard E. Fernow, *Economics of Forestry* (New York: Thomas Y. Crowell, 1902), 1.

9. Merk, *Economic History of Wisconsin*, 100, 105–8; Fries, *Empire in Pine*, 190, 286–8, 245. See also Paul W. Gates, *History of Public Land Law Development* (Washington, D.C.: Public Land Law Review Commission, 1968), 534–55; Lucile Kane, "Federal Protection of Public Timber in the Upper Great Lakes States," *Agricultural History* 23 (1949): 135–9.

10. Russell McKee, "Tombstones of a Lost Forest," *Audubon* 90 (March 1988): 68.

11. In 1871, the average daily wage of a skilled laborer in the United States was $2.58, and good pine stands could be obtained for $4.00 an acre. See Bureau of the Census, *The Statistical History of the United States: From Colonial Times to the Present* (New York: Basic Books, 1976), 165; Paul W. Gates, *The Wisconsin Pine Lands of Cornell University: A Study in Land Policy and Absentee Ownership*, 2d ed. (Madison: State Historical Society of Wisconsin, 1965), 214. During the Civil War, "the wages of loggers in the northwestern pineries of Wisconsin ranged from $3 to $4 per day including board." See Merk, *Economic History of Wisconsin*, 109.

12. Merk, *Economic History of Wisconsin*, 108.

13. Ibid., 70.

14. See Oscar Burt and Ronald G. Cummings, "Production and Investment in Natural Resource Industries," *American Economic Review* 60 (1970): 576–90; Howard Hotelling, "The Economics of Exhaustible Resources," *Journal of Political Economy* 39 (1931): 137–75; Robert M. Solow, "The Economics of Resources or the Resources of Economics," *American Economic Review* 64 (May 1974): 1–14.

15. This assumes that costs are not rising or falling. If they were, the price could rise or fall faster than the interest rate. Technically, it is the rental value of the resource that follows the interest rate.

16. See Johnson and Libecap, *Explorations in Economic History*, 379; Milton Friedman and Anna J. Schwartz, *A Monetary History of the United States* (Princeton, N.J.: Princeton University Press, 1963), 69.

17. George F. Warren and Frank A. Pearson, *Prices* (New York: John Wiley and Sons, 1933), 36.

18. By the turn of the century, timber from the South and the Far West was beginning to dominate the market. See Johnson and Libecap, *Explorations in Economic History*, 376–77; Larson, *History of the White Pine Industry*, 221, 396–8.

19. For a detailed description, see Olson, *The Depletion Myth*, 42–69.

20. See Terry L. Anderson and P. J. Hill, "The Race for Property Rights," *Journal of Law and Economics* 33 (April 1990): 177–97.

21. Richard N. Current, *Pine Logs and Politics: A Life of Philetus Sawyer, 1816–1900* (Madison: State Historical Society of Wisconsin, 1950), 22–25; Merk, *Economic History of Wisconsin*, 73; Johnson and Libecap, *Explorations in Economic History*, 375.

22. Current, *Pine Logs and Politics*, 23.

23. Gates, *Wisconsin Pine Lands*, 106, 237–9, 242, 243.

24. Olson, *The Depletion Myth*, 6.

25. Gates wrote that in 1852 "the territorial legislature of Minnesota stated that encouragement had been given to the establishment of sawmills in the territory but not an acre of pine land had been offered at public sale and none was open to preemption." The legislature further stated that the industry "would be willing and anxious to pay the government for the land. . . ." See Gates, *Wisconsin Pine Lands*, 538.

26. This was not accidental. The government understood the importance of private ownership in the protection of the timber resource. See Fries, *Empire in Pine*, 192.

27. See Fries, *Empire in Pine*, 195.

28. A. G. Ellis, "Upper Wisconsin Country," in *Collections of the State Historical Society of Wisconsin*, ed. Lyman C. Draper, vol. 3 (Madison: State Historical Society of Wisconsin, 1857), 445.

29. Larson, *History of the White Pine Industry*, 405.

30. Merk, *Economic History of Wisconsin*, 99.

31. Malcolm Rosholt, *The Wisconsin Logging Book* (Rosholt, Wisc.: Rosholt House, 1980), 282.

32. The Porcupine Mountains Wilderness State Park in Minnesota is particularly interesting because it was nearly logged due to Department of Defense

contracts during World War II. It should be noted that it was government demand rather than private market forces that finally made the timber valuable enough to consider for logging.

33. See Steven Karpiak, "The Establishment of Porcupine Mountains State Park," *Michigan Academician* 2 (1978): 135–9. For information on other tracts, see Fred Rydholm, "Upper Crust Camps," in *A Most Superior Land: Life in the Upper Peninsula of Michigan* (Lansing: Michigan Natural Resources Magazine, 1983). Additional information concerning the holdings of the Huron Mountain Club can be obtained from the Huron Mountain Wildlife Foundation in White Pigeon, Michigan.

34. Information on the Kingston Plains is from McKee, "Tombstones of a Lost Forest," and from conversations with people in the Great Lakes area.

35. The $20 figure is based on Gates, *Wisconsin Pine Lands*, 238. Interest rate sources are Friedman and Schwartz, *A Monetary History*, 640, and *Economic Report of the President—February 1988* (Washington, D.C.: U.S. Government Printing Office, 1988), 330.

36. See Warren Scoville, "Did Colonial Farmers 'Waste' Our Lands?" *Southern Economic Journal* 20 (1953): 178–81.

5

BUREAUCRACY VERSUS ENVIRONMENT

Although efforts to reserve millions of acres in the political domain were underway during the late nineteenth century, Mr. and Mrs. W. W. Beck were doing their part to preserve one little corner of the world on the outskirts of Seattle, Washington. In 1887, they bought several parcels of land with giant fir trees reaching 400 feet in height and 20 feet in diameter. The Becks built a pavilion for concerts and nature lectures and added paths, benches, and totem poles. Ravenna Park soon became immensely popular. Visitors paid 25 cents a day or $5 a year ($3 and $60 in 1990 dollars) to enter the park. Even with the fees, 8,000 to 10,000 people visited the park on a busy day.[1]

As the Seattle population grew and conservationist sentiment developed, residents began to lobby for acquiring more public parklands, including Ravenna Park. In 1911, the city bought Ravenna from the Becks for $135,663 following condemnation proceedings. Shortly after the city's acquisition, according to newspaper accounts, the giant firs began disappearing. The Seattle Federation of Women's Clubs confronted Park Superintendent J. W. Thompson with reports of tree cutting. He acknowledged that the large "Roosevelt Tree" had been cut down because it had posed a "threat to public safety." It had been cut into cordwood and sold, Thompson conceded, but only to facilitate its removal and to defray costs. The federation asked a University of

Washington forestry professor to investigate. When the women brought the professor's finding that a number of trees had been cut to the attention of the Park Board, the board expressed regret and promised that the cutting would stop. By 1925, however, all the giant fir trees in Ravenna had disappeared.[2]

Some people still blame the destruction of the trees on a 1925 windstorm; others blame automobiles and chimney smoke. But it was the bureaucracy that destroyed what the Becks had saved. Park employees took advantage of their access to the park and cut down trees to sell for firewood. Park Department records charge Superintendent Thompson with abuse of public funds, equipment, and personnel, plus the unauthorized sale of park property. Even if he and his subordinates were not the direct culprits, they had allowed the cutting to go on.

The Ravenna Park debacle occurred at a time when leaders of the early conservation movement were touting public ownership as the only way to conserve America's natural resources. In their view, the greed of private owners was an insurmountable obstacle to conservation. Yet, in Ravenna Park private owners protected natural treasures while public agents destroyed them. Even an outcry from public watchdogs could not prevent the eventual destruction of the giant fir trees. Today, Ravenna is just another city park with tennis courts and playgrounds.

Could similar controversies and results occur with political resources today? Unfortunately, the answer is yes, and on a much larger scale than the incident at Ravenna Park.

TIMBER BEASTS VERSUS TREE HUGGERS

The U.S. Forest Service, with an annual budget of around $2 billion and roughly 39,000 full-time employees, is the largest natural resource agency in the federal government. It oversees natural resource use on 191 million acres of national forests and is required by law to manage its lands for multiple uses, which include timber production, livestock grazing, mineral and energy production, fish and wildlife habitat, wilderness protection, and public recreation. During the past two decades, the agency has come under a barrage of criticism from environmentalists who feel that the agency has over-emphasized commodity production at the expense of environmental amenities and commodity interests that believe the agency gives wilderness values too much attention.[3]

Such controversy is typical on the seven national forests that make up the 14 million-acre Greater Yellowstone ecosystem, the "largest relatively intact ecosystem remaining in the lower 48 states."[4] The forests are valued for their recreational opportunities and their commodity production, including timber, but environmentalists insists that the Forest Service's timber program is highly destructive. They argue that the region's harsh climate and steep terrain are not good for producing commercial stands of timber. Because reforestation is slow and costly, wildlife populations are disturbed. When timber is harvested, too little emphasis has been given to the visual effects of clear-cutting. Environmentalists also contend that logging in roadless areas threatens to displace Yellowstone's grizzly bear population and that the water quality in streams known worldwide for their fishing is likely to decline from sedimentation associated with road construction and clear-cutting.[5] Logging interests counter that these problems will be worse if timber harvesting does not control the fuel load and minimize the effect of fires. They point out that the massive fires in the summer of 1988 had much smaller environmental effects and lower control costs in areas where logging had taken place.[6]

Added to the environmental debate are fiscal concerns. Virtually every aspect of national forest management loses money. The national forests surrounding Yellowstone National Park had losses from their timber programs ranging from $241,000 to $2.2 million per year from 1979 through 1984. According to Forest Service budgets, all seven national forests had losses in fiscal year 1988 totalling $7.15 million. Less well recognized are the losses on recreational services. The millions of people who fish, hike, and hunt on national forests generally do so for free. On the Gallatin National Forest alone, expenditures surpassed receipts in fiscal year 1988 by nearly $2 million, approximately twice the deficit from timber production.[7]

Yellowstone's ecosystem is not the only environmentally significant area mired in political controversy. Environmentalists argue that excessive logging and road building are also occurring on the Tongass National Forest in Alaska, the largest in the national forest system and "one of the last largely intact rain forests in the world's temperate latitudes."[8] Most of the trees in the Tongass are giant Sitka spruce and hemlock, some as old as 800 years. These trees also provide valuable habitat for Sitka black-tailed deer and for the greatest concentrations of bald eagles and grizzly bears in America. According to studies by the U.S. Fish and Wildlife Service and Alaska's Department of Fish and Game, it can take as long as 250 years before a logged area can provide suitable habitat for these species, so the Forest Service's planned harvest program will likely lead to substantial declines in these wildlife populations.[9] But the Forest Service continues to offer for sale nearly 450 million board feet a year, losing anywhere from fifteen to ninety-eight cents on every dollar spent.[10]

The fiscal and environmental problems that exist in the national forests are the result of institutions, not people. To expect forest managers in the bureaucracy to set aside self-interest and objectively weigh the benefits and costs of multiple-use management is to ignore the information and the incentives that confront them. Forest managers are not supposed to manage the public lands to maximize the economic return, but they can and do manage in ways that maximize their budgets. Bureaucrats in general have a propensity to expand their staffs and budgets because such expansions provide higher salaries, more prestige, and more power. In the case of the Forest Service, timber revenues are generated when trees are harvested with a percentage of the receipts retained by the bureaucracy. In addition, timber harvests mean larger road building staffs and more budget for timber management. With little revenue generated from recreational or environmental amenities and less staff required to manage wilderness, these values have received less attention than traditional commodities.

Organized wilderness advocates, however, are increasing pressure for making larger expenditures on recreational and environmental amenities and for devoting more land to these uses. The pendulum may swing toward these areas, but the controversy will not disappear. With the costs diffused among all taxpayers and with benefits concentrated, environmentalists consider no price to be too great for saving wilderness. For example, when a group of environmentalists and local landowners discovered that a timber company was planning to cut trees from four sections (2,560 acres) in the Greater Yellowstone ecosystem, they asked Congress to buy the property. With timberlands in the area worth approximately $500 per acre, the landowner was eager to sell if the group got the appropriation, which was equal to nearly $800 per acre. Such pressures will only increase Forest Service deficits and fuel the backlash from commodity interests whose jobs depend on the forests. The bureaucratic process does little to encourage either fiscal or environmental responsibility.

PLANT CONTROL ON THE RANGE

Like the national forests, our federal rangelands have multiple uses. They provide a seasonal or permanent home for some three thousand species of wildlife and fish, a source of energy reserves and hardrock minerals, rangeland for grazing livestock and wildlife, and free recreation for the public. And like our national forests, there is reason to question the government's management of these lands.

Consider the management tool known as chaining, where two crawler tractors drag 600 feet of anchor chain with links weighing 90 pounds between them to remove pinon pine and juniper trees. The BLM and the Forest Service used these tractors on hundreds of thousands of acres in the Southwest during the 1960s and 1970s and advocated chaining as an effective plant control program. Its application, they believed, had a variety of benefits, including restoring an area to its original grassland state, improving wildlife habitat, increasing watershed values, and increasing livestock forage.[11]

With the financial backing of the federal treasury, the BLM chained more than 250,000 acres in Utah and 43,000 acres in Nevada. The Forest Service chained over 77,000 acres in Utah's national forests and 6,000 acres in Nevada's Humboldt Forest. Reports of the extent of chaining are not complete, but when lands in Arizona and New Mexico are included the total area cleared by chaining is about 3 million acres.[12]

Little research supports the federal land managers' contention that chaining has a multiplicity of values. There is no solid evidence that pinon-juniper woodland areas represent an invasion of original grassland habitat; therefore, chaining cannot be considered an act of restoration. In addition, Forest Service scientists have found that chaining has no significant effect on water quality and does not increase water yield. As far as wildlife is concerned, removing woodland habitat eliminates an area of security for mule deer and, while it creates forage for deer, it does little for the deer population, since the limiting factor in the chained areas is habitat security. Finally, chaining did not help the Shoshone and Paiute Indians of Nevada, who depended on pinon pine nuts as a traditional source of winter food. The only real benefit from chaining was the creation of additional forage for livestock, which allowed those holding grazing leases on chained lands to receive the benefits while making no investment.[13]

THE "WATER" PORK BARREL

While chaining accommodated a few leaseholders, it pales in comparison to what the Bureau of Reclamation has done on behalf of western irrigators. Even though federal dam construction practically ground to a halt during the 1980s, costs are still being exacted on the treasury and the environment. One example of the environmental cost was revealed when contaminated drainage water forced the closing of California's Kesterson Wildlife Refuge, an important stopover for millions of migrating waterfowl. The culprit was an unusually high level of selenium, a naturally occurring chemical, that is benign at low levels but lethal at high levels. Biologists found that as a result of the selenium poisoning, wild duck eggs often did not hatch and when they did grotesque deformities were common. The source of the selenium-laced water that found its way to Kesterson was California's Central Valley Project, an irrigation project that provides subsidized water to farmers in the San Joaquin Valley. Further investigation has revealed that the selenium contamination extends to thousands of evaporation ponds in California's Central Valley and to the rivers that flow into San Francisco Bay.[14]

The effects of irrigation on wildlife are amplified when rivers and natural lakes are de-watered by subsidized federal water projects. In Nevada's Pyramid Lake and in the Stillwater National Refuge, for example, water levels have receded to unprecedented low levels. A system of dams and canals on the Carson and Truckee rivers has caused the drawdown by diverting water to irrigators in Nevada's Lahontan Valley. The water level at Pyramid Lake, home of the endangered cui-ui fish and the threatened Lahontan cutthroat trout, has dropped by sixty feet. The Stillwater Refuge, which in good years harbored 200,000 ducks, 6,000 geese, and 8,000 tundra swans, has lost almost 68 percent of its productive marsh.[15] In 1938, Winnemucca Lake, once a paradise for waterfowl on the Pacific Flyway, dried up. The same fate may be in store for Pyramid Lake and the Stillwater Refuge.

The situations in California and Nevada are the by-products of the federal government's water pork barrel. For eighty years, the Bureau of Reclamation, the federal agency responsible for making the "desert bloom like a rose," has spent tens of billions of taxpayers' dollars to bring subsidized water to western irrigators. Through interest-free loans and extended repayment schedules, western irrigators pay only a fraction of the cost of storing and delivering water. Irrigators whose runoff ended up in Kesterson, for example, pay less than 10 percent of the cost to store and deliver the water.[16] BuRec's efforts have resulted in engineering marvels like Glen Canyon Dam and Hoover Dam, but the water that continues to flow so cheaply into fields creates not only environmental tragedies, it also aggravates agricultural surpluses.

The fiscal and environmental problems inherent in federal water projects are not the fault of bad managers. They result from an institutional framework that does not discipline federal managers to be either fiscally or environmentally responsible. Moreover, the system builds an iron triangle among politicians, water users, and bureaucrats that is difficult to dismantle. If the discipline of free market environmentalism was at work, massive, subsidized projects would not be built, higher water prices would encourage efficiency, and polluters would be liable for the damage they produce.

A BIRD'S-EYE VIEW OF FARM POLICY

For sixty years, federal farm policy has set the tone for land management on a major portion of the 300 to 340 million acres of private farmland in the United States. Unfortunately, the program's track record of wildlife conservation has been abysmal. During the last thirty years, the population of small game animals such as ring-necked pheasants, ducks, cottontail rabbits, and bobwhite quail has been reduced to only a small fraction of what it was.[17] These birds and animals once thrived on farms with shelterbelts, shrubs along fence rows, and thick growths of cattails along streams and marshes. Today, this kind of habitat is more the exception than the rule. Farmers are now growing the same crop year after year, draining the remaining wetlands, converting upland cover to row crops, and drenching their fields with pesticides and herbicides. The result is a bland, repetitious countryside that offers minimal habitat for wildlife.

Federal agricultural programs are the major cause of this sterile landscape. They induce farmers to increase production by cultivating otherwise uneconomic land. For example, agriculture was responsible for 87 percent of wetland conversion between 1950 and 1980, and direct government subsidies were the main reason the conversions were undertaken.[18] The negative impact on the environment has been exacerbated by programs that support commodity prices and reduce risks by subsidizing insurance. With returns higher and costs lower than they would be in a free market, farmers plant more acres and produce more crops. To reduce the surpluses, federal programs require farmers to cut back on the acreage planted, but farmers attempt to circumvent such efforts by using more pesticides and fertilizers to increase output per acre.

Federal programs have also tried to retire land from production, but the programs have had virtually nothing to do with conservation. For example, annual surveys by wildlife personnel in twelve midwestern states and in Colorado and Pennsylvania indicated that from 20 to 56 percent of idled cropland was without cover for entire summers, thus providing little protection for animals. Land that did have cover was frequently disturbed by early summer mowing during the critical nesting period for birds. Ironically, annual set-aside acreage in the Midwest includes more than two-thirds of the acres previously converted from wetlands through federally subsidized drainage programs.[19]

Equally bad for wildlife is the farm program's "base acreage" concept. A farmer's subsidy payments are computed as a percentage of average acres planted in the previous five years. The more land that a farmer has in his acreage base, the larger his government payments are. This gives farmers a tremendous incentive to bring even poorer land into production, because it enlarges the cropland base and qualifies them for bigger government payments in the future.

Following passage of the 1985 Farm Act and the establishment of the Conservation Reserve Program, there was hope that farmers would return to practicing environmentally sensitive agriculture. Under the program, taxpayers pay farmers to take land out of production for ten years and provide financial assistance for planting a cover crop. After five years and an annual cost of $1.5 billion, however, the program has had disappointing results. Only a small percentage of the 30 million retired acres provide enough diversity of vegetation to help wildlife survive the elements. Moreover, most of the acreage is in tame grass, which the Department of Agriculture continually lets farmers remove in drought-hit regions.[20]

The Conservation Reserve Program is an example of a well-intentioned but ineffective effort to accomplish soil and wildlife conservation. The farmers who receive the largest payments are those who have cultivated the most erodible soil; farmers who have practiced good land conservation receive very little. A far more effective approach would be to remove the subsidies that create the incentives to destroy habitat in the first place, saving taxpayers money and improving soil and wildlife conservation.

CONCLUSION

And so the story goes. The Forest Service, the Bureau of Land Management, the Bureau of Reclamation, and the Department of Agriculture carry out policies that exact heavy tolls on the environment. What is the problem? Some critics of environmental and natural resource policy focus on the personalities in administrations. But such an approach overlooks the fact that environmental travesties have occurred under both Democratic and Republican administrations. The volume of logging on national forests and the resulting budget shortfalls have increased in every decade since the 1950s; federal water projects underwritten by taxpayers have spanned nearly a century; and subsidies for farm products and other federal inducements for destroying habitat have been taking place since the 1930s. Other critics argue that more money should be spent on environmental amenities. Yet, spending for pollution control alone totaled $739 billion in constant 1982 dollars from 1972 through 1984.[21]

The perverse results described in this chapter occur because of institutional failure. In government agencies, bureaucrats have incentives to provide constituents with the products and services they want at little or no cost to them. Entrepreneurs in this arena are rewarded with larger staffs, more authority, and larger budgets, but they do not face the reality check of profitability. Moreover, to the extent that they have a single constituency, such as farmers in the Department of Agriculture, there is little incentive for the bureaucracy to consider other values. Increasing farmers' incomes becomes the primary goal, even if there are perverse environmental consequences. Where there are multiple constituencies, such as in the Forest Service, the political arena becomes a battleground where development interests are pitted against environmental interests in a zero-sum game. Unfortunately, the process is costly to the groups themselves, to the taxpayer, to the economy, and often to the environment.

NOTES

1. Terry L. Anderson and Jane Shaw, "Grass Isn't Always Greener in a Public Park," *Wall Street Journal*, May 28, 1985, 30.

2. Ibid.

3. National Audubon Society, *Audubon Wildlife Report 1968* (New York: National Audubon Society, 1986), 1–156.

4. Rick Reese, *Greater Yellowstone: The National Park and Adjacent Lands* (Helena: Montana Magazine, 1984), 36.

5. The Wilderness Society, *Management Directions for the National Forests of the Greater Yellowstone Ecosystem* (Washington, D.C.: The Wilderness Society, 1987), 13–14.

6. Letter to Donald Leal from Doug Crandall, March 4, 1990. Crandall is manager of Brand S. Corporation, a logging company in the Greater Yellowstone area.

7. The Wilderness Society, *Management Directions*, 22; U.S. Forest Service, *Timber Sale Program Annual Report: Fiscal Year 1988* (Washington, D.C.: U.S. Forest Service, 1989); Gallatin National Forest recreational budget for fiscal year 1988.

8. The Wilderness Society, *America's Vanishing Rail Forest (Executive Summary)* (Washington, D.C.: The Wilderness Society, 1986), 1.

9. John W. Shoen, Matthew Kirchoff, and Michael Thomas, "Seasonal Distribution and Habitat Use by Sitka Blacktailed Deer in Southeastern Alaska" (Alaska Department of Fish and Game, Juneau, 1985); J. I. Hodges, James G. King, and Fred C. Robards, "Resurvey of the Bald Eagle Breeding Population in Southeast Alaska," *Journal of Wildlife Management* 43 (January 1979): 219–21.

10. U.S. Forest Service, Region 10, "Statement of Obligations" (Juneau, Alaska, 1984). See also U.S. Forest Service, *Timber Sale Program Annual Report*.

11. Ronald M. Lanner, "Chained to the Bottom," in *Bureaucracy vs. the Environment*, ed. John Baden and Richard L. Stroup (Ann Arbor: University of Michigan Press, 1981), 154–69. Although chaining is no longer practiced to the extent that it was, the disruption of thousands of acres remains.

12. Richard S. Aro, "Pinion-Juniper Woodland Manipulation with Mechanical Methods," *The Pinion-Juniper Ecosystem: A Symposium*, ed. Gerald F. Gifford and Frank E. Busby (Logan: Utah State University, 1975), 67–75, 156.

13. Lanner, "Chained to the Bottom," 158; Warren P. Clary et al., "Effects of Pinion-Juniper Removal on Natural Resource Products and Use in Arizona," Research Paper RM–120 (Washington, D.C.: U.S. Forest Service, 1974), 163.

14. Richard W. Wahl, *Markets for Federal Water: Subsidies, Property Rights, and the Bureau of Reclamation* (Washington, D.C.: Resources for the Future, 1989), 197–219; Kathleen Rude, "Ponded Poisons," *Ducks Unlimited* 54 (January–February 1990): 14–18.

15. Kathleen Rude, "Heavenly Water, Earthly Waste," *Ducks Unlimited* 50 (May–June 1986): 41–45.

16. Richard W. Wahl, "Cleaning Up Kesterson," *Resources*, no. 83 (Spring 1986): 12.

17. Robert B. Dahlgren, "Distribution and Abundance of the Ring–Necked Pheasant in North America," in *Pheasants: Symptoms of Wildlife Problems on Agricultural Lands*, ed. D. L. Hallett, W. R. Edwards, and G. V. Burger (Bloomington, Ind.: North Central Section of The Wildlife Society, 1988), 29–43.

18. Secretary of the Interior, *The Impact of Federal Programs on Wetlands: Vol. I. The Lower Mississippi Alluvial Plain and the Prairie Pothole Region* (Washington, D.C.: Government Printing Office, 1988), 3–5.

19. A. H. Berner, "Federal Pheasants: Impact of Federal Agricultural Programs on Pheasant Habitat, 1934–1985," in *Pheasants*, 60.

20. U.S. Department of Agriculture, Agricultural Stabilization and Conservation Service, *Conservation Reserve Program: Ninth Signup Results* (Washington, D.C.: Government Printing Office, January 1990); U.S. Department of Agriculture, News Division, "Yeutter Announced Additional Drought Assistance: CRP Opened for Haying and Grazing" (news release, Washington, D.C., July 1989).

21. *State of the Environment: A View Toward the Nineties* (Washington, D.C.: The Conservation Foundation, 1987), 23.

6

INSIDE OUR OUTDOOR POLICY

Recreational opportunities and environmental amenities are income elastic; that is, the demand for them rises with income. Since World War II, incomes for United States citizens have been rising dramatically, increasing the willingness of Americans to pay more for outdoor opportunities. Comparing figures from 1960 and 1985, average expenditures per individual increased, in real terms, 200 percent for fishing and 400 percent for hunting.[1] Total visits to Yellowstone National Park in 1987 were 8 percent higher than in 1986; during the same period, entrance fees rose from two dollars to five dollars per vehicle.[2] At the same time, a growing number of farmers and ranchers in the United States have found that hunters are willing to pay for the opportunity to hunt on their land.[3]

Increased ability to pay for outdoor recreation means that there are more opportunities for profit and more recreation-related products. Sales for outdoor equipment reached over $25 billion in 1987, and the latest U.S. Fish and Wildlife survey on wildlife-related recreation revealed that recreationists spent $21.5 billion on travel, food, and lodging in 1985.[4] In response, producers have introduced a host of innovative products, from electronic fishfinders to weather-resistant, featherweight clothing.

Until recently, however, a relatively small amount of private money has been spent on the land, water, and other natural resources necessary for outdoor recreation. Exceptions include Kampgrounds of America, founded in 1962 as a response to a growing demand for camping facilities along major highways; hunting and fishing clubs in the East and in California that have leased lands for many years and hiking clubs that built trails and huts with private initiative; youth camps that provide facilities for a variety of outdoor activities; and ski slopes and lifts that were built on both private and public lands with private funds.

One reason for the low level of private response to growing recreational and environmental demands is that one-third of the land in the continental United States is controlled by the federal government and is subject to politics. Politicians interested in obtaining votes give their constituents outputs from these political lands at no cost or at nominal fees. For most national forests, therefore, below-cost recreation costs millions of dollars each year, often exceeding below-cost timber sales by a factor of two. As a result, the private sector has had to compete with a supplier of recreational and environmental amenities that does not have to face the discipline of a profit-and-loss statement.[5]

As with any good, low or zero fees for federally controlled resources increase the demand and result in overcrowding and diminished quality. In the West, where federal land is pervasive, a growing number of recreationists are finding that the quality of their recreational experience is decreasing and they are turning to the private sector.[6] Unfortunately, the extent of public landownership combined with the federal government's long history of providing recreational opportunities has created an inertia that is difficult to overcome.

In 1962, John F. Kennedy appointed the first presidential commission on outdoor recreation, an early example of the public's role in providing recreational opportunities. The principal recommendations of the Outdoor Recreation Resources Review Commission emphasized a dominant role for the federal government and led to the creation of several federal programs, including the Wilderness Preservation System, which has some 89 million acres of wilderness lands; the Wild and Scenic River System, which has designated 72 rivers totalling 7,365 miles; and the National Trails System, which has produced about 23,500 miles of scenic and historic trails.[7] A subsequent President's Commission on Americans Outdoors in 1987 carried on with this inertia. Charged by President Ronald Reagan in 1985 with reviewing "outdoor recreation policies, programs and opportunities" for the public and private sectors, the commission focused primarily on a single component of recreation: the federal "outdoor estate." Some proposals in the commission's report could set the stage for a vast expansion of public landownership and federal controls on land use over the next two decades. These include a $15 billion trust fund, which would generate "an absolute minimum" of $1 billion per year to acquire, develop, and protect open space; a nationwide network of public greenways connecting existing and new parks, forests, and other open spaces; and a scenic byways project that would use restrictive zoning and require $200 million per year to protect scenic viewsheds along roadways. In 1987, the president of the Conservation Foundation, William K. Reilly, judged that the commission has "affirmed a crucial federal role in funding, leadership, and resource husbandry."[8]

The recommendation that government take an even larger role in supplying recreation assumes that the private sector is unable to provide the optimal amount of recreational services and resource husbandry to meet the public's demand and that government is the better producer. A dismayed Jacqueline Schafer, member of the President's Council on Environmental Quality, has pointed out that the Commission on Americans Outdoors does not emphasize people and the ways they create opportunities. She interpreted the commission's report as saying "you can't have [recreational] opportunity unless you have land guaranteed by the government."[9]

But this view ignores how critical private lands are to realizing the full potential of our outdoor resources, particularly wildlife. Private lands "constitute 60 percent of the 1.35 billion acres of America's forests and rangelands," and they provide some of the best habitat for game and nongame wildlife in the United States.[10] Also ignored is the federal government's record of stewardship, which has not always been good. With a mounting federal debt forcing us to seek ways to reduce the size of government and lessen the burden on taxpayers, we should encourage the private sector to assume more responsibility for providing outdoor recreation through free market environmentalism.

THE ECONOMICS OF OUTDOOR RECREATION

To understand how the private sector can provide more outdoor recreation, it is necessary to recognize that individuals respond to prices. Consumers move away from buying relatively high priced goods by finding substitutes. If recreational opportunities are available at low or zero prices, then consumers can be expected to take advantage of those opportunities and use them to the point where the additional value in consumption is equal to the additional cost. At the same time, producers will *not* shift resources away from alternative productive uses, such as farming or ranching, and into recreation when prices for such activities are not high enough to yield positive returns.

Product substitution is often ignored in the formulation of natural resource policy because prices faced by decision makers are often zero or nominal. For example, the Gallatin National Forest in southwestern Montana attracts thousands of fishermen, hunters, hikers, and campers every year. Yet, the Forest Service has failed to monetize the value that recreationists place on the area. The fees charged are so low that revenue from recreation amounted to $191,318 in fiscal year 1988 and the costs of provision, including trail and road construction and maintenance, campgrounds, and administration, totaled $2,021,000.[11] At these low prices, there is no signal that recreational resources are scarce and little incentive for consumers to consider substitutes.

The same set of conditions holds for producers. A rancher who owns land along a trout stream could significantly improve fishing by keeping cattle away from the stream, thus reducing bank erosion and increasing bank vegetation. The capital cost of fencing out the cattle may be quite low, but if the rancher is prevented from charging fishermen an access fee and from making a profit, he has little incentive to put up the fence. Improving fishing opportunities would only encourage fishermen to enter the rancher's property, reducing his privacy and exposing him to liability.[12]

Environmentalists tend to argue that there is no (or, at least, very little) substitution between traditional commodities produced from land and water and environmental amenities. For example, the Department of the Interior has proposed to permit oil exploration in the 1.5 million-acre coastal plain of the Arctic National Wildlife Refuge, which represents about 8 percent of the nation's largest preserve. Environmentalists have fought to keep the coastal plain closed, however, and have given little room for compromise: "Where's the compromise? It's the type of an issue where you don't think compromise. You drive a stake in the sand and say, 'You don't cross the Canning River [the western edge of the refuge's coastal plain].'"[13]

Yet, in some cases, traditional outputs and environmental amenities *can be* jointly produced with only a small disturbance to the environment. In fact, certain arrangements can be mutually supportive to both environmental and developmental interests. On the Audubon Society's privately owned Rainey Preserve in Louisiana, for example, petroleum development operates under carefully controlled conditions in an environmentally sensitive area, a sanctuary for wildlife. At Rainey, developers produce gas from a large reserve and owners of the sanctuary receive royalties from the activity, providing them with additional resources to purchase other sensitive lands.

In other cases, amenities and recreation can be jointly produced with traditional commodities using the same inputs. In these cases, a rise or decline in the supply of traditional commodities will result in a corresponding rise or decline in the supply of amenities. Agriculture and open space are an example of jointly produced outputs. About 1.5 billion acres in crop, forest, and pasture/range production provide a substantial part of the open space in the United States.[14]

Recreation and timber can also be jointly produced. Growing timber helps provide natural water storage for streams and rivers and ensures stable flows throughout the warmer months. These conditions support the burgeoning demand for water-related activities, such as fishing and white-water rafting, as well as pleasing settings for camping and hiking. These areas also provide valuable habitat for big game species, such as elk, deer, and bighorn sheep, and important habitat for endangered and threatened species, including grizzly bears and peregrine falcons. Timber removal, however, can impose costs on recreation if it is not managed to minimize the impact on watersheds, riparian zones, and cover for wildlife.

IS THERE MARKET FAILURE?

From the standpoint of supplying both traditional commodities and outdoor recreation, the important public policy question is whether markets accurately reflect recreational and environmental values (or costs) to consumers and producers. The answer to this question depends on the nature of property rights to inputs and outputs.

Cattle ranching provides one example of how property rights enable markets to work effectively to provide meat. Combining a consumer willingness to pay a price that makes beef production profitable with well-defined and enforced property rights ensures that producers can capture the profits from cattle production. In this way, the enabling mechanisms for property rights include: (1) fencing, which defines the owner's land and grass used in production; (2) a brand, which identifies ownership of the cattle; and (3) a legal and political system, which enforces the owner's claim to the inputs and the output.

The same elements of property rights are necessary for private provision of wildlife. Economist Harold Demsetz used the example of the Montagnais Indians in the Labrador Peninsula who established beaver trapping territories during the early 1600s to show how these property rights can work.[15] Before white trappers and traders arrived in the region, the Montagnais hunted beaver communally. But as the demand from new markets grew, the value of the beaver increased and more pressure was put on the resource. To avoid complete depletion of the beaver population, the Montagnais established private hunting grounds and successfully managed the beaver on a sustained-yield basis. The costs of defining and enforcing private property rights were the time and resources used to identify territories for individual hunters and to exclude others from those territories. When the value of the beaver was high enough, it was worth the cost of establishing rights to the animals.

Property rights are equally crucial today in the private provision of wildlife hatibat. For a farmer, this provision of habitat can entail leaving a marsh for nesting waterfowl instead of converting it to cropland. For a rancher, it can entail establishing no-grazing riparian zones to protect streamside habitat for white-tailed deer and ruffed grouse. Capturing a return from recreationists who may be willing to pay enough to yield a profit from producing wildlife, however, requires that landowners can control access and exclude those unwilling to pay. Owners can thus claim the rewards of producing wildlife on their land. But if trespass laws are weakened so that landowners cannot exclude nonpayers, then they have little economic incentive to provide wildlife habitat.

It is possible to provide even greater incentives for landowners to produce wildlife. Under current arrangements, landowners control access to their property, but the state regulates the taking of wildlife. In some cases, this bifurcation of control prevents better wildlife management. Suppose that an extended hunting season on a ranch would be possible if the rancher improved habitat. The extra days of hunting would allow the rancher to collect additional revenue and capitalize on improvements. But the regulatory rigidity in most states prevents landowners from receiving this kind of compensation.

Those who oppose the free operation of markets for wildlife focus on the theme of exploitation. They argue that, in the absence of government ownership, "commercialism" of the bison almost led to its extinction. The problem, however, was that there were no private property rights to the bison. Herds were left for everyone to use, allowing individuals to kill the animals without having to face the full costs of depleting the herd. Historically, wildlife exploitation can be linked to an *inability* to establish private property rights rather than to market failure.[16]

The same misguided view of markets for wildlife is evident in the recent push by some conservationists for a worldwide ban on trading ivory. They interpret the high demand for ivory as the culprit in the substantial decline of the African elephant population. In Kenya alone, poaching has reduced the number of elephants from 65,000 to 19,000 over the last ten years. To stop the killing, conservation groups such as the World Wildlife Fund and the United Nations–sponsored Convention on International Trade in Endangered Species called for a ban on the trading of ivory. But the evidence strongly suggests that the ban will only accelerate the destruction of African elephants. Kenya has had a ban on most uses of ivory ever since its elephant population began to decline. But even with restrictions, the illegal killing has continued. In Zimbabwe and Botswana, however, where ivory trading is legal, the elephant population has thrived, increasing at a rate of 5 percent a year. In those countries, local people have a strong economic interest to protect the elephants and prevent poaching. In Zimbabwe, the revenue from the tusks and hides and a portion of the money made from selling hunting permits go to nearby communities. While Kenya's elephant population has plummeted, Zimbabwe's elephant population has grown from 30,000 to 40,000.[17] The Zimbabwe experience demonstrates how effective economic incentives can be in promoting the recovery of the African elephant.

Similarly, when landowners in the United States are compensated for the wildlife on their property, the views of wildlife can change dramatically. Montana rancher Franklin Grosfield was tired of losing hay to wildlife and of being awakened in the middle of the night by hunters seeking permission to hunt on his land. But his attitude toward these costs changed when he decided to lease his land to a hunting club. The hunters provide Grosfield with revenue to supplement his cattle operation, and, as he put it, "I've taken one of our worst liabilities [wildlife] and turned it into an asset."[18]

If ranchers cannot capture benefits from producing environmental amenities, those amenities may become liabilities. Rancher Michael Curran identified one of the factors that influence landowners' decisions to produce wildlife and habitat:

> We feed 250 elk for six months, and 500 deer and about 300 antelope for an entire year. . . . We've figured that if the Montana Fish and Game Department paid us for the forage consumed, they'd owe us $6,500 every year.[19]

With no compensation, the presence of elk on private land is often seen as a liability rather than an asset. Some western landowners still consider deer, antelope, and elk a costly nuisance because they consume forage, destroy fences, and attract trespassers. One Wyoming rancher went so far as to construct a "six-foot high, 27-mile, antelope-proof fence" to protect his range. The fencing had tragic consequences for antelope during the winter of 1984:

> Many antelope, stymied by the tightly woven wire, bunched up against the fence, becoming vulnerable to slow death by starvation and freezing. A few of the weak ones made it into the town of Rawlins, only to be chased and killed by dogs.[20]

Even in the public sector, returns from wildlife relative to traditional commodity uses affect resource decisions. On the national forests surrounding Yellowstone National Park, for example, a high level of logging and road building has reduced habitat that provides shelter for elk during harsh winters and a means of escape from hunting pressure. In this region, the Forest Service derives most of its revenue from logging and road building on the national forests. There are no user fees for elk hunting on these forests, and the Forest Service simply has no economic incentive to maintain elk habitat.[21]

Not only does the political sector fail to monetize the value of elk and elk habitat on public lands, but it also reduces the value of these resources on nearby private lands. Timber companies with large landholdings in the West could provide significant recreational opportunities, but they cannot compete with the zero prices the government has set for fishing and hunting on adjacent national forests. As a result, timber companies in this region spend little or nothing to enforce their property rights in amenities, and they tend to ignore these values in management decisions.

MARKETS AT WORK

The story is much different in the East and the South where there is less public land and where private landowners manage for land values other than timber. The International Paper Company's wildlife program is a prime example. International Paper employs specialists to oversee wildlife and recreation on its lands, including the 16,000-acre Southlands Experiment Forest located near Bainbridge, Georgia. At Southlands, researchers develop forest management practices that enhance wildlife populations as well as profits. White-tailed deer, turkeys, rabbits, bobwhite quail, mourning dove, and other species are beginning to reap the benefits of these new management techniques. Habitat is improved by controlled burning, buffer zones along streams, and tree-cutting practices that leave wildlife cover and plenty of forage.[22]

According to company officials, investing in wildlife research and habitat production makes sound business sense. On its 1.65 million acres in Texas, Louisiana, and Arkansas, in 1988 International Paper charged an average of 83 cents per acre for hunting clubs and 62 cents per acre for individual hunters. Company officials see a good possibility that the return could go as high as ten dollars per acre as more hunters seek the better hunting conditions available on its lands. International Paper's 3,500-acre Cherokee Game Management Area in east Texas already earns six dollars a year per acre. For the nation's largest private landowner, ten dollars an acre is a considerable incentive.[23]

In terms of responding to recreational demands, North Main Woods, Inc. offers another interesting contrast to public land management. A non-profit association formed by twenty landowners, North Main Woods manages recreation on 2.8 million acres (about twice the size of Delaware) of mostly private commercial forests. The area includes two of the wildest rivers in New England, the Upper St. John and the Allagash, both of which have numerous stretches of white water. The area also has abundant wildlife, including moose, white-tailed deer, black bear, and partridge. With 252 lakes and ponds and miles of brooks and streams, the area is noted particularly for its excellent fishing for brook trout, lake trout, landlocked salmon, and whitefish. Most of the area is not considered a wilderness because it is managed for timber production and is interlaced with logging roads, but it still provides a high quality outdoor experience. Visitor days in the area grew from 121,000 in 1974 to 189,000 in 1984.[24]

Landowners formed North Maine Woods, Inc. when they began to experience problems from recreational use. They were suffering the costs of soil erosion and safety on private roads, overcrowding and overuse of camping areas, littering, and the ever-present threat of forest fires. The association's primary goal was to develop a program to manage public use on their lands and to find ways to fund it. North Maine Woods now controls access to the area through seventeen checkpoints and access roads, where visitors are required to register, pay fees for different types of use, and obtain permits for campsites. In 1984, the fees ranged from two dollars per day to seventeen dollars for an all-season permit; the association used the revenue to construct and improve campsites, run a trash collection system, and run public education programs. Although the organization's initial efforts were resisted by those who were accustomed to free, unrestricted access, the less crowded, clean, well-organized system of recreational management is promoting cooperation between landowners and recreationists.[25]

Even smaller landowners are looking for ways to capture returns from non-traditional land attributes. In the past, recreational amenities were often viewed as liabilities or nuisances because of gates left open, roads torn up, and litter left on the property. The fee-hunting alternative opens new opportunities.

In these days of posted farmland, shrinking public access, and growing hordes of hunters, a hunting preserve membership is an absolute guarantee that you will have a place to hunt and a place to take junior, and you won't have to spend half of the day looking for a landowner whose permission to hunt may not come readily. . . . The bottom line is better hunting, more shooting, and a happier end to each excursion. What more can the sportsman ask for?[26]

In Texas, where over 85 percent of the land is privately owned, deer hunters in 1980 purchased leases ranging from $100 to $2,000 per individual, depending on the quality and quantity of the game and the facilities and services offered by the landowner. The net returns from deer leases often "equal or exceed the annual net returns from livestock operations in many areas of the state," providing a powerful incentive for landowners to provide quality hunting opportunities.[27]

Consumers have also attempted to develop opportunities for recreation and to discover innovative ways of marketing them. A number of sportsmen's organizations offer ways to bring hunters and private landowners together by offering benefits to both. The National Outdoors Association, for example, registers private land in Nebraska, Iowa, South Dakota, Washington, Ohio, Florida, and New York that is available to its members. For twenty dollars a year, each member receives a list of cooperating landowners and a five hundred thousand dollar liability insurance policy. The organization also monitors the conduct of its members.[28]

Sandhills Outfitters, Inc. got started by offering a new line of business to ranchers who were in danger of losing their ranches in the Sandhill country of Nebraska. Sandhills Outfitters offered to lease hunting rights, and ranchers reeling from plummeting cattle prices were more than willing to listen. In 1987, the organization leased more than one hundred thousand acres of prime waterfowl, pheasant, sharp-tailed grouse, and prairie chicken habitat and offered guided hunts on private land, complete with room and board. In the interest of helping as many area ranchers as possible, Sandhills Outfitters also lists individual ranchers who want to accommodate hunters and open their lands to guests.[29]

Land conservation efforts at the local level provide a different twist on markets: they are used to protect the environment rather than to make pecuniary profits. The success of these private organizations runs counter to the critics' assumption that voluntary markets will not work because the natural environment forever remains a public good.[30] Using primarily volunteer initiative and private funds, these organizations have grown rapidly during the past three decades. In 1950, only 36 conservation organizations existed in the United States; by 1975, there were 173; and by 1982 there were 404 groups representing over 250,000 members. In 1989, local conservation organizations reported that they controlled over two million acres of valuable resource lands throughout the United States, Puerto Rico, and the Virgin Islands.[31] Land conservation trusts are generally established with tax exempt status for the purpose of preserving land for its amenity values and for keeping land in agricultural uses. Funds are raised by soliciting members who pay a small fee per year and by soliciting grants from foundations and corporations. Land trusts use these funds to buy land in fee simple title or to purchase conservation easements.

Land conservation organizations have an incentive to charge fees for access to their property because the revenues can be used to further their goals. In sharp contrast, government resource agencies fail to capture the returns that would be available if they charged realistic user fees; thus they fail to protect or enhance recreational values. Speaking for the Trustees of Reservations in Massachusetts, Gordon Abbott, Jr., stated: "We're also fortunate that user demand enables us to raise 35 percent of our operating income from admission fees and that these can be adjusted within reason to catch up with inflation. We're great believers in the fairness of users paying their way."[32]

At the national and international levels, The Nature Conservancy leads the way. As of 1990, it owned and managed over 2.5 million acres of private nature preserves in the United States and Canada. The Conservancy is also a pacesetter in finding ways to raise money to cover the operating expenses of its preserves. On the 13,000-acre Pine Butte Preserve in northwestern Montana, for example, the Conservancy offers nature tours through the last lowland grizzly bear stronghold in the lower forty-eight states. It oversees cattle grazing on select areas of the preserve, where grazing fees netted $10,000 in revenue in 1986. The Conservancy also started a guest ranch business, offering guided nature tours and access to hiking trails, fishing, and horseback riding. The revenues from the ranch help offset the cost of operating the preserve.[33]

GOVERNMENT INTERFERENCE

These examples suggest that it is not a lack of entrepreneurship that is preventing the private sector from producing more outdoor recreational and environmental amenities. As these goods rise in value, entrepreneurs will make efforts to capitalize on profit opportunities by establishing property rights. In many cases, however, government interferes with the private sector's potential by distorting markets and erecting institutions that make it prohibitively costly to establish private property rights to natural resources.

Free public hunting provides an example of government's distortion of prices in the market for outdoor recreation. On lands owned by International Paper in the South, where the company's recreational sales from hunting leases and other fee programs more than tripled in the

1980s, over one million acres are leased for recreation. On its timber holdings in the Pacific Northwest, however, where most of the surrounding timberland is national forest, International Paper has no recreational fee system and it pays little attention to recreational values.

In other cases, government subsidies for traditional commodity outputs distort prices and hinder the private production of environmental amenities. The farm program provides a case in point. For decades the federal government has paid farmers to grow crops such as wheat, corn, cotton, and rice, encouraging farmers to convert most of their land to cropland. Populations of ducks, pheasants, quail, and cottontail rabbits have drastically declined over the last forty years because their habitat has been lost to subsidized crops.[34] Ironically, under pure market conditions, farmers would not be able to farm areas of poor quality and make a profit, but the subsidies provided by the federal government have enabled them to ignore economic reality.

Legal restrictions on private property rights provide another example of institutional impediments to the private provision of amenities. Consider the provision of stream habitat for fishing. On the one hand, if a riparian landowner tried to fence off a large section of a navigable river, the technological costs of enforcing rights would likely be quite high. On the other hand, it is feasible to fence off a small stream and charge a trespass fee. But if the law allows free and open trespass for recreationists on streams, then the institutional costs are prohibitive in either case.

The public trust doctrine creates such an institutional cost. Evolving from English common law, which prevented the crown from excluding citizens from using navigable waterways, tidal areas, and beaches, the public trust doctrine holds that rights to water and riparian land are subject to the state's responsibility to protect resources. Until 1984, the doctrine applied mainly to larger, navigable rivers, but in that year the Montana Supreme Court extended the doctrine to all streams, and in 1985 the state legislature codified free access between the "high water marks."[35] Because it is now more difficult to control access, landowners have less incentive to care for the streams that run through their property. They are now in a position where they can capture fewer of the benefits from improving streams and adjacent habitat for fishing and hunting. Any improvements would only attract more visitors, thus reducing privacy and inviting liability.

A similar barrier results from the legal and moral opposition to fee hunting and fishing. Wildlife is the property of the state and cannot be sold or regulated for hunting by anyone other than the state. This legal formality is circumvented by charging trespass or access fees. Although free access to wildlife is not guaranteed by the public trust doctrine, some argue that a publicly owned resource such as wildlife should never be subject to access or user fees.[36] Pressure is mounting to extend the concept of free access as codified in Montana's stream access legislation. Sportsmen organizations are lobbying in Montana and Wyoming to open access across private land to reach public lands, and some feel that free access should be extended to the wildlife whether it is on public or private land. This would raise the cost of enforcing property rights to wildlife and remove incentives for landowners to improve habitat.

In contrast, Colorado, California, and Utah have developed "ranching-for-wildlife" programs that encourage landowners to invest in improving wildlife habitat on their properties. For example, a rancher might improve brush cover for upland game birds or plant willows to provide habitat for white-tailed deer. In return, the state allows a modification of hunting regulations on the ranch properties so that landowners can raise additional revenues from wildlife production. This typically includes extending the hunting season, raising the limit on game taken, or selling permits directly to hunters without going through the state lottery system.[37]

Perversely, the government sometimes penalizes landowners for improving habitat. Dayton Hyde, who put 25 percent of his ranch into marshes for wildlife, initiated research on the sandhill crane and built a lake with three and a half miles of shoreline for wildlife. But he paid a price:

> My lands have been zoned. I am being regulated for wetlands that weren't there before I created them. Like most of my neighbors I can save myself from financial disaster only by some creative land management, but the state legislature has cut out most of my options.[38]

As founder of Operation Stronghold, an international organization of private landowners practicing conservation on their land, Hyde is serious about wildlife conservation. But his efforts rest on the cooperation of thousands of private landowners, who could go a lot further if government would refrain from imposing costly zoning restrictions. Hyde has found that some ranchers are reluctant to join. As one landowner put it: "Look, you don't understand. We would like to do our share for wildlife but we are afraid if we create something worthwhile the public will want what we have. It's just plain easier and a lot safer to sterilize the land."[39] Because the willingness of the private sector to improve habitat or create recreational opportunity depends on the incentives landowners face, we cannot expect a positive response from the private sector if landowners are penalized for improving habitat.

Another legal barrier prevents the private production of stream amenities. As a way of validating water rights, states apply the rule of beneficial use, which says that rights to water will be lost if it is not withdrawn from the stream for beneficial use. Unfortunately, beneficial *private* use often excludes instream flows. In other words, if a right-holder decides not to divert all the water to which he is entitled and instead leaves some of it in the stream for fish, he loses his claim to it because that use is not considered beneficial. In 1917, a Utah court found it

> utterly inconceivable that a valid appropriation of water can be made under the laws of this state, when the beneficial use of which, after the appropriation is made, will belong equally to every human being who seeks to enjoy it. . . . [We] are decidedly of the opinion that the beneficial use contemplated in making the appropriation must be one that inures to the exclusive benefit of the appropriator and subject to his dominion and control.[40]

The result of this "use it or lose it" approach was manifested on Montana's Ruby River in May 1987. Minimal snowpack, little spring rain, and a heavy demand for irrigation had reduced a 1.5-mile section of the Ruby to a trickle. Hundreds of trout were stranded in overheated pools and eventually died.[41] Sadly, the water needed to keep the river flowing was of low value in other uses. As fish were dying in the Ruby River, six inches of water were standing in nearby fields. The problem could have been avoided if only small amounts of water had been transferred from irrigation to instream flows. Montana's Department of Natural Resources and Conservation did eventually persuade local irrigators to leave approximately a hundred cubic feet per second flowing in the stream, but the effort was too little and too late for the trout. And the department had to depend on the good graces of the irrigators; legal action by the state agency would have undoubtedly resulted in litigation. With the low snowpack, the de-watering problem was not unexpected, and it would have been easy for a private conservation group like Trout Unlimited to lease water from the irrigators. The amount of water necessary to have prevented the kill could have been rented for less than $4,000. With 50,000 members and an annual budget of over several million dollars, Trout Unlimited had access to the necessary resources to purchase the water, had it been permitted to do so.[42]

WHERE DO WE GO FROM HERE?

Since the first presidential commission on outdoor recreation promulgated its recommendations in 1962, more and more responsibility for recreation has been turned over to the political sector. As a direct result, millions of acres have been added to the public domain and countless regulations have been imposed on private landowners. The second presidential commission in 1987 took the same position, calling for more acquisitions to the "federal estate" and more restrictions on private landowners. There was little recognition that the private sector can create new opportunities in outdoor recreation. If proponents of current policy would only realize the potential in the private sector, they would not continue making naive and shortsighted recommendations that clearly hamper innovative responses from private individuals and organizations.

There are six policy initiatives that would encourage the private sector to participate more in providing wildlife habitat and outdoor recreational opportunities and would force government to be more fiscally responsible. These initiatives are best referred to as the "path of least resistance." For reasons of political feasibility, they do not include beneficial initiatives such as selling off or leasing public lands to the private sector, although resistance to such a move may well diminish in the future if the following proposals are implemented:

1. State agencies and courts must remove legal restrictions to the private provision of instream flows. This means removing legalities that restrict private water use to water diversions for "beneficial" purposes, that require users to divert all the water allocated to them, and that prevent users from freely selling or leasing a portion of their allocation to interested parties. This would enable private parties to protect stream habitat as well as encourage greater cooperation with other water users.

2. The courts must stop expanding the public trust doctrine in ways that erode private ownership and discourage private protection of amenity values. The use of this doctrine to prevent landowners from restricting public access to their property might provide a free lunch to special interests, but it also sends a clear message to landowners that fish and wildlife are a liability, not an asset. Landowners will act to reduce the production of fish and wildlife on their property to discourage the public's interest in their land.

3. State and local governments must cease applying so-called environmental zoning laws and other land-use restrictions on private owners who improve fish and wildlife habitat. Intrusive zoning laws can squash private initiative. The use of conservation easements provides an ex-

ample of how it is possible to achieve environmental protection and work with landowners.

4. State and federal wildlife officials must institute fish and game laws that are compatible with access fees. Current game laws are set by state and federal agencies, typically on a statewide or regional basis. By working with landowners in setting seasons and bag limits on an individual basis, economic incentives can be created that will achieve greater productivity in fish and wildlife habitat. This will encourage improved wildlife populations and greater recreational access on private lands.

5. Federal land agencies must implement a realistic user-fee program on national forests, BLM rangelands, wildlife refuges, and national parks.[43] Zero or token fees result in crowding, abuse of resources, and reduced incentives for the private sector to provide similar activities. The move to higher recreational user fees eliminates fiscal problems caused by subsidized recreation and gives the private sector a chance to compete on an equal footing when it attempts to provide similar forms of recreation.

6. Congress must cancel government programs that subsidize the destruction of recreational and environmental amenities. Environmentalists and fiscal conservatives have much to gain by working together in putting an end to farm subsidies, below-cost timber sales (see Chapter 4), and below-cost recreation.

The President's Commission on Americans Outdoors clung to an outdated agenda of bigger government. Encouraging greater participation from the private sector can reduce pressure on public resources and create greater diversity. Rising values of recreational and environmental amenities will provide an incentive for entrepreneurs to develop new technologies and institutions for producing and marketing these goods. At the very least, we must ensure that legislation and government agencies do not stand in the way.

NOTES

1. Figures for 1960 are from *Statistical Abstract of the United States, 1987*, Table 380, 219; figures for 1985 are from Lee Sabler, ed. *Ducks Unlimited* 51 (July–August 1987): 17. Increases are adjusted for CPI increase from 1960 through 1985.

2. This increase is based on preliminary figures reported by Mike Pflaum, a Park Service ranger in charge of visitation information at Yellowstone National Park.

3. Kenneth E. Solomon, "South Dakota Fee Hunting: More Headaches or More Pheasants," in *Pheasants: Symptoms of Wildlife Problems on Agricultural*

Lands, ed. D. L. Hallett, W. R. Edwards, and G. V. Burger (Bloomington, Ind.: North Central Section of The Wildlife Society, 1988), 229–38; Jim Robbins, "Ranchers Finding Profit in Wildlife," *New York Times*, December 13, 1987.

4. Sporting goods sales figures are from *Statistical Abstract of the United States, 1989*, 222, Table 379; travel expenses for wildlife-related recreation are from U.S. Department of the Interior, U.S. Fish and Wildlife Service, *1985 National Survey of Fishing, Hunting, and Wildlife-Associated Recreation* (Washington, D.C.: U.S. Fish and Wildlife Service, 1988), 137.

5. The exception is in the East and in the mid-South region, where federal land is less pervasive, and in the provision of facilities such as ski runs or campgrounds, where additional capital investment is necessary and the private sector has responded.

6. Robbins, "Ranchers Finding Profit."

7. The Conservation Foundation, *National Parks for a Generation: Visions, Realities, Prospects* (Washington, D.C.: The Conservation Foundation, 1983), 65–66; President's Commission on Americans Outdoors, *Americans Outdoors: The Legacy, the Challenge* (Washington, D.C.: Island Press, 1987), 153.

8. President's Commission on Americans Outdoors, *Americans Outdoors*, xi.

9. Terry L. Anderson, "Camped Out in Another Era," *Wall Street Journal*, January 14, 1987.

10. Task Force on Recreation on Private Lands, *Recreation on Private Lands: Issues and Opportunities* (proceedings from a workshop sponsored by the President's Commission on Americans Outdoors, Washington, D.C., March 10, 1986), 1.

11. These figures were derived by Ross MacPherson using 1988 Forest Service data and applying the same accounting techniques used to compute net returns from timber sales on the Gallatin National Forest.

12. In many situations, liability protection is considered a normal cost of the activity. Businesses elect to buy liability insurance because the expected costs of a lawsuit exceed the insurance costs. These insurance premiums become a cost of doing business and are reflected in prices. If consumers are not willing to pay the price, including insurance costs, then the product will not be supplied. If ranchers are precluded from charging for fishing on their property, then they are not adequately compensated for the increased liability and, therefore, they supply less recreational opportunities.

13. Donald Woutat, "Stakes Are High in the Battle Over Oil Exploration in Alaska National Wildlife Refuge," *Bozeman Daily Chronicle* (Montana), November 5, 1987.

14. Victor H. Ashe, "Needs and Opportunities for Outdoor Recreation," in *Transactions of the Fifty-first North American Wildlife and Natural Resources Conference*, ed. Richard E. McCabe (Washington, D.C.: Wildlife Management Institute, 1986), 14.

15. Harold Demsetz, "Toward a Theory of Property Rights," *American Economic Review* 57 (May 1967): 348.

16. In the natural resource arena, the traditional arguments against the market provision of natural resource amenities have focused on public goods

and common property arguments. Public goods are cases where existing property rights do not allow exclusion to capture the real demand for the good. Common property is a case where property rights simply do not exist. The common property arguments do not go far enough in asking what obstacles stand in the way of establishing private property rights.

17. Randy Simmons and Urs Kreuter, "Save an Elephant—Buy Ivory," *Washington Post*, October 1, 1989.

18. "As the Cattle Business Weakens, Ranchers Turn Their Land Over to Recreational Use," *Wall Street Journal*, August 27, 1985, 33.

19. Tom Blood and John Baden, "Wildlife Habitat and Economic Institutions: Feast or Famine for Hunters and Game," *Western Wildlands* 10 (Spring 1984): 13.

20. "Where the Antelope Roam," *National Wildlife Federation: Annual Report, 1984* (Washington, D.C.: National Wildlife Federation, 1984), 8.

21. L. Jack Lyon et al., *Coordinating Elk and Timber Management: Final Report of the Montana Cooperative Elk-Logging Study, 1970–1985* (Bozeman: Montana Department of Fish, Wildlife, and Parks, 1985), 37–48; Donald Leal, "Saving an Ecosystem: From Buffer Zone to Private Initiatives," in *The Yellowstone Primer: Land and Resource Management in the Greater Yellowstone Ecosystem*, ed. John A. Baden and Donald Leal (San Francisco, Calif.: Pacific Research Institute for Public Policy, 1990), 35.

22. President's Council on Environmental Quality, *Environmental Quality: 15th Annual Report of the Council on Environmental Quality* (Washington, D.C.: U.S. Government Printing Office, 1984), 426.

23. Blood and Baden, "Wildlife Habitats," 11.

24. President's Council on Environmental Quality, *Environmental Quality*, 381, 384.

25. Ibid., 383, 384.

26. "Private Clubs Provide Choice Shooting," *Fishing and Hunting News* 12 (April 1982): 2.

27. Robert C. Taylor, Bruce Beattie, and Kerry R. Livengood, "Public vs. Private Systems for Big Game Hunting" (paper presented at conference on Property Rights and Natural Resources, Center for Political Economy and Natural Resources, Bozeman, Montana, December 1980).

28. Kit Harrison, "Group Solicits Landowner Help," *Sports Afield* 193 (March 1985): 29.

29. Jerome B. Robinson, "Sandhill Ducks," *Sports Afield* 198 (September 1987): 144.

30. They assume that the natural environment remains a public good and, therefore, is incapable of attracting sufficient private investment for protection, because it would be too costly to exclude those who do not contribute from enjoying the benefits of protection. But before we assume away markets, we must look at what aspect of the natural environment is being considered. Certainly, the public-good tendency for clean air is apparent, but the so-called public good tendency of wildlife, wilderness, and endangered species habitat is not so apparent in the face of today's rising recreational and environmental demands.

31. *1989 National Directory of Conservation Land Trusts* (Alexandria, Va.: Land Trust Exchange, 1989), iv–v.

32. Gordon Abbott Jr., "Long-Term Management: Problems and Opportunities," in *Private Options: Tools and Concepts for Land Conservation*, ed. Barbara Rusmore, Alexandra Swaney, and Allan D. Spader (Covello, Calif.: Island Press, 1982), 207.

33. Sue E. Dodge, ed., *The Nature Conservancy Magazine* 40 (March–April 1990): 3, 33.

34. M. Rupert Cutler, "Integrating Wildlife Habitat Features in Agricultural Programs," in *Transactions*, 132–40.

35. Terry L. Anderson and Allen Freemeyer, "The Public Trust Doctrine: Recreationalists' Free Lunch," *Institute Perspective*, vol. 4 (Logan, Utah: Institute of Political Economy, n.d.), 2.

36. Jo Kwong, "Private Hunting Provides Public Benefits," *Wall Street Journal*, June 19, 1987.

37. Ibid.

38. Dayton O. Hyde, "Recreation and Wildlife on Private Lands," in *Recreation on Private Lands*, 25.

39. Ibid., 26.

40. *Lake Shore Duck Club* v. *Lake View Duck Club*, 50 Utah 76, 309 (1917).

41. Eric Wiltse, "Irrigation Spells Death for Hundreds of Ruby River Trout," *Bozeman Daily Chronicle*, May 12, 1987.

42. Terry L. Anderson and Donald R. Leal, "A Private Fix for Leaky Trout Streams," *Fly Fisherman* 19 (June 1988): 28–31.

43. Forest analyst Randal O'Toole has proposed a recreational user fee program for the national forests. He suggested a daily fee for dispersed recreation on all national forests, as well as higher fees for high-demand activities unique to individual forests. He also proposed decentralizing the national forest system, an approach that includes retaining recreational user fees and income from production of commodities, such as timber and minerals, by each national forest and an end to appropriations from Congress. See Randal O'Toole, *Reforming the Forest Service* (Washington, D.C.: Island Press, 1988).

7

ECOLOGY AND ENERGY

Prospecting for Harmony

When energy resources are controlled by the political sector, environmentalists are pitted against exploration and development companies in a setting that encourages confrontation. This problem became especially acute during the 1970s when the energy crisis focused a great deal of attention on the overthrust belt in the Rocky Mountains, where the federal government controls nearly half of the land. Even though the energy crisis lessened during the 1980s, exploration efforts on public land continue to fuel the fires of environmental confrontation.

The controversy has reached a high pitch in the battle over whether to allow exploration and development in the Arctic National Wildlife Refuge's 1.5 million-acre coastal plain. Geologists believe that the coastal plain contains between 600 million and 9.2 billion barrels of economically recoverable oil, with a mean estimate of 3.2 billion barrels.[1] The area is also an important habitat for wildlife, including 500 musk oxen, 100 brown bears, a few dozen wolves, 325,000 geese, 300,000 other wildfowl, 62 marine species, and, for brief periods during the summer, more than 100,000 caribou of the Porcupine herd. In response to a 1986 Department of the Interior report recommending that the area be made available to oil and gas development, environmentalists mounted an effective campaign to block final approval in Congress. The debate is still raging.

Although these kinds of confrontations suggest that exploration and development of oil and natural gas necessarily lead to environmental damage, this need not be the case. In fact, there are approaches that enable development to be carried out in a sensitive manner. For example, under certain conditions developers can use directional or slant drilling to prevent disturbance to fragile surface areas such as swamps and marshlands. This approach has been used successfully on the Michigan Audubon Society's Bernard W. Baker Sanctuary. Special applications, such as highly insulated platforms, have also been used to mitigate disturbances to fragile Arctic environments. Continued field research in the tundra region of Alaska's North Slope, the coastal marshes of Louisiana, and the steep mountainous areas of the Rockies has led to new ways of minimizing the effects of oil and gas activities on wildlife and habitat.

Yet, environmental groups continue to battle companies over oil and gas exploration. We will argue that greater harmony between environmental amenities and oil and gas development is often prevented by government policies that give each side strong incentives to engage in a wasteful battle over the control of public resources. We will also suggest policy alternatives that promote cooperation by satisfying the goals of both economic efficiency and environmental integrity.

COSTS ARE SUBJECTIVE

There is no question that oil exploration and production can have adverse effects on the environment. Noise, lights, moving earth, oil spills, and blowouts are only a few of the concerns environmentalists have when exploration and development take place in environmentally sensitive areas. But reducing the likelihood of these effects increases the costs of exploration and production. Slant drilling, quiet mufflers, and interruptions in drilling schedules to accommodate wildlife are costs that oil companies have not been accustomed to taking into account.

What are the environmental costs from exploration and production, and how should the risks of incurring higher costs from accidents be considered? To address these questions, we must understand that an environmental cost results from the *actual* environmental damage and from the values individuals place on affected resources. Damages such as noise from machinery or displacement of land can be reduced significantly by using devices such as mufflers to reduce noise or by reclaiming land to restore the site to its original condition. The likelihood of damages from an oil spill or a blowout will depend on the precautionary measures that developers take. Environmentalists and developers have such conflicting perspectives that they will see the risks of avoiding accidental damage very differently. Developers, striving to keep production costs low in order to maximize profits, prefer lower precautionary costs and are willing to take higher risks for accidental damage. At the same time, if they face the full costs of damage, they are held accountable for their decisions and must weigh the savings of less precaution with the possibility of paying higher costs if damage occurs. Environmentalists prefer a lower probability of environmental damage and, hence, higher production costs. But unless risk abatement represents an actual cost to them, they sacrifice nothing in demanding the lowest possible risk and highest possible cost of production. In the extreme, this means no exploration or production.

While such preferences are understandable, the important question is whether all costs are internalized among decision makers so that efficient levels of oil production and environmental amenities are chosen. The information necessary to assess the appropriate level of environmental damage abatement will vary considerably from location to location and from time to time. Although experts can assess the time- and place-specific environmental and technological constraints, all costs ultimately are subjective and depend on the values that individuals place on resources. Even if everyone could agree on the probability of environmental damage associated with oil development, there is still the problem of agreeing on what the *subjective costs* are.

Consider oil exploration on public land near Yellowstone National Park. For one person, a drilling rig might represent nothing but noise and visual pollution that significantly reduces the value of a visit to the park. For another, the close-up view of the massive, lighted derrick drilling 24,000 feet below the Earth's surface may represent a fascinating contrast between impressive technology and beautiful scenery. And for the "roughneck" whose job depends on oil exploration, pristine mountains or impressive technology may be irrelevant. None of these values is right or wrong; each simply represents a *special interest*.

THE POLITICAL CHOICE

The problem is getting individuals with diverse preferences to accurately and honestly reveal their values in the political setting. A person who considers the drilling site as a form of pollution will most likely claim that "*no* drilling is acceptable in a pristine mountain setting." The person whose job depends on oil exploration may contend that a pristine environment is of little value if he is unemployed or if gasoline is not available to transport people to the woods.

But talk is cheap. If an environmental group successfully curtails oil exploration, then it captures the "profits" associated with the pristine environment but bears none (or only a small share) of the opportunity cost of forgone energy production. An oil company that is allowed to explore for oil without concern for the environment reaps the profits from oil production without bearing the opportunity cost of forgone environmental amenities. Neither side has to face opportunity costs, and both are locked into a zero-sum game (one party's gain is the other's loss). In a political setting, trade-offs between the environment and energy are necessarily confrontational.

Recognizing that politics will determine the distribution of profits from energy resources, both sides will invest time and money lobbying government.[2] But lobbying does not create wealth; it only redistributes it through political action. With so many decisions on natural resource use placed in the hands of state and federal bureaucrats, the transfer game has become extremely important for both oil company executives and environmental leaders who realize that their wealth is affected by bureaucratic decisions.

While this explains the demand for wealth transfers, the role of politicians and bureaucrats explains its supply. Just as entrepreneurs in the marketplace recognize and fill demands for goods and services, politicians and bureaucrats discover opportunities to meet the demands of their constituencies. The constraints on each, however, are very different. Private entrepreneurs provide new goods and services only when they expect the benefits to exceed the opportunity cost of inputs used in their production. Entrepreneurial politicians and bureaucrats also provide new goods and services, but they do not necessarily face the full opportunity cost of their choices. And while environmentalists have argued that we cannot put a "price tag" on wilderness, the fact remains that when the government declares millions of acres off-limits to development there are opportunity costs in terms of forgone minerals, motorized recreation, and other uses valued by individuals.

Consider how these choices are made when a potential drilling site is located in the middle of a private 100,000-acre ranch where the mineral rights are intact. Assume that the ranch has been in the same family for four generations and that the owner has a strong environmental ethic, which means that he cares about the productive capacity of the land as well as its environmental values. An oil company believes there is great potential for oil to be discovered and developed on the ranch. As long as the rights to explore and produce oil on the land are well defined and enforced, it is unlikely that the parties will battle over the right to drill, even though strong opposing preferences may prevail. The owner of the ranch has veto power over energy development, but

84   *Ecology and Energy*

TABLE 7.1   Wilderness Acres Managed by the Federal Government

Agency	Designated Wilderness	Recommended for Wilderness	Under Study for Wilderness
Bureau of Land Management	369,000	400,000	22,400,000
Fish & Wildlife Service	19,300,000	3,400,000	58,000,000
Forest Service	32,100,000	2,500,000	9,300,000
National Park Service	36,800,000	8,900,000	28,600,000
Totals	88,569,000	15,200,000	118,300,000

Source: American Petroleum Institute, *Should Federal Onshore Oil and Gas Be Put Off Limits?* (Washington, D.C.: American Petroleum Institute, 1986), p. 9.

a decision not to allow drilling carries an opportunity cost in the form of forgone royalties. The energy company has an incentive to keep the rancher happy by offering to develop the site in ways that are less harmful to the productive or environmental values of the land; otherwise, it is unlikely to get permission to explore.

The difference between the political and private determination of energy exploration and development is that in politics one side's losses are the other side's gains; with private control, each side stands to gain by satisfying the other's desires. Cooperation replaces political conflict as both sides prospect for harmony.

THE ALL-OR-NOTHING APPROACH

With political choice ruling our federal lands, millions of acres have been closed to "prospecting for harmony." The amount of federal onshore acres that have been *permanently* removed from energy exploration by wilderness legislation has grown from 9 million in 1964 (the year the Wilderness Act was enacted) to nearly 89 million. Add to this the amount of lands removed indefinitely from exploration because of wilderness study classification, and the total reaches over 222 million acres (see Table 7.1). When we include national parks, wildlife refuges, Alaskan set-asides, and miscellaneous federal lands, the total acres withdrawn from exploration stands at 319 million, or 45 percent of the total onshore federal estate.[3]

Much the same pattern has occurred on offshore areas. Not long after the Reagan administration unveiled its five-year offshore leasing program in 1982, a series of congressional moratoria removed from the program millions of acres off the coasts of California and New England. Since then, lawsuits have led to the removal of millions of acres, including some of the best known offshore prospects.

The opportunity costs of removing areas from energy development may be quite high. For example, a 1986 Department of the Interior study reports an expected present value of the net economic benefits from petroleum development in the Arctic National Wildlife Refuge of $2.98 billion. Alternatively, using updated oil price projections and revised tax and financial assumptions, a simulation model applied by the Wilderness Society projects an expected present value of net economic benefits between $32 million and $1.39 billion. The lower yields, which assume a larger number of dry holes, reflect the lower level of optimism by environmental interests. It is evident from the enormous differences in projected net benefits that reaching agreement on energy potential is extremely difficult.[4]

The debate over energy development has taken an all-or-nothing approach that often ignores expected costs. Hundreds of thousands of acres are being either opened or closed to development, with no provision being made for developing small increments of land under carefully controlled conditions. In this setting, it is not surprising that cooperation between environmentalists and developers is virtually non-existent. If environmentalists do not oppose development, they lose wildlands and gain no revenues. If developers succumb to environmental opposition, they lose revenues. The game is essentially zero sum.

Federal oil and gas leasing has also fallen victim to litigation. Legal disputes add to energy costs as federal environmental assessments of proposed exploration and development are challenged in the courts.[5] Under the 1969 National Environmental Protection Act, federal agencies are required to prepare an environmental impact statement for any "major federal action significantly affecting the quality of the human environment."[6] The EIS requirement alone resulted in lawsuits, lengthy delays, and judicial set-asides.

Even though development brings increased economic activity, higher incomes, and a higher tax base, local constituencies still oppose development. The reason for opposition is that the benefits must be weighed against the costs of public services, including increased police and fire protection, roads, and hospitals. For example, in their 1981 study of the regional impact on Alaska of federal offshore oil and gas leasing, Porter and Huskey estimated that the total net burden on the people living in the area before leasing began was between $917 and $2,309 per capita.[7] And this burden often increases when oil development activities decline. Given such a trade-off and given the risks that drilling poses to commercial fishing and tourism, local opposition is understandable.

Federal policy has been extremely ineffective in mollifying state and local opposition to offshore activity. Since 1983, the Georges Bank area off the coast of New England has been closed to leasing by congressional moratorium. In early 1988, a bill was placed in Congress to continue the moratorium indefinitely. Leasing sales off the California coast have also have been held up since 1984 by congressional moratoria and litigation. And offshore exploration was ground to a halt in Alaska by lawsuits brought by coastal communities and environmentalists.[8]

Since the federal offshore leasing program began in 1954, 30.7 million offshore acres—only 3 percent of the federal offshore acreage—have been leased.[9] During the earlier years, this small fraction may have been due to low energy prices and technological constraints. During the last fifteen years, however, significant improvements in technology have made ocean drilling more profitable. Nevertheless, the program continues at a snail-like pace compared to foreign offshore efforts. Since 1964, the United Kingdom has leased 66 million acres of offshore area (including the huge oil discovery in the North Sea) and Canada has leased some 900 million offshore acres.

Current policy under the 1972 Coastal Zone Management Act may do more to exacerbate problems with offshore leasing. The act is, in part, a grant-in-aid program, making available federal funds and technical assistance for the development and implementation of state coastal zone management programs. During fiscal years 1974 through 1982, the federal government distributed more than $489 million to states and territories to help them develop and implement their coastal zone management programs.[10] The legislation also offers states leverage over federal leasing decisions. Section 307 of the act and its implementing regulations require oil companies seeking a federal license or permit to carry out activities that affect land and water uses in a state's coastal zone to present an approved plan before it can obtain a "federal consistency certification."[11] This document must state that the proposed activity complies with and will be conducted in a manner consistent with the program of the affected state. The same requirement applies to a company seeking Department of the Interior approval of an offshore exploration or production plan.

The consistency provision has been used to delay offshore lease sales. In a 1982 lawsuit, the state of California contended that even the act of issuing a lease sets into motion a chain of events that results in oil and gas development, which directly affects the state-controlled coastal zone. A federal district court and the court of appeals for the Ninth Circuit agreed and ordered the Department of the Interior not to issue certain disputed leases in the Santa Maria Basin on which bids had been opened in May 1981. On January 11, 1984, the U.S. Supreme Court reversed the lower courts by ruling that the mere act of issuing a lease has no direct effect on coastal areas and that a consistency review is not required before a lease can be sold.[12]

Opposition to offshore leasing stems primarily from the costs and risks imposed on coastal communities. Development does entail local benefits of increased economic activity, additional jobs, and a higher tax base, but this may not be enough to offset the higher costs of public services that accompany such activity, as Porter and Huskey found for Alaska's offshore development program.[13] At the same time, offshore activity poses some risk of oil spillage and can be potentially damaging to coastal resources and the enterprises that depend on them, such as fishing and tourism.

Strong liability rules for offshore damage provide one approach for reducing the effects of offshore development. If private operators know they will be held liable for the *total costs* of damaging the environment and related activities, such as commercial fishing and tourism, then they will find ways to mitigate their exposure to the risk of costly damage payments. Unfortunately, government has softened the rules of liability, making it less compelling for the private sector to employ safer methods in their oil and gas activities.[14] Victim compensation from public funds and the protection of operators through bankruptcy produce incentives that further lessen vigilance over safety. Until third parties have some assurance that strict liability will be enforced, opposition to offshore drilling and oil shipping is likely to persist.

Sharing oil and gas revenues among the federal government, coastal states, and local communities has the potential to mitigate state and local opposition to offshore drilling. Communities must be compensated in some way to offset the increases in infrastructure, police and fire protection, schools, and so forth that accompany a rise in offshore development activities. There are proposals for the federal government to share the revenues of offshore development with states. Revenue sharing must also include compensation to local communities that bear the costs of additional public services from offshore activities.

THE POTENTIAL FOR SENSITIVE DEVELOPMENT

Ironically, at the same time that restrictions on and delays of federal leasing are increasing, there is growing evidence for the viability of environmentally sensitive development of oil-producing areas. For example, James Knight, Jr., has found that exploration and development caused "only short-term localized impacts" to elk in Michigan's Pigeon River Country State Forest. The elk tended to return to drilling areas two weeks to a month after drilling was completed, and they tolerated production more than they did exploratory drilling. Lightly traveled

roads did not appear to threaten the animals.[15] Knight also found that
seismic investigations caused more disturbance to elk than exploratory
drilling and that serious impact was likely if the animals are disturbed
during rutting and calving periods, suggesting that timing can also
mitigate harm.

Another set of studies focused on caribou and moose. Research on
caribou originated several years ago out of concern that migration
routes and calving grounds would be irreparably harmed by the trans-
Alaska pipeline and by energy development in Prudoe Bay. Although
these studies have not resolved the controversy on Alaska's North Slope,
there are indications that although oil and gas operations have altered
animal behavior and movement, they have not significantly reduced
caribou populations, as pre-development critics had predicted. In fact,
caribou populations have increased and the moose have not been
harmed.[16] Studies of other arctic wildlife, including bears, small mammals, birds, and fish, have shown some habitat shifts but no significant
population changes. Certainly the level and approach of these operations
must be carefully monitored and controlled to ensure safety to the
wildlife in the Arctic region, but it is important to recognize that a
low-disturbance operation *is* possible.

Numerous procedures can be used to maintain the environmental
integrity of drilling sites and the surrounding area. Extremely fragile
areas, such as marshes, can be protected through directional drilling,
a technique that allows drilling on a site at some distance from the
target. The Petite Anse 82 well on Avery Island, which is privately
owned by the McIlhenny family, was drilled vertically for about a mile,
then angled horizontally for about twelve thousand feet to protect the
surface environment.[17] At the drilling site, the drilling fluid used to
lubricate the drill bit and circulate rock cuttings to the surface also
sealed off and protected the penetrated rock strata from contamination,
as well as controlled pressures in the well. Protective pipe and casing
were used to prevent contamination of aquifers and other strata within
several hundred feet of the surface. The space between the casing and
the rock sides of the hole was filled with cement to prevent communication between strata, ensuring that fresh water zones were not damaged by zones containing saline water.

Surface effects can be minimized by keeping the drilling pad small
(from one to five acres) and self-contained. Noise and air emissions
can be strictly controlled, safety valves and seals can be installed to
stop the flow of unwanted fluids or gases from reaching the surface,
and dikes and protective liners can be placed to control spills. If the
well is dry, then the hole can be sealed, all equipment removed, and
the site reclaimed, including restoring the original contours of the land,

replacing topsoil, and reseeding with native vegetation. When all this is done, it is very difficult to find an abandoned well.

In offshore operations, tanker operations pose the largest risk of damage to the marine environment. Between 1974 and 1982, accidents costing over $250,000 (in 1987 dollars) for cleanup costs and damage awards averaged seventeen per year. Between 1974 and 1988, seven accidents cost over $10 million. Before 1989, one of the costliest spills was the Amoco *Cadiz,* which occurred in 1978 off the coast of Brittany, France. A federal judge in Chicago ordered Amoco to pay $85.2 million in damages and interest to private and public claimants affected by the accident.[18] The judgment may be reduced, however, because the long-term effects have not proved to be as bad as expected. In ten years, the coastal environment has recuperated.

The costliest transport oil spill in the United States occurred in the spring of 1989 when the Exxon *Valdez* spilled 10,836,000 gallons of oil in Alaska's wildlife-rich Prince William Sound. Exxon spent $1.28 billion (after-tax cost) on cleanup efforts but recovered only 1,604,000 gallons of the oil. In addition to cleanup costs and unresolved private claims, Exxon faces potentially huge fines and penalties under numerous state and federal statutes governing water pollution.[19]

In contrast to oil transport operations, the record of U.S. offshore development indicates that the chance of a major oil spill from a platform or pipeline accident is extremely small. Of the more than thirty thousand offshore wells drilled during the last fifteen years, there has been only one offshore platform accident—the 1969 Santa Barbara spill—that resulted in a significant oil spill. The implication is that by preventing domestic offshore development for the sake of environmental "protection," a greater reliance is placed on ocean tanker deliveries importing oil from overseas—and a greater environmental risk is imposed.[20]

The Santa Barbara spill was dramatic and costly (causing $16.4 million, in 1969 dollars, of damage), but the long-term consequences have not been as negative as expected. First, scientific studies on the flora and fauna of the area have been conducted in the aftermath of the spill and no long-term effects are apparent. Second, the oil industry has developed safety measures for offshore development. Blowout preventers are now used to close off wells if an unexpected change in well pressure occurs. Generally, a series of three or more blowout preventers is connected to the top of the well casing string. Another safety device consists of choke and kill lines, which permit drill operators to control pressures in a well if a blowout is threatened. These lines enable the operator to alter drilling fluid composition and flow in the well.[21]

In addition to high safety standards, expanding research and field testing indicate that offshore oil structures can offer something more than environmental coexistence. Fishery biologists know that fish can be attracted in marine waters by installing artificial reefs, and the construction and placement of such structures are common practices around the world. The Japanese, for example, have been building artificial reefs for over two hundred years to improve coastal fishing. Tenneco towed a retired oil platform from its original site south of Morgan City, Louisiana, to a site 275 miles southeast of Pensacola, Florida, and sank it in 175 feet of water. The Tenneco platform affords a high profile that attracts mid-water as well as bottom-dwelling fish and a large surface area for attachment sites for crustaceans. In addition, active platforms in offshore Louisiana and southern California waters have proven to be excellent attractors for fish and fishermen. Some of the most diverse marine communities in the Gulf of Mexico congregate around these platforms. Oysters, clams, lobsters, crabs, snappers, and many other species desired by commercial and sport fishermen can be found in abundance at the base of these platforms.[22]

FROM PRIVATE TO PUBLIC HARMONY

Cooperation is possible when there are private, tradeable property rights. An example of this is the National Audubon Society's Rainey Wildlife Sanctuary in Louisiana. The Audubon Society, a group opposed to oil and gas development in most wilderness settings, acted differently when it owned the land and mineral rights. The Rainey sanctuary is home for deer, armadillo, muskrat, otter, mink, thousands of geese, and many other birds, and it would seem unlikely that Audubon would allow natural gas production there. But since the 1960s there have been "oil wells in Rainey which are a potential source of pollution, yet Audubon experience in the past few decades indicates that oil can be extracted without measurable damage to the marsh. Extra precautions to prevent pollution have proven effective."[23] In return for allowing Consolidated Oil and Gas to produce on the sanctuary, Audubon receives royalties. Because the Society cares about the environment, they impose strict contractual restrictions on how the gas can be extracted; and because these restrictions cost the oil company more, Audubon receives lower royalties. That is the price they pay for caring for the environment.

The Rainey sanctuary is not the only example of cooperation with industry in the Audubon system. Oil exploration and discovery brought the Michigan Audubon Society's Bernard W. Baker Sanctuary to the attention of Mobil Oil Corporation. In 1975, Mobil Oil approached

Michigan Audubon with a proposition to explore and drill for oil in the Big Marsh. They offered a potential income of up to $100,000 per well with the possibility of four or five wells. Fiscal pragmatists in Audubon argued that Mobil offered a solution to the Society's growing deficits. Others argued that the nesting grounds for the sandhill crane could not be disturbed at any price. When the members voted in October 1976 on a proposed amendment to the bylaws that would have prohibited mineral extraction in all Michigan Audubon Society sanctuaries, a majority of the 2,301 votes favored the amendment. But the majority was not the two-thirds necessary for passage. Then Mobil Oil withdrew its offer.

Five years later things had changed. An article in the May 1981 issue of *Audubon* describes the scene at Big Marsh Lake:

> They had just broken ground for the drilling pad, last time I went out to Big Marsh Lake. . . . Three or four weeks probably, and a sky full of sandhill cranes would be splashing down out there in the marsh. That's why the hardhats were in a hurry. They had to get the pad in, and find what they were looking for beneath the marsh, and get out themselves for a while, before the cranes returned. That's the way it was written in the contract. There was this timeclock, and when the cranes punched in, the hardhats would have to punch out.[24]

Given an operating deficit of $14,000 and the technical capabilities of directional drilling, the Michigan Audubon Society decided to allow Michigan Petroleum Exploration to explore the marsh. Michigan Petroleum was required to drill from a pad a half-mile from the marsh, use high efficiency mufflers to minimize noise, contain drilling fluids, and finance studies of possible environmental problems. The Society expected and received royalties of approximately $1 million, probably less than they could have obtained had they not demanded strict environmental controls. In conversation with Audubon's David Reed, manager of the refuge, John Mitchell captured how thinking has changed:

> We talked into the evening, Reed and I. He said he had come a far piece from Earth Day. I said, so had I. Once in an unguarded moment, he allowed as how he liked the idea of cooperating with industry in a situation where it was likely there would be no adverse impact on the biotic community. And I said that maybe if that kind of situation wasn't on the scarcer side of rare—well, then probably we would find more preservationists behaving like pragmatists. Or at least beginning to think that way.[25]

Unfortunately, with energy resources controlled by politics, examples of such harmony are difficult to find. Extreme groups such as Earth

First! use confrontational tactics to stop development in the national forests, but given the zero-sum nature of development on public lands, even the more mainline organizations are unlikely to be "cooperating with industry." Instead, the rhetoric runs high as both sides battle for the spoils of political allocation.

The problem for public resource managers is that it is difficult to know what values are being traded off in development decisions. Basically, the federal lands (on or offshore) produce two categories of goods: (1) commodities, such as timber, forage, oil, gas, coal, minerals, and commercial fish, and (2) amenities, such as wilderness, free-flowing rivers, endangered species habitat, marine sanctuaries, and other environmental values. For the onshore estate, federal laws such as the Federal Land Policy and Management Act and the National Forest Management Act require that land other than official wilderness be managed for multiple use. Maximization of multiple-use values necessitates equating the additional value from one use to another. If one value is greater, then that use should be expanded relative to others. The implementation of this "equi-marginal" principle, however, requires that decision makers have information on the value of alternative uses. For a rancher trading off wheat production against barley production, the task is not difficult. It is not even hard if the trade-off involves energy because there are market values that provide information. In the absence of market information, however, such rational trade-offs became impossible. If we cannot determine the relative values of amenities and commodities, then there is no way of knowing whether more of one or the other should be provided. Hence, federal statutes requiring multiple-use management and regulation will have to be implemented without the benefit of realistic value information. Opinion polls and surveys are used as proxies, but they do not provide reliable information about the value of environmental amenities because individuals are not faced with actual trade-offs. The respondents bear no actual costs from saying that they oppose development.

Obtaining better information about competing values requires policies that focus on market mechanisms. The first of these mechanisms is the pricing of goods produced from public lands. A host of studies have documented the problems with below-cost timber and grazing activities that are prevalent on many national forests and rangelands.[26] Removing government subsidies for timber and forage extraction would not only reduce government spending but would also enhance the environment. Further, user fees for recreational outputs are either token or nonexistent. Forest analyst Randal O'Toole has proposed user fees for a variety of recreational activities, including hunting, fishing, wilderness hiking, rafting, and camping. Receipts collected for recreation on the 190 million-acre national forest system totaled $30 million in 1986 out of total receipts of $1 billion. But, O'Toole says,

> Most forests could produce fees averaging $3 per visitor day. . . . At this rate, recreation would be the main source of national forest income throughout the Rocky Mountain and Intermountain regions, Alaska, the New England and Midwestern forests, and the Southern mountain forests. . . . At $3 per visitor day, total income from recreation will exceed $900 million in 1990.[27]

O'Toole's figure of $3.00 compares with an average fee of $3.50 per visitor day charged by North Maine Woods, Inc. (see Chapter 6) for similar recreational uses on its land.

If the price of recreational goods reflected demand and supply, then decision makers would have the information they need to determine what combination of outputs maximizes benefits. Setting fees in the public sector to reflect actual demand in recreational goods, however, does pose problems. Consumers always want lower prices for things they consume, and even if prices could be set near the market-clearing level, it would be very difficult to adjust those prices with changing levels of scarcity. People will use the political process to fight adjustments upward and to implement adjustments downward. Finally, without the competition and profits that provide discipline in the private sector, there is no way of really knowing if prices are correct.

Truly innovative solutions to the problem of evaluating and making trade-offs among the many uses of political lands must come in the form of free market environmentalism. Private options for dealing with onshore lands range from variations on leasing to complete privatization. Many researchers and commentators have detailed the advantages and disadvantages of these options, but most have focused on commodity leasing.[28]

If market-based values for environmental amenities are to enter the equation, the leasing and sale options must be expanded to allow environmental groups to lease lands. Under current leasing arrangements, the only way environmentalists can get their voice heard is through politics. If environmental groups could compete to purchase or lease public resources, then their voices might be heard in the marketplace. For example, when a federal tract is opened for energy leasing, environmental groups should be allowed to bid. The groups may want to preclude all development on the land, but they will have to realistically evaluate the opportunity costs. Alternatively, they can sublease for development under their own terms, in which case they have control of the environmental consequences.

TABLE 7.2   Annual Revenue for Selected Environmental Organizations
in the United States

Organization	Annual Revenue
The Nature Conservancy	$109,604,000[a]
National Wildlife Federation	78,753,000[a]
Ducks Unlimited	70,594,099[b]
Sierra Club and subsidiaries	39,282,479[b]
Greenpeace, U.S.A.	33,930,747[b]
National Audubon Society	33,601,514[a]
Natural Resources Defense Council	13,475,075[a]
Environmental Defense Fund	12,902,741[a]
The Wilderness Society	10,928,494[b]
Defenders of Wildlife	4,082,459[b]
National Parks and Conservation Association	3,361,200[c]
Izaak Walton League	1,554,000[b]
Trout Unlimited	2,538,176[b]
Total	$414,607,984

[a]Fiscal year 1989
[b]Fiscal year 1988
[c]Fiscal year 1987
Sources: Figures taken from annual reports.

A common objection to this proposal is that environmental groups cannot compete with giant corporations who can profit from the resources. This argument misses two points. First, purchasing the equivalent of conservation easements on energy resources may not be that expensive. Groups can either accept lower royalties if they win the lease or they can pay development companies to use more costly methods that mitigate environmental impacts. This may be far less expensive for both sides than expensive litigation or lobbying. Second, environmental groups and their members are not necessarily poor. Table 7.2 shows the annual budgets for a number of large environmental groups. Allocating funds in excess of $414 million to leasing or purchasing public lands could give these groups much more control and reduce the acrimony.

Another argument against market competition for public land resources is that a value cannot be placed on environmental amenities. But when the government reserves land from development, a value is being placed on the reservation; the political process has decided that it is worth at least the opportunity cost of the resources left undeveloped. Moreover, expenditures on litigation and lobbying reflect a minimum value for the environmental amenities in question. If environmental groups were using their funds for market competition instead of for transfer activity, then market prices would reflect these values.

A third argument against placing public resources in private hands is that there is a free-rider problem associated with many amenity values. For example, if people who never visit a wilderness area derive pleasure from knowing that it exists, then it would be difficult to directly charge them for the existence value they enjoy. The logic of the argument may be correct, but there is a lot of evidence that people make significant contributions to environmental groups even when they could free ride. These contributions may understate the value of the resource, but there is no way of knowing whether the efficiency effects of an understatement will be greater than those of an overstatement in the political arena where the provision of amenities is subsidized.

Although leasing or selling public lands is the preferable free-market alternative for harmonizing trade-offs, there are alternatives that would overcome objections to a competitive auction of lands with wilderness characteristics. Richard Stroup and John Baden have suggested that wilderness endowment boards be established to take over ownership of some unique environmental assets (the Arctic National Wildlife Refuge's coastal plain would be an example).[29] These boards, comprised of members approved by Congress, would have a narrowly defined mission of protecting and enhancing wilderness values. Each board would have a fiduciary responsibility under common law to carry out a single mission, and it would have the option of allowing alternative uses in an area as long as those uses enhanced the board's overall mission. The example of the Audubon Society's Rainey preserve suggests how energy values might be traded off against amenity values, since marginal adjustments to minimize damage to the environment can be made while generating revenues to support an environmental cause. There is no reason why oil exploration and development could not take place in small, well-controlled parts of existing wilderness areas. A wilderness endowment board would have the incentive to consider what such development is worth and how revenue from it could be used to purchase additional wilderness lands. Furthermore, the boards would have final authority over the restrictions placed on development.

CONCLUSION

Oil and gas leasing as well as other commodity production on public lands has become a casualty of the zero-sum game. Environmentalists, development companies, and state and local interests have been at growing odds with federal authorities over how public resources should be divided. Current policy fosters acrimony rather than cooperation among disparate users of natural resources. Free market environmentalism, with its emphasis on well-defined and enforced property rights, provides an alternative. In the political arena, rights are up for grabs and special interests will compete for them. The inherent conflict in this process can only be eliminated by moving in the direction of privatizing surface and subsurface rights to the federal estate.

NOTES

1. U.S. Department of the Interior, Fish and Wildlife Service, *Draft Arctic National Wildlife Refuge, Alaska, Coastal Plain Resource Assessment: Report and Recommendation to the Congress of the United States and Legislative Environmental Impact Statement* (Washington, D.C.: Government Printing Office, 1986).

2. See Terry L. Anderson and Peter J. Hill, *The Birth of a Transfer Society* (Stanford, Calif.: Hoover Institution Press, 1980); Gordon Tullock, "The Welfare Costs of Tariffs, Monopolies, and Theft," *Western Economic Journal* 5 (June 1967): 242–32.

3. American Petroleum Institute, *Should Federal Onshore Oil and Gas Be Put Off Limits?* (Washington, D.C.: American Petroleum Institute, August 1985), 7, 9.

4. See Anderson and Hill, *Birth of a Transfer Society*; Tullock, "Welfare Costs of Tariffs." The model used by the Wilderness Society used cost data based on a study published by the National Petroleum Council, *U.S. Arctic Oil and Gas* (Washington, D.C.: National Petroleum Council, 1981). A real oil price growth rate of one percent from the 1987 base price of $18 per barrel is employed in half of the trials, and growth rates of zero and 2 percent each are used in 25 percent of the trials for the base-price scenarios.

5. For example, since 1985 oil and gas leases on Montana's Gallatin and Flathead national forests have been set aside because a district court judge ruled that the environmental assessment carried out by the Forest Service was inadequate. See Lettie M. Wenner, *The Environmental Decade in Court* (Bloomington: Indiana University Press, 1982); American Petroleum Institute, *Should Federal Onshore Oil and Gas Be Put Off Limits?* 43.

6. 42 U.S.C. Sec. 4321.

7. Ed Porter and Lee Huskey, "The Regional Economic Effect of Federal OCS Leasing: The Case of Alaska," *Land Economics* 57 (November 1981): 594.

8. Richard Martin, "Resisting an Oil Rig Invasion," *Insight*, March 14, 1988, 17–18; Ken Wells, "U.S. Oil Leasing Plan Is Challenged by Eskimos Trying to Protect Their Culture at World's Edge," *Wall Street Journal*, March 12, 1986.

9. American Petroleum Institute, *Should Federal Onshore Oil and Gas Be Put Off Limits?* 16.

10. Data provided by the U.S. Department of Commerce, Office of Coastal Zone Management.

11. Coastal Zone Management Act (as amended), Section 307, 43 U.S.C. 1456.

12. 52 U.S.L.W. 4063, *Secretary of the Interior et al.* v. *California et al.* (U.S. January 11, 1984), 683 F. 2d 1253 reversed (9th Cir. 1982).

13. Porter and Huskey, "Regional Economic Effect," 594.

14. For example, section 311 of the Clean Air Act limits the liability of responsible parties to $50 million per incident of spillage unless willful negligence or willful misconduct on the part of the operator can be proven in a court of law.

15. James Everett Knight Jr., "Effect of Hydrocarbon Development on Elk Movements and Distribution in Northern Michigan" (Ph.D. diss., University of Michigan, Ann Arbor, 1980).

16. American Petroleum Institute, *Compatibility of Oil and Gas Operations on Federal Onshore Lands with Environmental and Rural Community Values* (Washington, D.C.: American Petroleum Institute, 1984), 57; V. Van Ballenberghe, "Final Report on the Effects of the Trans-Alaska Pipeline on Moose Movements," Special Report 1 (Joint State/Federal Fish and Wildlife Advisory Team, Anchorage, Alaska, 1976); Stering Eide and Miller Sterling, "Effects of the Trans-Alaska Pipeline on Moose Movements" (Alaska Department of Fish and Game, Juneau, June 1979).

17. The National Institute for Urban Wildlife, *Environmental Conservation and the Petroleum Industry* (Washington, D.C.: American Petroleum Institute, n.d.), 5.

18. H. Smets, "Compensation for Exceptional Environmental Damage Caused by Industrial Activities," in *Insuring and Managing Hazardous Risks: From Seveso to Bhopal and Beyond*, ed. Paul R. Kleindorfer and Howard C. Kunreuther (Berlin, Germany: Springer-Verlag, 1987), 80; Bill Richards, "Amoco Ordered to Pay Award of $85.2 Million," *Wall Street Journal*, January 12, 1988.

19. "Alaska After," *Newsweek*, September 18, 1989, 50–62.

20. American Petroleum Institute, *Should Offshore Oil Be Put Off Limits?* 119. The National Academy of Sciences estimated that U.S. offshore oil and natural gas operations are responsible for only five one-hundredths of one percent of the oil that gets into the world's oceans. Tankers and other transportation forms account for 20 percent, and natural oil seeps account for 15 percent. See U.S. Department of the Interior, Minerals Management Service, "Offshore Oil Production Accounts for Little of World's Ocean Pollution" (news release, Washington, D.C., July 26, 1983).

21. Walter J. Mead and Philip E. Sorenson, "The Economic Cost of Santa Barbara Oil Spill," in *Santa Barbara Oil Spill: An Environmental Inquiry* (Santa Barbara: California Marine Science Institute, University of California at Santa Barbara, 1972); American Petroleum Institute, *Should Offshore Oil Be Put Off Limits?* 124–5, 134–5.

22. The National Institute for Urban Wildlife, *Environmental Conservation and the Petroleum Industry*, 13–15.

23. John Baden and Richard Stroup, "Saving the Wilderness," *Reason* 13 (July 1981): 28–36.

24. John G. Mitchell, "The Oil Below," *Audubon* 83 (May 1981): 16–17.

25. Ibid.

26. See *Forests of the Future* (Washington, D.C.: The Wilderness Society, 1987); "Restoring Degraded Riparian Areas on Western Rangeland," Report no. GAO/T-RCED–88–20 (Washington, D.C.: General Accounting Office, March 1988).

27. Randal O'Toole, *Reforming the Forest Service* (Washington, D.C.: Island Press, 1987), 191.

28. See Marion Clawson, *The Federal Lands Revisited* (Washington, D.C.: Resources for the Future, 1983).

29. Richard L. Stroup and John A. Baden, "Endowment Areas: A Clearing in the Policy Wilderness," *Cato Journal* 2 (Winter 1982): 691–708.

8

GOING WITH THE FLOW

Expanding Water Markets

"Whiskey is for drinkin' and water is for fightin'," Mark Twain wrote. In the arid West, where water is the lifeblood of agriculture, this adage has become especially appropriate as municipal, industrial, and environmental demands for water have come into more conflict. Traditionally, growing demands have been met with structural solutions, such as the Central Arizona Project that cost billions of dollars to deliver water primarily to municipal users in Phoenix and Tucson. But fiscal and environmental reality is forcing westerners to recognize that the days of solving water problems with concrete and steel are over. Colorado Governor Richard D. Lamm described the change:

> When I was elected governor in 1974, the West had a well-established water system. . . . Bureau [of Reclamation] officials and local irrigation districts selected reservoir sites and determined water availability. With members of the western congressional delegation, they obtained project authorization and funding. Governors supported proposals, appearing before congressional committees to request new projects, and we participated in dam completion ceremonies.
>
> In 1986, the picture is quite different. The boom in western resources development has fizzled. . . . Congress . . . has to worry about how to cut spending, not which [water] projects to fund. . . . Farmers are trying to stay

in business and are recognizing that their water is often worth more than their crops. Policy-makers recognize that the natural environment must be protected because it is a major economic asset in the region.[1]

This political, social, and economic climate ushered in a new era in managing water resources in the West. In the face of efforts to curtail government spending and protect the environment, the customary and legal institutions that govern water allocation must foster the conservation and efficient allocation of existing supplies and take water's growing recreational and environmental value into account. These institutions evolved during an era when federal outlays to fund huge water projects made trade-offs unnecessary, however, and they are not up to the task.

For most of the twentieth century, the federal government financed the construction and maintenance of water storage and delivery projects designed to make the western desert "bloom like a rose." The Bureau of Reclamation and the Army Corps of Engineers administer the use of the water from these projects, providing nearly 90 percent of it to agricultural users who pay only a fraction of what it costs to store and deliver it. The artificially low prices for federal water promote waste at a time when water supplies are coming under increasing stress from industrial, municipal, and environmental demands. And despite these demands, the political allocation of federal water has been unresponsive, with few transfers of water made to other uses. What we have learned from the stronghold that agricultural interests exert on federal water is that if water runs uphill to money, it gushes uphill to politics.

The 1980s, however, have seen a major change in water policy. Free market environmental principles have become a coalescing theme among environmentalists and fiscal conservatives who oppose water projects that are both uneconomical and environmentally destructive. This theme was instrumental in defeating the 1982 Peripheral Canal initiative, a project to divert northern California water to southern California. Opponents successfully convinced voters of the high costs of the project as well as the detrimental environmental effects of draining fresh water from the Sacramento delta. Following the initiative's defeat, Thomas Graff, general counsel for the California Environmental Defense Fund, asked: "Has all future water-project development been choked off by a new conservationist-conservative alliance. . . ?"[2] The answer appears to be yes. During the 1980s, new, large-scale federal water projects have come to a virtual halt.

Water marketing can provide a basis for extending the alliance into the 1990s, by encouraging efficient use, discouraging detrimental environmental effects, and reducing the drain on government budgets. Equally important, water marketing can release the creative power of individuals in the marketplace, enabling water users to bring to bear specific knowledge to respond to growing scarcities. As economist Rodney Smith explained, with water marketing "a farmer can apply his first-hand knowledge of his land, local hydrology, irrigation technology, and relative profitability of alternative crops to decide how much water to apply and which crops to grow on his land."[3]

THE PRIOR APPROPRIATION DOCTRINE

As with all aspects of free market environmentalism, water marketing depends on well-specified water rights; that is, rights must be clearly defined, enforceable, and transferable. Clearly defined and enforced water rights reduce uncertainty and assure that the benefits of water are captured. Transferable rights force users to face the full cost of water, including its value in other uses. If alternative uses are more valuable, then current users have the incentive to reallocate scarce water by selling or leasing it. Unfortunately, well-specified water rights are conspicuously absent from the legal institutions that govern the use of the resource. Governmental restrictions produce uncertainty of ownership, stymie water transfers, and promote waste and inefficiency in water use.

By removing these governmental restrictions and adhering more closely to the prior appropriation doctrine, water marketing can provide a mechanism for improving efficiency and environmental quality. The prior appropriation doctrine evolved on the western frontier, where water was scarce and agricultural and mining operations required users to transport water considerable distances from the stream. Responding to the special conditions in the West, early California gold miners devised their own system for allocating water. They recorded each claimant's right to divert a specific quantity of water from a stream and assigned it a priority according to the principle of "first in time, first in right." Under this system, a market for water quickly evolved in the late nineteenth century, but it was short-lived.[4]

In 1902, the system for managing water in the West changed dramatically. The Newlands Reclamation Act ushered in massive subsidies to the storage and delivery of water and sent signals, especially to the agricultural sector, that water was inexpensive and, therefore, less valuable. The act established funding to construct and operate projects that would deliver water to arid western lands. Western irrigators were to repay the costs of the projects through ten-year, interest-free loans. In subsequent years, the value of the loan subsidy was significantly increased when the government extended repayment periods, granted periods of no payment, and used revenues from hydroelectric projects to pay part of irrigation costs. As a result, farmers used the low-priced water to make the desert bloom, and the Bureau of Reclamation expanded to meet the farmers' insatiable demand for water. Massive dam projects were built or proposed for nearly every major river in the West, with little consideration given to realistic benefit-cost analyses. As long as there were potential dam locations on free-flowing streams and as long as Congress continued to supply the funds, scarcity was not a problem.

Today, however, with budget limitations and few undammed streams, new ways must be found to allocate scarce water among competing uses. Water marketing provides a compelling solution. Consider the situation in southern California, where growing metropolitan areas are demanding significantly more water for municipal and industrial uses but are facing restricted supplies. In 1985, with the opening of the Central Arizona Project, water from the Colorado River to southern California's Metropolitan Water District was reduced by 500,000 acre-feet a year.[5] Unless new sources of water for the region can be found, the district is forecasting significant shortages in the 1990s. But there is a solution: some of the water used to irrigate 4.5 million acres in central California's San Joaquin Valley could be delivered to municipal uses.

Transferring water from the San Joaquin Valley could also help solve water quality problems. Encouraged by decades of federal price supports and subsidized water prices, farmers have applied massive amounts of water to their land. As a result, soil quality in the San Joaquin Valley has steadily deteriorated, as water has brought salts to the surface. Trace elements, such as selenium, have been leached from the soil and carried in drainage water. This effect is graphically demonstrated at the Kesterson Wildlife Refuge, where pollution has killed largemouth and striped bass, catfish, and carp and has caused newly hatched water birds to develop crippling deformities. Over the years, the reservoir has been transformed from a fish and wildlife sanctuary into an environmental disaster.[6]

Solving the problems of deteriorating water and soil quality will require significant investments in water conservation and cleanup, with costs ranging from $10 an acre-foot for recycling tailwater to $175 an acre-foot for using drip-sprinkler systems. But none of those investments makes economic sense to the region's farmers, who currently pay as little as $5 an acre-foot for irrigation water delivered by state and federal water projects.[7]

The solution lies in a proposed sale of water from the San Joaquin Valley to southern California cities, which currently pay $200 an acre-foot for water. These cities, which expect to pay as much as $500 an acre-foot for water from any new storage and diversion facilities, could continue to pay $200 an acre-foot if they purchased water from San Joaquin farmers, using water that farmers save through conservation. At $200 an acre-foot, farmers could make a profit even if they invested $175 an acre-foot in drip-sprinkler systems. They could also improve the environment by taking damaged land out of production and eliminating the toxic runoff from agricultural chemicals.[8]

Unfortunately, federal policy has discouraged such transactions. The Bureau of Reclamation controls the water, and San Joaquin farmers cannot sell it without the Bureau's consent. The Bureau has funded massive projects that supply 35 percent of the West's delivered water and holds contracts that govern the use of the water, most of which is sold to irrigators at heavily subsidized prices. Irrigators in the San Joaquin Valley, for example, pay only about 15 percent of the cost of their delivered water. Conservationists argue that such subsidies have led to a large over-investment in water storage and delivery, wasteful water management practices, and the over-cultivation of farmland.

It is becoming increasingly clear that the Bureau's subsidies and its ability to veto transfers are standing in the way of efficient water allocation. A 1986 report to the Western Governors' Association concluded that a fundamental change is needed:

> Essentially the Bureau must make a transition from an agency whose workload has been constructing large water projects to an agency that assists the West to make better use of the waters the Bureau already provides. It can facilitate this transition by providing support for voluntary transfers of Bureau–provided water.[9]

But the change is coming slowly, because the Bureau of Reclamation has traditionally depended on expensive structural solutions to sustain its budget and its discretionary power. Supporting water transfers would reduce the size of the pork barrel and threaten the Bureau's power to control western water management. The alliance among the Bureau, Congress, and farmers may be strongest in the context of western water, and it does not appear that it will weaken until new coalitions are formed.

In all likelihood, state legislatures will spearhead any major changes in the system. The 1986 report to western governors recommended that western states take

> significant steps towards the encouragement of water use efficiency . . . in terms of meeting in-state demands for water at the least cost, with due

regard for community and environmental values in water . . . [and] consider implementing a comprehensive program, going beyond water pricing reform, to encourage conservation and salvage of water through markets.[10]

States are already moving in that direction. New Mexico, Colorado, Utah, and California have made it legal for a person or an agency to temporarily transfer surface-water rights to another and reclaim those rights in the future. California's legislature also encourages voluntary water conservation by "vesting the senior right to saved water in the user who saves the water. The law enables him to dispose of that water as he wishes, subject to basic transfer legislation."[11]

There are many indications that water-market solutions are being taken seriously in the policy studies arena. At a 1987 symposium on water policy, one water expert stated that "regulatory and pricing measures can be contrasted with what promises to be a more effective approach, namely facilitating voluntary market transfers of water." Furthermore, "the nation is approaching limits of what can be achieved by increasing supply. . . . This means introducing market devices into the equation."[12] Market allocation of surface-water use is clearly an idea whose time has come.

EXTENDING THE PARADIGM

The same insights that have helped to refocus the debate on the efficacy of markets in the allocation of surface water can be extended to the more complex tasks of allocating instream flows and groundwater. America's environmental awakening and a burgeoning demand for recreational facilities, coupled with the declining quality of many streams, have drawn attention to the importance of instream flows. In many areas of the West, the depletion of groundwater supplies and water contamination due to toxic wastes have raised new concerns about groundwater. Both instream flows and groundwater are thus prime candidates for free market environmentalism.

Instream Flows

At one time, the management of instream flows was restricted to the maintenance of flow levels sufficient for navigation and power generation; today, however, water must meet a broader range of instream uses. For example, adequate instream flow levels must be maintained to sustain fish and wildlife habitats. Maintaining adequate flow levels can assimilate pollutants that remain a threat to many inland waters. The demand for instream recreational opportunities is also growing. A

1985 study by the U.S. Fish and Wildlife Service found that the sport fishing population increased by 27 percent between 1970 and 1980; at that rate, the sport fishing population is projected to reach nearly 70 million by the year 2000.[13] With the value of instream flows rising, the problem is to facilitate reallocation from off-stream uses.

The protection of instream flows is currently regarded as a responsibility of state agencies, which must balance competing uses. This is difficult. Traditional off-stream uses can de-water streams, which can "adversely affect and in some cases destroy valuable in-place commercial and recreational water uses."[14] Understandably, state agencies hesitate to reserve instream flows when such allocations would collide with existing diversion rights in fully appropriated (or nearly so) watersheds. The water efficiency task force for the Western Governors' Association pointed out:

> States are reluctant to try to use their power to regulate to protect and enhance instream flow values on such streams because to do so may invite litigation. Additionally, where states have the authority to acquire existing water rights and to transfer them to instream flow rights, this authority has not usually been exercised because of budgetary constraints. . . . The gap in protection of instream flows on streams approaching full allocation and the absence of protection of these flows in some states, together with water code provisions that encourage consumptive uses, [leaves] instream flows only partially protected in western states.[15]

Given the problems with political water allocation, it is appropriate to ask whether water markets could do better.[16] While property rights to instream flows have not been well defined, remember that the definition process is costly. As the value of instream flows rises and the technologies for monitoring water use improve, the likelihood of having rights to instream flows will increase. A comparison between instream flows and nineteenth-century grazing land is illustrative.

> Sophisticated technologies of streamflow monitoring can serve the law of instream flow rights just as the technology of barbed wire served the nineteenth-century law of private rights in grazing land. Defining the parameters of a right to instream flows is no more difficult than defining the parameters of a right to divert water for agriculture or industry.[17]

One important consideration in the definition of instream flow rights must be their impact on third parties. Particularly important is the effect that instream flow rights could have on off-stream water markets. To appreciate the potential impact of instream flow rights on transfers, consider the hypothetical stream illustrated in Figure 8.1. At the head

106

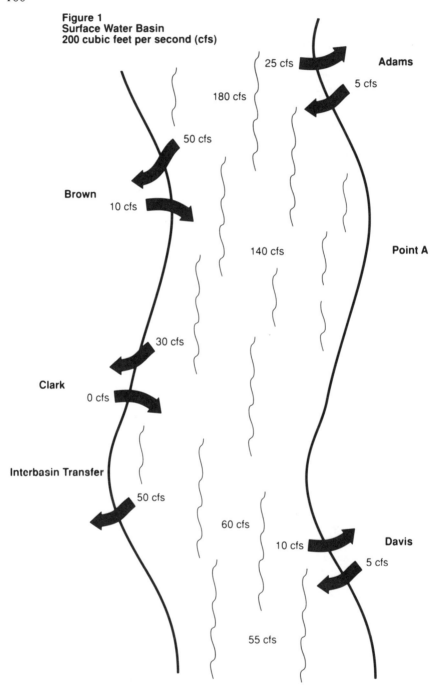

Figure 8.1   Surface Water Basin: 200 cubic feet per second (cfs).

of the relevant portion of the stream, the flow is 200 cubic feet a second (cfs). The stream is fully appropriated; that is, all landowners along the stream have well-established rights to divert the flow amounts shown, provided that they return the amounts shown. For example, Farmer Adams has a right to divert 25 cfs as long as he returns 5 cfs, and Farmer Brown has a right to divert 50 cfs as long as he returns 10 cfs. But if Farmer Davis wishes to sell his flow-use right to someone upstream, he can only sell 5 cfs, his consumption right. If he sold his diversion right, 10 cfs, and all of it was consumed, then the rights of users downstream would be impaired.

The binding flow constraint becomes operative when a claim for 140 cfs instream flow is introduced at point A. If Clark sells his consumption right, 30 cfs, to Adams or Brown, then the instream flow at point A will be reduced to 110 cfs and the instream flow claim will be impaired. The claimant whose rights are enforceable and whose grievance is upheld can capture some of the gains from the transaction between Clark and Adams or Brown. If many claims to instream flows were in place, then the problem would multiply, because each instream claimant could potentially hold up exchanges.

The problems stemming from the binding flow constraint, however, are not unique to instream flows. If Davis and Clark move their consumption rights far enough upstream, then Brown's rights will be impaired. But courts in the West have confronted such problems and have resolved them by considering priority dates and transfer rights. The binding flow constraint has not deprived the prior appropriation doctrine of its utility.

Furthermore, several factors could mitigate the problems stemming from the binding flow constraint. Claims to instream flows in the upper reaches of a river would create fewer problems, because diversions could take place at fewer upstream points. Likewise, claims to instream flows near the mouth of a river would have little impact because they would be subject to the consumption rights of those upstream. Finally, the problems would be mitigated if consumption rights could be transferred without impairing the claimants' rights to instream flows. For example, suppose that Adams wanted to increase his consumption of water and he can purchase a consumption right from Clark or Brown. If he purchases it from Brown, there will be no impairment. Therefore, if many users hold consumption rights between the desired point of consumption and the instream flow claim, there would be little reason to acquire the rights to flows at lower points.

A way for claimants of instream flows to avoid problems with upstream transfers is to purchase upstream diversions and sell them to users downstream. As long as users could not divert water between the point of purchase upstream and the point of sale downstream, the flows between the two points would be enhanced. Such purchases would have a lower value, of course, because the purchasers would have to refrain from reselling the water to users upstream, but that would be the price of preserving instream flows.

Opponents of proposals to establish rights to instream flows also argue that it would be too costly to prevent free riders from enjoying the resulting benefits, which might include scenic value, fishing experiences, and improved wildlife habitat. Nonpayers could reap the existence value, the critics point out; that is, they would have the satisfaction derived from simply knowing that an amenity exists, even if they do not consume or use it. For example, a Bostonian might be happy knowing that the Snake River in Idaho is free-flowing, even if he has no intention of looking at it or rafting on it. Hence, those who try to invest in instream flow rights would have a tendency to underinvest because of the free-rider problem.

All goods have some potential for free riding, and the free-rider problem has not precluded the private provision of some instream flows. With increasing frequency, private groups have moved to secure protection and enhancement of instream flows. During the winter of 1989, for example, irrigators, The Nature Conservancy, and the Trumpeter Swan Society made such an effort on the Henry's Fork of the Snake River in Idaho. The resident population of trumpeter swans on the river was near starvation, its aquatic food supply cut off by river ice. Additional water from the upstream dam was desperately needed to clear a channel and allow the birds access to their food. Through donations, an estimated $20,000 to $40,000 worth of additional water was acquired to help avert the birds' starvation.[18]

The market process can foster solutions to the free-rider problem because free riders represent opportunities for entrepreneurs who can devise ways of collecting from them. Environmental entrepreneurs in organizations such as The Nature Conservancy and Trout Unlimited play an important role in creating private rights and capturing the benefits of environmental amenities of instream flows. With the right incentives, entrepreneurs in ranching and farming can accomplish similar results. Suppose that a rancher who owns riparian land is deciding whether to increase cattle grazing, which reduces fish habitat by destroying bank vegetation and causing siltation. Motivated by profit, the rancher is unlikely to give up grazing to preserve fish habitat unless he can profit from fishing.

For small streams, the cost of excluding non-paying fishermen is relatively low, making a fee fishing system viable. In the Yellowstone River Valley, south of Livingston, Montana, spring creeks offer some of the world's greatest trout fishing, and sportsmen from all over the world try their hand at fly-fishing on those challenging creeks. Because the creeks begin and end on private property, many of the legal restrictions on private control of fishing access do not apply and upstream diverters do not exist. The private owners, who can collect a fee of between $30 and $35 a day from each angler, have a strong incentive to provide high-quality fishing. Grazing on the stream banks is limited and fishing access is controlled so that wildlife and land are protected, fish populations are sustained, and the fishermen enjoy uncrowded conditions. Comparable experiences are hard to find in areas under public control. On a potentially productive state-owned spring creek in Lewistown, Montana, for example, "free" access has produced the inevitable crowding and a reduced fish population.

A major stumbling block to the private provision of instream flows is the legal precedent for postulating a relationship between diversion and beneficial use. In frontier mining camps, an appropriation could be made by anyone who was willing to use the water, but judicial and administrative bodies gradually established diversion as a prerequisite for beneficial use. In the absence of diversion, they have rejected all private appropriation claims. In a 1917 ruling against a claim to appropriate water for a duck habitat, the Utah Supreme Court concluded that it was

> utterly inconceivable that a valid appropriation of water can be made under the laws of this state, when the beneficial use of which, after the appropriation is made, will belong equally to every human being who seeks to enjoy it. . . . We are decidedly of the opinion that the beneficial use contemplated in making the appropriation must be one that inures to the exclusive benefit of the appropriator and subject to his domain and control.[19]

In 1915, *Colorado River Water Conservation District* v. *Rocky Mountain Power Company* also emphasized diversion. The conservation district had sought to establish the right to appropriate instream flows for the propagation of fish, but in 1965 the Colorado Supreme Court found that there was

> no support in the law of this state for the proposition that a minimum flow of water may be "appropriated" in a natural stream for piscatorial purposes without diversion of any portion of the water "appropriated" from the natural course of the stream.[20]

In 1979, instream flow claims in California were even denied to a state agency and a nonprofit public-interest corporation.[21] In both cases, the

California Supreme Court argued that there was no evidence that there would be a diversion of or physical control over the water.

Having been denied the option of private appropriations, states have undertaken to reserve flows by other means. Idaho appropriates flows through its Water Resources Board, which responds to requests from the private sector, but the political nature of the board makes it difficult for private conservationists to reserve flows at sites where there is interest in future water development. Washington has attempted to maintain its instream flows by giving its Department of Ecology the power to deny or grant conditional permits for water appropriation. The department bases its decisions on scientific criteria, completely ignoring economic factors. Moreover, the monumental task of analyzing data and trying to set base flow levels for all rivers and streams in the state has hindered the department's ability to process appropriation claims; in 1980, it acted on only one of the twenty-six requests it received.

Montana has maintained instream flows by reserving water through public appropriations. The 1973 Water Use Act "authorizes the United States, the state, and [the state's] political subdivisions to apply for water reservations for existing or future beneficial uses or to maintain minimum flows, levels, or quality of water."[22] Water reservations are placed with the state's Department of Natural Resources and Conservation, as are applications to appropriate water. Reservations are reviewed every ten years, but there does not appear to be much flexibility once the reservations are established.

Although most states have agencies with the power to claim unappropriated water or reserve water for instream flows, the Colorado Water Conservation Board must apply for rights in unappropriated flows or purchase existing rights (state law forbids the board to acquire such rights through eminent domain). In addition, the board must provide evidence that each of its requests for water would involve a beneficial use. It can purchase rights at market rates, but because state revenues are used for such purchases, decision makers are able to ignore the full opportunity costs of their actions.[23]

Nearly all states have disallowed private ownership of instream flows, but pressures are building to change this. Notwithstanding the free-rider argument, innovative contractual arrangements can overcome the problems with privately providing public goods, as Ducks Unlimited, Trout Unlimited, and The Nature Conservancy have demonstrated. To maintain adequate instream flows, The Nature Conservancy purchased and retired the diversion rights for Boulder Creek in Colorado (it then had to turn the rights over to the Colorado Water Conservation Board because of the prohibition on private ownership of instream flows). The

Nature Conservancy has also been diligently bargaining for rights to instream flows to help preserve the endangered humpback chub on the Gunnison River and the squawfish on the Yampa River. In the Gunnison River case,

> agreement has already been reached with Pittsburgh and Midway Coal Company (P&M) for the donation of a large conditional water right to the Conservancy for instream flow, and a covenant is in effect preventing development of the remaining P&M water rights in the Gunnison Gorge. When the donation is completed, the Conservancy will apply to the state water court for a change in use from commercial to instream flow.[24]

But the right will have to be turned over to the Colorado Water Conservation Board. If The Nature Conservancy was allowed to hold the right, considerable flexibility in responding to changing requirements could be added to the water allocation process. The Conservancy could more easily change the location of the right through transfers or use it in bargaining for future habitat needs without the burden of political constraints.

Claimants of private instream flows could purchase consumption rights to flows upstream from the minimum flow point and sell them to parties downstream. They could also purchase and release stored upstream water during low flow periods. During a recent drought in Texas, for example, resort owners along the Guadalupe River jointly purchased water from an upstream authority and agreed to release enough water from an upstream lake to increase the river's instream flow from 20 to 100 cfs. Another example occurred in 1987, when senior rights holders de-watered the Ruby River in southwestern Montana, causing a major fish kill. The state's Department of Natural Resources and Conservation eventually increased the flow, but that solution was temporary and has created conflicts. A market for instream flow rights would have improved the situation.[25]

The amount of flow needed to prevent the fish kill on the Ruby was relatively small—150 cfs—and the marginal value of such water, even during a drought, is fairly low. In fact, while the fish were dying, local irrigators had water standing in their fields. If an organization such as Trout Unlimited had been able to purchase some of the standing water, the farmers would have had a very different incentive. But Montana's water laws stood in the way. If an individual or an organization had purchased water and left it in the river, then junior rights holders whose claims had not been fully met could have diverted it. Under the current system, would-be instream flow claimants have no way to exercise their demands, and senior diverters have no incentive to leave marginal water in the river. The experience on the Ruby followed by another drought year led a coalition of environmentalists and recreationists to support legislation to allow the Montana Department of Fish, Wildlife, and Parks to lease water on a short-term basis. If the leasing system works, it may clear the path for private groups to lease water and expand water marketing for instream flows.

The use of markets has been more pervasive in England and Scotland, where scarcity has encouraged the development of property rights to fishing sites. With the demand for fishing opportunities rising, "there are few landowners . . . who can afford to ignore the commercial aspect of the sporting rights which they own."[26] It has become worthwhile for British landowners to incur the costs of specifying and enforcing contractual arrangements that govern fishing. As a result, many private, voluntary associations have been formed to purchase fishing access rights.

> In the 1960s and 1970s, smaller, privately managed fisheries that offered exclusivity in exchange for higher rod fees began to break out like an aquatic rash around [England]. Now every city and major town . . . has first-rate trout fishing within easy reach and at an affordable price.[27]

In Scotland, "virtually every inch of every major river and most minor ones is privately owned or leased, and while trespassing isn't quite as serious a crime as first-degree murder or high treason, it isn't taken lightly."[28] As of 1981, a fisherman in Grantown-on-Spey, England, could

> join the local angling association by paying a weekly fee of about $25 and be free to fish any of seven miles of association water. Sometimes, too, hotels and inns own or lease a stretch of river for their guests or make arrangements with the local owner of fishing rights.[29]

In Great Britain, angling is an accessory right to riparian ownership, and fishing rights can be leased to nonriparian landowners. The recent successes there suggest that the riparian doctrine still has merit as a means of limiting access to streams and protecting fish and wildlife habitats. The British system serves to enhance recreational opportunities, because such instream activities as fishing involve real opportunity costs that decision makers are forced to take into account when they consider the merits of water uses.

Unfortunately, the possibility of using the British system in the United States and increasing the recreational and environmental value of instream flows is precluded by adherence to the public trust doctrine. That doctrine attenuates landowner rights, obstructs the provision of the use of private instream flows, and destabilizes the system for appropriating diversion rights, all in the name of public rights held in trust by the government. Because the premise of the doctrine is that the public possesses rights superior to any private claims, private rights are subjugated to public rights. The people retain sovereignty over public resources and the use of such resources; therefore, the state can neither exercise that sovereignty nor delegate authority to individuals in the form of property rights.

The rationale for the public trust doctrine initially made economic sense. If anyone had been able to claim a right to a one-foot strip of land across the Mississippi River, he would have had the power to control commerce on the river. Thus, early courts disallowed such claims in the interest of promoting commerce and navigation and preventing monopolies. Until 1983, the doctrine was applied almost exclusively to issues involving navigable waterways. But in that year, in *National Audubon Society* v. *Superior Court of Alpine County, California* was forced to restrict diversions from the Mono Lake watershed on the grounds that the state had a public trust relationship to the environment and wildlife of the lake.[30] The California Supreme Court's decision gave environmentalists and recreationists a precedent for establishing public rights through the public trust doctrine.

In 1984, two Montana Supreme Court decisions applied the doctrine in a way that has had a significant impact on the conflict between private property rights and governmental power. *Montana Coalition for Stream Access* v. *Curran* and *Montana Coalition for Stream Access* v. *Hildreth* paved the way for legislation that has opened all streams in the state to public access. The first decision stated that

> streambed ownership by a private party is irrelevant. If the waters are owned by the state and held in trust for the people by the state, no private party may bar use of those waters by the people. The Constitution and the public trust doctrine do not permit a private party to interfere with the public's right to recreational use of the surface of the state's waters.[31]

Through these two decisions and subsequent legislation, the state effectively deprived riparian landowners of the right to restrict access to their streams and obscured the criteria for recreational use. A compromise bill, passed in 1985, designated 17,000 miles of Montana waters for public access and put the regulation of the property in the hands of the Department of Fish, Wildlife and Parks.

The application of the public trust doctrine enunciated in the Mono Lake decision and extended in the Montana legislation has been creeping into legal findings and laws all over the West. Instead of being given incentives to cooperate and to create fish and wildlife habitats and recreation facilities, landowners and recreationalists are being pitted against each other in bitter, no-win struggles. The public trust doctrine is being used to circumvent established property rights in water diversion and to preempt the prior appropriation doctrine. Its current application stifles the possibility of using water markets to allocate off-stream diversions and thwarts the prospects for the private preservation of instream flows.

Groundwater

As with the allocation of instream flows, there has been practically no opportunity for the market to play a role in allocating groundwater in the United States. Free market environmentalism helps explain what has hindered market application and how markets could alleviate problems in the allocation of that resource.

Groundwater use has been steadily increasing for forty years. In the West, groundwater accounts for 46 percent of the municipal and 44 percent of the industrial water supplies. Due to the rising demand, extraction now exceeds natural recharge in most of the West's groundwater basins. Kenneth Frederick has estimated that withdrawal in western aquifers exceeds resupply by more than 22 million acre-feet each year. Groundwater depletion is occurring in urban as well as rural parts of the United States. In Tucson, Arizona, the largest American city that is entirely dependent on groundwater, the water table has fallen by 50 meters since 1960; the water table beneath Dallas–Fort Worth has fallen by 150 meters. Similar conditions exist in California's San Joaquin Valley, in Houston, Texas, and in Savannah, Georgia. One of the most dramatic cases of depletion is occurring in the Ogallala aquifer, which stretches from South Dakota to northwest Texas. Since 1940, that enormous subsurface reserve has been tapped for irrigation, and withdrawal in northern Texas and southwestern Oklahoma exceeds recharge by 22 percent in normal years and by 161 percent in dry years. Withdrawal for the North Platte basin exceeds recharge by 40 percent; in the South Platte, the figure is 60 percent.[32]

Does such groundwater depletion make good economic sense? From an efficiency standpoint, the answer may be yes.[33] "Mining" a basin is appropriate if the future value of the water is expected to be lower than the current value. The real problem in groundwater management is to induce users to optimize the rate of extraction. Optimization occurs when the net marginal value of the water being extracted is equal to the net marginal value of the water being left in a basin for future extraction.

A major difficulty in allocating groundwater is that the future value of water left in a basin is not captured solely by individuals who decide to conserve. Water left for the future is a fugitive resource; that is, its value can be captured by anyone. Suppose that an individual must decide whether to leave water in a basin in order to offset future shortfalls in precipitation or surface-water availability. Even if he believes that the current consumption value is less than the discounted future insurance value, his incentive to leave water in the basin is reduced by the knowledge that other users can pump the water immediately. Each individual realizes that anything he leaves behind may be consumed by others. In the absence of secure ownership claims, future value gets zero weight in the calculus.

Groundwater users cannot optimize the rate of extraction unless the rights to water in a basin are clearly defined by water institutions and the courts. Only then can users accurately calculate the current and future value of groundwater supplies. Thus, the first step in solving the problem of depletion is to secure well-defined rights in groundwater use, which in turn will facilitate market transfers.

To gain an understanding of the present property rights structure, it is important to realize that the underpinnings of groundwater law are found in English common law. Because little was known about the hydrology of groundwater, rights to groundwater were assigned to the owner of the overlying land. As Frank Trelease has pointed out, "It was in the light of this scientific and judicial ignorance that the overlying landowner was given total dominion over his 'property,' that is, a free hand to do as he pleased with water found within his land, without accounting for damage."[34] When groundwater rights either are not assigned or are assigned on the basis of overlying land, the common-pool problems can become severe. Each individual achieves the greatest net benefits by pumping water earlier than the others, because the lift costs increase as the level is lowered. The "tragedy of the commons" occurs because each individual has an incentive to pump water earlier than everyone else, so the supply is rapidly depleted.

Such poorly defined rights were harmless as long as there was little demand for groundwater; but as demand increased, the changes that were made to manage the resource did not lead to efficient groundwater use. For example, owners of overlying land have been granted rights to groundwater on the basis of "reasonable use." The problem with the rule of reasonable use is that the interpretation of reasonableness has been subjected to the whims of judges and administrators, which has made the tenure of rights uncertain. In addition, the equal rights provision has usually been interpreted to mean that water use was restricted to overlying land and could not be transferred elsewhere.

Conservation could be served if a system of property rights in groundwater was developed that was similar to the prior appropriation doctrine. Economist Vernon Smith has taken us a step in this direction with his proposal to issue property deeds for two rights: a share of the total water stock in a basin and a share of the average annual recharge flow of the basin. The maximum initial allocations of each component would be proportional to users' pumping rates during a prior period. In the Tucson Basin in Arizona, using a base period of 1975, the initial allocations would be a function of the 224,600 acre-feet of water extracted during that year. If an individual had used $x(i)$ acre-feet, his proportion, $P(i)$, would be $x(i)/224,600$. He would thus be entitled to receive a property deed for a stock right in proportion, $P(i)$, to the Tucson Basin's total water stock, which was approximately 30 million acre-feet in 1975, and a property deed for a flow right in proportion, $P(i)$, to the basin's average annual recharge flow, 74,600 acre-feet. Basing the initial allocations on prior use, however, could promote water waste, as potential rights holders would be encouraged to race to the pump house.[35] To prevent this, the initial allocations could be based on the proportion of a user's land that overlies an aquifer rather than on prior use.

In order to enforce the newly defined rights, metered pumps could be used and periodic readings taken. At the end of each year, an adjustment could be made by subtracting a user's share of the total recharge flow from the amount he had used. Stream flows or other sources of recharge could be used to estimate the total recharge flow for a given year. Those who pumped more water than they owned could be fined or could have their overdraw subtracted from future entitlements with interest charged.

Allowing transfers of property rights in stocks and flows would promote efficiency, because users would have an incentive to compare the opportunity costs of various uses. Furthermore, groundwater users would have a greater opportunity to stabilize water levels if they could make exchanges with outside suppliers, which users of surface water in certain states are already permitted to do. They could adjust their stocks and flows by making purchases during dry years and by selling temporary shares during wet years. As with surface-water exchanges, groundwater exchanges would have to be based on consumption criteria in order to protect buyers and sellers against third-party effects. An additional benefit of the exchange system is that the risk of dry years would be distributed among many producers and consumers. Risk-averse parties would have an incentive to acquire or hold greater shares in groundwater stocks and flows. The water market would thus incorporate a voluntary savings plan that permitted users to guard against water shortages.

But the assignment of property rights in stocks and flows would not necessarily solve all the common-pool problems. A holder of a title to a stock of water could still face high extraction costs imposed by the usage rates of other pumpers. Such third-party effects could be lessened through unitization, a contractual arrangement that evolved in oil recovery to mitigate common-pool problems.[36] Under such an arrangement, all parties would contract to use agreed-upon methods of extraction and delivery and to share the costs. Some wells would be shut down and others would remain operational. Those wells left open would be strategically chosen to prevent the cone-of-depression problem, wherein pumping from one well draws water from adjacent wells. Each party's share of the lift costs would be based on his usage rate. For that reason, unitization might entail higher delivery costs, but it would also foster increased water conservation and thus lower lift costs.

Of course, because unitization would require the cooperation of all shareholders of groundwater, negotiating such agreements would entail higher transaction costs than negotiating two-party contracts. Increases in the value of groundwater and the cost of excessive water withdrawals, however, might justify proceeding with unitization, at least for small basins. What is important at this stage is to remove and to refrain from creating legal obstructions to the evolution of such arrangements. That means getting rid of restrictions on overlying land and criteria for reasonable use and choosing a set of rules that would enhance the specificity, enforceability, and transferability of property rights.

CONCLUSION

During the 1980s, the management of water in the West entered a new era. Demands for limited water supplies, environmental concerns, the federal debt, and the incidence of legal conflicts over water have all increased, and a troubled farm economy was cursed with over-production. By far, the biggest impetus for change in water institutions has been the increase in environmental and recreational demand. As Environmental Defense Fund economist Zach Willey put it, "We've had 100 years of [water] development, and the environment's been kicked around pretty bad." But trying to rehabilitate the environment means recognizing all water interests. Willey concluded: "You're not going to do it by wholesale taking away of resources from industry and farmers. . . . You're going to do it through a system of incentives." Willey's approach is to "go out and make some deals," but before that can be accomplished institutional reforms are needed.[37] The Bureau of Reclamation holds claim to 35 percent of the water delivered in the West, which is being supplied at highly subsidized prices. To make matters worse, trade that would transfer water to higher-valued alternatives is being stymied. Neither of those conditions is compatible with conservation or efficient allocation.

In order to reap the advantages of the market, policy makers must find ways to define property rights in water, enforce them, and make them transferable—and then guard against doctrines that erode these principles. The prior appropriation doctrine supports these principles, but the public trust doctrine is eroding them. By limiting the application of the public trust doctrine, by extending the application of the prior appropriation doctrine to instream flows, by unitizing extraction efforts and instituting clearly defined property rights in groundwater basins, and by reducing the impediments to exchange, policy makers could vastly improve the nation's water allocation system. The development of coalitions that could bring about the necessary institutional reforms would be enhanced by the realization that efficient water markets could reduce not only environmental degradation but also budget deficits and the role of government.

NOTES

1. Richard D. Lamm, "Foreword," in *Western Water: Tuning the System*, by Bruce Driver (Denver: Western Governors' Association, 1986), ii.

2. Thomas J. Graff, "Future Water Plans Need a Trickle-Up Economizing," *Los Angeles Times*, June 14, 1982, V-2.

3. Rodney T. Smith, *Trading Water: The Legal and Economic Framework for Water Marketing* (Claremont, Calif.: Claremont McKenna College, Center for Study of Law Structures, 1986), 26.

4. See Terry L. Anderson, "Institutional Underpinnings of the Water Crisis," *Cato Journal* 2 (Winter 1983): 759–92.

5. Timothy H. Quinn, "Water Exchanges and Transfers to Meet Future Water Demands in Southern California" (paper presented at conference on Water Marketing, Lowell Thomas Law Center, Denver, September 24–26, 1986), 2.

6. Richard W. Wahl, *Markets for Federal Water: Subsidies, Property Rights and the Bureau of Reclamation* (Washington, D.C.: Resources for the Future, 1989), 197–219.

7. Zach Willey, "Economic Common Sense Can Defuse the Water Crisis," *EDF Letter* (Environmental Defense Fund), March 1987, 7.

8. Ibid. See also B. Delworth Gardner, "Assessing Salinity and Toxic-element Disposal Problems in the San Joaquin Valley," *Applied Agricultural Research* 2, no. 1 (1987): 20–31.

9. Driver, *Western Water*, xi.

10. Ibid., viii–ix.

11. Ibid., 29.

12. Richard W. Wahl, "Voluntary Market Transfers of Federally Supplied Water" (paper presented at symposium on Evolving Issues in Water Policy, Congressional Research Service, Washington, D.C., February 13, 1987), 2; Kenneth D. Frederick, "The Legacy of Cheap Water" (paper presented at symposium on Evolving Issues in Water Policy, Congressional Research Service, Washington, D.C., February 13, 1987), 4.

13. Zach Taylor, "Hunting and Fishing in the Year 2000," *Sports Afield* 195 (February 1986): 81.

14. R. W. Johnson, "Public Trust Protection for Stream Flows and Lake Levels," *University of California at Davis Law Review* 14 (1980): 256–7.

15. Driver, 33–34.

16. See Terry L. Anderson and Ronald N. Johnson, "The Problem of Instream Flows," *Economic Inquiry* 24 (October 1986): 535–54.

17. James Huffman, "Instream Uses: Public and Private Alternatives," in *Water Rights: Scarce Resource Allocation, Bureaucracy, and the Environment*, ed. Terry L. Anderson (San Francisco: Pacific Institute for Public Policy Research, 1983), 275.

18. Terry L. Anderson, "Trumpeting Water Markets," *Orvis News* (1989). See also Ken Wiley, "Untying the Western Water Knot," *The Nature Conservancy Magazine* 40 (March–April 1990): 5–13.

19. *Lake Shore Duck Club* v. *Lake View Duck Club*, 50 Utah 76, 166, p. 309 (1917).

20. 158 Colo. 331, 406 P. 2d 798 (1965).

21. *Fullerton* v. *California State Water Resources Control Board*, 90 Cal. App. 3d 590, 153 Cal. Rptr. 518 (1979); *California Trout, Inc.* v. *State Water Resources Control Board*, 90 Cal. App. 3d 816, 153 Cal. Rptr. 672 (1979).

22. Huffman, "Instream Uses," 254–5.

23. John Baden and Rodney Fort, "Natural Resources and Bureaucratic Predators," *Policy Review* 11 (Winter 1980): 69–82.

24. Steven J. Shupe and John A. Folk-Williams, "Public Interest Perspective: Instream Flow Acquisitions by the Nature Conservancy," *Water Market Update* (March 1980), 10.

25. *Dallas Times Herald*, July 16, 1984, B3; Eric Wiltse, "Irrigation Spells Death for Hundreds of Ruby River Trout," *Bozeman Daily Chronicle* (Montana), May 12, 1987, 3.

26. Douglas Southerland, *The Landowner* (London: Anthony Bond, 1968), 110.

27. Brian Clarke, "The Nymph in Still Water," in *The Masters of the Nymph*, ed. J. M. Migel and L. M. Wright (New York: Nick Lyons, 1979), 219.

28. Ed Zern, "By Yon Bonny Banks," *Field and Stream* 86 (September 1981): 120.

29. Ibid., 120, 136.

30. 33 Cal. 3d 419, 658 P. 2d 709 (1983).

31. 682 P. 2d 170 (Mont. 1984); 684 P. 2d 1088 (Mont. 1984).

32. Kenneth D. Frederick, "The Future of Western Irrigation," *Southwestern Review of Management* 7 (Spring 1981): 21; Stephen Fenichell, "The Dry Season," *Northwest Orient* (August 1986): 16; Bruce Beattie, "Irrigated Agriculture and the Great Plains: Problems and Policy Alternatives," *Western Journal of Agricultural Economics* 6 (December 1981): 291.

33. See Terry L. Anderson, Oscar Burt, and David Fractor, "Privatizing Groundwater Basins: A Model and Its Applications," in *Water Rights.*

34. Frank J. Trelease, "Developments on Groundwater Law," in *Advances in Groundwater 'Mining' in the Southwestern States*, ed. Z. A. Saleem (Minneapolis: American Water Resources Association, 1976), 272.

35. Terry L. Anderson and Peter J. Hill, "Privatizing the Commons: An Improvement?" *Southern Economics Journal* 50 (October 1983): 438–50.

36. Stephen N. Wiggins and Gary D. Libecap, "Oil Field Unitization: Contractual Failure in the Presence of Imperfect Information," *American Economic Review* 75 (June 1985): 370.

37. Quoted in Richard Conniff, "A Deal That Might Save a Sierra Gem," *Time*, April 3, 1989.

9

HOMESTEADING THE OCEANS

As one of the world's largest commons, the oceans provide a challenge for free market environmental solutions. Outside the territorial limits of sovereign countries, only weak treaties limit the use of ocean resources for fishing, mineral or energy development, shipping, and garbage disposal. With few restrictions on entry, a tragedy of the commons occurs, resulting in pollution and the depletion of fish populations. Moreover, pressure on the commons is increasing, as new technologies raise the returns to exploiting ocean resources. For example, new drilling techniques make ocean oil exploration more feasible; shipping technologies are increasing the size of oil tankers and the potential for pollution; and refrigeration, sonar, and on-board processing allow fishing fleets to deplete fisheries.

Common fisheries are also being exploited by recreational fishing. The Sport Fishing Institute reported that the number of days devoted to marine recreational angling each year in the United States nearly tripled between 1955 and 1985. In fact, scientists contend that the catch of some species by sport fishermen has had a greater impact on population size than the activities of commercial fishermen. The growing influence of saltwater sport fishing coupled with commercial harvesting has intensified pressure on ocean fish.[1]

These rising demands and new technologies are creating pressures to change the rules governing access to ocean resources. Historically, access to resources beyond territorial waters was open to anyone for the taking. Gradually, however, coastal nations have begun to exert greater control over resources lying farther off their shores. The move to "fence" ocean resources began in 1945, when President Harry Truman claimed that the United States had exclusive rights to mineral and hydrocarbon resources lying on or under its continental shelf. What followed was a steady procession of declarations by coastal nations to extend claims to resources lying within 200 miles from shore. These claims have converted coastal waters "from a regime of largely open access and high seas freedoms to one with significant national controls over resource uses."[2]

Like the evolution of property rights to land and water on the American frontier, extending territorial limits is not the final solution to the problem of open access to ocean resources. As economist Ross Eckert pointed out, the conversion from strictly open access to limited access "does not guarantee the improved allocation of ocean resources" but is "only a first step for removing the inefficiencies that result from communal rights." Data from the National Marine Fisheries Service show that all major coastal fisheries in the United States continue to suffer from over-exploitation. Fisheries off the Northeast coast, for example, have experienced some of the worst problems, with a 53 percent decrease in the stock of Atlantic cod and significant declines in haddock, flounder, and pollack.[3]

Table 9.1 lists species in United States coastal waters that were either fully utilized or over-fished according to the criteria of maximum sustainable yield. Of the over-fished species, seven were fished by foreign fleets and six by United States fleets. The declines can no longer be blamed on foreign vessels, however, because their numbers have dropped dramatically during the last eight years.[4] At the same time, total catch has risen, putting pressure on the reproductive capacity of fisheries. After decades of regulation, the striking result has been the continued decline of fish populations. As with reforms in land resource policy, the key to effective fishery policy lies in a property rights approach.

THE OCEAN COMMONS

Ocean fisheries provide the classic case of the tragedy of the commons, because many species of fish are mobile and access is difficult to monitor. Therefore, the rule of capture dominates: any fish left by one fisherman is available to another. Rather than leaving fish to grow and reproduce, the incentive is to harvest the stock before others do. With each fisherman facing this incentive, the end result is for the fish stock to be over-exploited. Whether the population of fish ends up becoming extinct ultimately depends on the cost of capturing the last fish in the

TABLE 9.1   Status of Selected United States Fisheries, June 1974

Fully Utilized

Atlantic Mackerel	Pacific Hake
Red Hake	Atlantic Cod
Silver Hake	Atlantic Ocean Perch
Atlantic Herring	Bluefish
Atlantic Squid	Menhaden
Bering Sea Cod	American Lobster
King Crab	Gulf Shrimp
Tanner Crab	Eastern Tropical Pacific
Yellowfin Tuna	

Overfished

Yellowfin Sole (Foreign)	Haddock (Foreign)
Alaska Pollock (Foreign)	Yellowtail Flounder (U.S./Foreign)
Pacific Ocean Perch (Foreign)	California Sardine (U.S.)
Pacific Halibut (U.S.)	Pacific Mackerel (U.S.)
Atlantic Halibut (Foreign)	Atlantic Sea Scallop (U.S.)
Bering Sea Herring (Foreign)	Northwest Atlantic Shrimp (U.S.)
Bering Sea Shrimp (Foreign)	Atlantic Bluefin Tuna (U.S.)

Source: U.S. Senate, Committee on Commerce and National Ocean Policy Study, *A Legislative History of the Fishery Conservation and Management Act of 1976*, 94th Congress, 2d session (Washington, D.C., October 1976), pp. 358–59.

stock. Because these costs tend to rise exponentially, declining fisheries have historically reached commercial extinction before biological extinction; that is, the additional costs of capturing the few remaining fish exceed the returns, so that it has become unprofitable to continue fishing.[5]

Nonetheless, open access to the resource results in a lower than optimal (if not total depletion of) stock and an over-investment in fishing effort. As long as the cost of taking an additional fish is less than the value of the fish, a profit can be earned. But with open access, not all costs will be taken into account. Another fish taken from the stock can reduce the reproductive capacity of the fishery and raise search and capture costs for other fishermen. Because these added costs are external to an individual fisherman who considers only his costs and benefits, over time there will be too many fishermen in the fishery. In addition, open access encourages a rate of exploitation that will be too rapid. Being the first to exploit the fishery allows the highest returns, because the costs of finding and catching fish will be lowest. This race to the best fishing grounds is often manifest in the form of over-capitalization in radar, sonar, faster boats, and larger nets. The result is lower profits for the too many fishermen investing in too much capital to catch too few fish.

Economist Frederick Bell provided one of the first empirical verifications of over-exploitation of an open-access fishery. In his examination of New England's northern lobster fishery in 1966, he found that an efficient output of lobster would have occurred at 17.2 million pounds. To attain this output, the efficient number of lobster traps would have been 433,000 traps. During 1966, the observed number of traps was roughly double this amount, leading Bell to conclude that "over 50 percent of the capital and labor employed in lobstering represent an uneconomic use of factors."[6]

Oyster fisheries along the United States coast offer a useful contrast of how property rights can improve resource allocation. Using data from oyster fisheries in Maryland, Virginia, Louisiana, and Mississippi from 1945 to 1970, economists Agnello and Donnelley tested the hypotheses that private ownership of oyster beds would generate more conservation and higher returns for fishermen than open-access beds.[7] Under open access, we would expect fishermen to take as many oysters as early as possible, with the result being diminishing returns later in the season. Agnello and Donnelley found that the ratio of harvest during the earlier part of the season to the later part was 1.35 for open-access oyster beds and 1.01 for private beds. After controlling for other variables, they also found that fishermen in the private leasing state of Louisiana earned $3,207, while their counterparts in the common-property state of Mississippi earned $807. These findings support the expectation that private property rights solve the open-access problem.

Could property rights be established for fisheries on the high seas? This kind of approach is not costless, and federal and state governments have overruled groups of fishermen who have attempted to limit entry to their fisheries. Economists Johnson and Libecap observed that even though private territorial rights were missing, fishermen have historically "resorted to informal contracting and the use of unions and trade associations to mitigate open access conditions."[8] Fishing unions were particularly active from the 1930s through the 1950s, implementing policies along the Gulf Coast to limit entry, conserve shrimp stocks, and increase members' incomes. Such efforts by unions and fishing associations eventually met their demise in the courts, which refused to exempt the collective actions of associations and unions from antitrust prosecution.

> A cooperative association of boat owners is not freed from the restrictive provisions of the Sherman Antitrust Act . . . because it professes, in the interest of the conservation of important food fish, to regulate the price and the manner of taking fish unauthorized by legislation and uncontrolled by proper authority.[9]

Although scarcity and competition limit the effectiveness of unions and associations, they can provide an alternative "to limit entry and negotiate price agreements with wholesalers and canneries."[10] For a short time, they succeeded in internalizing the cost of regulation and conserving shrimp stocks. But as this situation revealed, any agreement establishing property rights to resources is difficult to maintain if the government declares it illegal.

REGULATING THE OCEAN FISHERY

Instead of relying on a property rights solution, government regulation has been the traditional mechanism for controlling over-exploitation of the ocean commons. Unfortunately, there are inherent problems with regulation, because the regulators do not own the resource and do not face economic incentives to manage it efficiently. For the fishery, most regulatory schemes have focused on sustaining the maximum yield of a fishery, that is, in allowing the largest quantity of fish that can be caught year after year without depleting the stock. Economists argue that this yield is usually not the yield that maximizes profits, however, because it ignores economic variables such as discounted returns of future catches and the costs of present and future extraction.[11]

On the whole, regulatory schemes focusing on maximum sustained yield and ignoring economic factors have led to lower profits and economic wastes in United States fisheries. Regulatory policies in the United States before 1976, for example, attempted to reduce catch and maximize sustainable yield by raising the cost of fishing. In the Pacific salmon fishery, regulators prohibited the use of traps that were first perfected by the Indians who caught the salmon when the fish returned to spawn. With the elimination of traps, fishermen turned to chasing the salmon in the open ocean. The substitute for traps became very expensive with sophisticated equipment that still allowed fishermen to over-exploit the resource. When the number of fishermen and the length of the season were restricted, entrepreneurs bought bigger boats, sonar, and more efficient nets. To plug these holes in the dike, regulators then established other layers of regulations controlling seasonal limits. The salmon catch was ultimately curtailed, but the approach generated economic inefficiency, as more labor and capital were applied to catch fewer fish. As fishermen were forced to fish longer in less productive areas with more expensive equipment, economic waste reduced the net value of the fishery. In 1965, Francis T. Christy, Jr., estimated that the over-capitalization and over-use of labor in American fisheries cost $300 million per year or, at a 6 percent interest rate, $5 billion in perpetuity.[12]

In addition to the over-capitalization caused by regulations, resources are invested in the regulatory process to favor one group of fishermen over another or owners of one type of equipment over another. The result is often absurd regulation. For example, Maryland oystermen at one time could use dredges but had to tow them behind sailboats on all but two days of the week, when motorized boats were allowed.[13] As economist James Crutchfield observed, the regulatory process has "generated an ever-increasing mass of restrictive legislation, most of it clothed in the shining garments of conservation, but bearing the clear marks of pressure politics."[14] The combined costs of regulations led Robert Higgs to conclude:

> The social resource waste has therefore grown steadily larger over time. Today, from a comprehensive point of view, the Washington salmon fishery almost certainly makes a negative contribution to net national product. The opportunity costs of the *socially unnecessary* resources employed there, plus the *socially unnecessary* costs of governmental research, management, and regulation, are greater than the *total value added* by all the labor and capital employed in the fishery.[15]

Meanwhile, despite these costs, many fisheries in United States coastal waters during the early 1970s were either in trouble or on the verge of it.

The Magnuson Fishery Conservation and Management Act of 1976 tried to remove some of these regulatory inefficiencies by setting a new direction for fishery policy. It extended the nation's marine management jurisdiction from three to 200 miles offshore and encouraged the development of domestic fisheries. Eight regional councils were established with the authority to manage fisheries under their jurisdiction. Notably, the act does not mandate the standard of maximum sustainable yield, but rather stipulates that fishery management plans may "establish a system for limiting access to the fishery in order to achieve optimum yield."[16] Optimum yield in this case must take into account economic variables, such as interest rates, fish values, and the cost of alternative technologies.

While the Magnuson legislation was a step in the right direction, significant problems remain for regulators. The legislation encouraged licensing entrants as a way of limiting the number of fishermen or vessels in a fishery, but limiting entrants "cannot prevent crowding, congestion, strategic fishery behavior, racing, and capital stuffing." Controlling the intensity of effort remains a thorny problem, because fishermen are substituting fewer larger boats for more smaller sized boats. The result is that "rising fish prices constrained by a limited number

TABLE 9.2   Representative List of Stocks Under Management

Geographic Area	Overfished	Overcapitalized
New England	haddock, yellowtail flounder, sea scallops	haddock, yellowtail flounder, American lobster
Mid-Atlantic	swordfish, scallops	swordfish, scallops, surf clams, ocean quahogs
South Atlantic	Spanish mackerel	Atlantic shrimp
Gulf of Mexico	Spanish mackerel, king mackerel, Gulf of Mexico reef fish (notably red snapper)	spiny lobster, shrimp, stone crab
Caribbean	shallow water reef (Nassau grouper and possibly certain trunkfishes)	spiny lobster
Pacific	chinook and coho salmon (selected stocks), Pacific ocean perch	chinook and coho salmon, groundfish (except Pacific whiting)
North Pacific	red king and gulf croaker, Tanner crab, Pacific ocean perch	sablefish, halibut, high seas salmon, king and Tanner crab
Western Pacific	seamount groundfish	bottomfish, lobster

Source: U.S. Department of Commerce, *NOAA Fishery Management Study* (Washington, D.C., 1986).

of vessels, and unconstrained by any sort of territorial limit, has led to vastly increased individual fishing capacity." Even with licensing, regulators find that a few powerful fishing vessels can do in a few minutes what used to take days. The bottom line is that the Magnuson act has not rebuilt the declining fisheries in United States waters. According to the 1986 "Calio study" (named after Anthony Calio, then head of the National Oceanic and Atmospheric Administration), twenty-two fisheries have an allowable catch that could be caught by fewer vessels. This excess catch capacity has also resulted in many fisheries being severely over-fished (see Table 9.2). The study also concluded that the ten most favored species, which have traditionally accounted for three-quarters of the total value of American commercial fisheries, remain significantly below historical levels and continue to be over-fished.[17]

Complicating the regulation of commercial fishing is recreational or sport fishing. With the recent rise in recreational fishing, several fish stocks have come under pressure, forcing regulators in some instances to take drastic action. For example, in 1987 the National Marine Fisheries Service banned commercial fishing of king mackerel after recreational fishermen from Texas through southeast Florida exceeded a 740,000-pound catch limit. Meanwhile, tension has grown between recreational fishermen and commercial interests. Commercial fishermen fear that recreational fishermen under the guise of conservation have become highly influential in setting policy at both the state and federal levels. Recreational fishermen complain that fisheries must not be managed solely for commercial interests and that they have as much right to the resource as commercial interests do. The management districts for both the South Atlantic and Gulf Coast fisheries are experiencing intense pressures from these the two groups.[18]

The conflicts between commercial and sport interests have led to concerted efforts by both groups to gain stronger footholds in regional fisheries management councils. Historically, the regional councils of the National Marine Fisheries Service were dominated by representatives from commercial fishing interests. This dominance may be changing as recreational interests have managed to gain more political influence. Meanwhile, the turf battles have left questions concerning the regional councils' effectiveness in managing fish stocks.

> As the battle between user groups has intensified, many observers have questioned whether NFMS and the councils, in their desire to satisfy every demand for a piece of the resource pie, have lost sight of their fundamental responsibility to protect the health of fish stocks.[19]

POLICY ALTERNATIVES

The preferred free market environmentalism approach to the fishery problem is to allow the establishment of property rights. This approach is certainly not new. Robert Higgs found that Indians along the Columbia River had well-established rights to fishing sites long before whites came to the area.[20] The Indians developed effective technologies for catching the salmon and avoided over-exploitation through intertribal agreements to allow sufficient upstream migration and to ensure sustained spawning. "Legally induced technical regress" resulted from legislation that outlawed traps and effectively eliminated fishing rights. This legislation ran counter to British common law, which had a place for private rights to coastal fisheries.

. . . when we consider that there were already, in 1200 AD, in tidal waters, territorial fishing rights in England and a form of territorial salmon right throughout the world in the 19th century, the legislative process can only be said to have reduced the characteristics of individual fishing rights.[21]

The tradition of property rights is gaining popularity with the growth of aquaculture. With aquaculture, there is potential for increasing fish production while reducing pressure on wild stocks. Because investment in aquaculture requires secure property rights and because property rights are more likely to evolve where the costs of establishing rights are lower, sessile species, such as oysters, have the most promise. As noted earlier, private rights to oyster beds in some states have led to greater productivity.

The emergence of salmon ranching indicates that a solution based on property rights can also be applied to anadromous species that return to their original spawning ground. But before salmon ranching can realize its full potential, property rights problems have to be worked out. For example, a ranch operator has control over his stock only while the salmon are in captivity—before they are released and after they return for spawning. Otherwise, the salmon reside in the open sea beyond the rancher's control. Under conditions of the "open range," the rancher may lose a substantial portion of his investment to natural mortality and commercial and sport fishermen. Some of these problems can be overcome if there is better coordination between ranchers and commercial fishermen. For example, economists Anderson and Wilen demonstrated that "restrictive ocean fishing season, depleted stocks of other species and low public smolt release levels raise the profitability from private aquaculture." They concluded that salmon ranchers would be willing to pay for a reduced season length and for reduced public smolt releases in return for receiving compensation from those who catch ranch fish in the ocean.[22]

This problem is similar to the one faced by British salmon sport fishermen. In many cases, the fishermen own fishing rights on streams, but they are disturbed by the alarmingly depleted salmon stocks that return to spawn. The reductions are the result of increased commercial harvests, especially by fishermen who have netting rights at the mouths of rivers.[23] To combat the problem, the Atlantic Salmon Conservation Trust of Scotland has been buying up netting rights. Most have been purchased from private owners, but some have even come from the crown. The idea of this buy-out program began in Canada, where the federal government bought and retired commercial netting rights in New Brunswick, Nova Scotia, and Quebec. Because the buy-out program is working so well, private interests in Iceland are exploring the possibility of buying the Greenland and Faeroese fisheries and shutting them down completely. The key to this solution is the transferability of fishing rights.

Another approach that eliminates interactions between fish ranchers and fishermen is based on raising salmon in pens. When the salmon reside in pens for their entire lives, there are no losses due to commercial and sport fishing in the open ocean. This method has proven highly successful for the Norwegians, who are the leading international producers of Atlantic salmon. Salmon farmers and ranchers in the United States still face political opposition from commercial fishermen, who have sought government protection of their markets, and from environmentalists who fear that salmon farming will lead to more pollution of bays and inland waters. In 1987, commercial fishermen in the Pacific Northwest convinced the Alaskan government to impose a one-year moratorium on net-pen salmon farms, and protests from local environmentalists in Washington have led the state to impose stringent guidelines in siting salmon farms.[24]

Institutional roadblocks also stand in the way of other private operations. In Maryland, out of some 9,000 acres of privately leased oyster grounds, only 1,000 are in production; 280,000 acres remain public. Privatizing Maryland's Chesapeake Bay oyster fishery faces the problem of weak enforcement of private leases. "It's hard to find an oyster ground that hasn't been poached upon," complained a planter on the Tred Avon River. "It's the main reason why so many people are reluctant to take their ground and invest their money in it."[25] Obviously, to realize the full potential of aquaculture in the United States, institutional barriers must be removed and the defense of private property rights must be strengthened.

Japan has led the race in establishing private property rights in fisheries. The Japanese took bold steps to allow the privatization of the commons because access to foreign fishing grounds was being more and more restricted by legislation such as the Magnuson act. The Japanese government now initiates the property rights process by designating areas that are eligible for aquaculture. The fishermen's cooperative associations are then given the responsibility of partitioning these areas and assigning them to individual fishermen for their exclusive use. Exclusive use allows the owner to invest in improvements and to capture the benefits of their investment.

Another mechanism for assigning rights to fisheries is to establish individual tradable quotas, or ITQs. An individual quota entitles the holder to catch a specified percentage of the total allowable catch. This system is attractive for several reasons. First, each quota holder faces greater certainty that his share of the catch will not be taken by someone else. Under the current system, total allowable catch is established, but the share is determined by who is best at capturing the fugitive resources. With ITQs, holders do not compete for the shares, so there is less incentive to race other fishermen. Second, transferability allows quotas to end up in the hands of the most efficient fishermen—that is, those with the lowest costs and who can pay the highest price for the ITQs. Less efficient producers and inputs move to other industries. As a corollary, ITQs encourage progress in reducing the cost of catching fish. Fishermen who adopt new cost-reducing methods make more money with their quotas and are in a better position to purchase quotas from those who are less efficient. This is in marked contrast to the current regulatory system, which encourages over-investment in the race for fugitive resources.

Several countries, most notably Australia and New Zealand, have implemented ITQs for handling fisheries where regulations have failed. Australia is using the ITQ system for the southern bluefin tuna fishery. Globally, the southern bluefin tuna population had declined from an estimated 650,000 metric tons prior to 1950 to about 160,000 metric tons in 1980. Scientists have concluded that to maintain the 1980 level, the world catch of the fish needed to be stabilized at about 32,000 metric tons, down from the previous level of 40,000 metric tons. To achieve this level, given an expected Japanese catch of 15,000 metric tons, the Australian catch had to be reduced from 21,000 metric tons to less than 10,000 metric tons. In addition, the Australian southern bluefin tuna fishery had so much over-capacity and over-capitalization that it remained unprofitable while taking record catches.

The results from implementing ITQs were very positive. After six months, the fleet capacity in the fishery had been reduced by 60 percent, as those who intended to stay in the fishery bought quotas from those who could earn more by leaving. There was also an increase in the average size of the catch, as operators with access to larger fish bought out operators with access to smaller fish. After the government established the ITQs, the improvements were achieved in the marketplace, without the government determining who could fish, what size fish could be kept, and what methods could be used. As an indication of increased value of the fishery, ITQs began selling for just under $1,000 per ton on October 1, 1984; they sold for $2,000 per ton five and one-half months later.[26]

CONCLUSION

While ITQs offer considerable advantages, determining the size of the total catch remains a governmental function. Fishery regulators determine total catch based on biological sustainability and economic factors. Unfortunately, regulators are susceptible to political pressures from the special interest groups they regulate, who then become important bureaucratic constituents in the budgetary process. The incentive for pleasing such groups by maintaining an inefficient industry size can be strong enough to overshadow the objectives of efficient production and sustainable future catches.

Establishing property rights to the ocean commons will not be easy, but, like the frontier West, we can expect increasing efforts at definition and enforcement. ITQ systems offer a step toward facilitating property rights solutions. In New Zealand, ITQs for the abalone fishery off the Chatham Islands are showing signs of eliminating the commons problem that have plagued the fishery for years. With more secure rights to future harvests, the value of ITQs rose in value by nearly a factor of six from 1988 to 1989. Furthermore, fishermen with more secure rights have formed a cooperative into which its members put one percent of their annual sales for a program to rear and plant young abalone.[27] ITQs make it "easier and cheaper" for fishermen holding quotas "to act collectively" in managing the size of their catch.[28]

Unfortunately, the success of ITQs and collective action by fishing associations stimulate political action by special interest groups who want a share of the growing pie. In the New Zealand case, government officials argue that part of the income from the abalone fishery is a "windfall" to quota holders and belongs to the government. And several indigenous groups argue that their rights to the fishery supersede non-indigenous quota holders and, therefore, the quotas should be turned over to them.[29] Unfortunately, these conflicts focus only on how to carve up the pie, not how to make it even larger. Removing judicial roadblocks to collective action by voluntary fishing associations, implementing ITQ systems, and refraining from further governmental redistribution of fishing rights can move us a long way toward a free market environmental solution to the ocean commons problem.

NOTES

1. Nelson Bryant, "Fishing Licenses Are At Issue," *New York Times*, February 5, 1989; Gina Maranto, "Caught in Conflict," *Sea Frontiers* 35 (May–June 1988): 144–51.

2. Ross Eckert, *The Enclosure of Ocean Resources* (Stanford, Calif.: Hoover Institution Press, 1979), 4.

3. Ibid., 16; U.S. Department of Commerce, National Oceanic and Atmospheric Administration, National Marine Fisheries Service, *Fisheries of the United States, 1986*, Current Fishery Statistics no. 8385 (April 1987); Jennifer

A. Kingston, "Northeast Fishermen Catch Everything, and That's a Problem," *New York Times*, November 13, 1988.

4. U.S. Department of Commerce, National Oceanic and Atmospheric Administration, National Marine Fisheries Service, *Fisheries of the United States, 1986 (Supplemental)* (Washington, D.C.: National Marine Fisheries Service, April 1987).

5. For a classic article on the commons problem, see H. Scott Gordon, "The Economic Theory of a Common Property Resource: The Fishery," *Journal of Political Economy* 62 (April 1954): 124–42. See also Colin W. Clark, "Profit Maximization and the Extinction of Animal Species," *Journal of Political Economy* 81 (August 1981): 950–60.

6. Frederick W. Bell, "Technological Externalities and Common-Property Resources: An Empirical Study of the U.S. Northern Lobster Fishery," *Journal of Political Economy* 80 (January–February 1972): 156.

7. Richard J. Agnello and Lawrence P. Donnelley, "Prices and Property Rights in the Fisheries," *Southern Economic Journal* 42 (October 1979): 253–62.

8. Ronald N. Johnson and Gary D. Libecap, "Contracting Problems and Regulation: The Case of the Fishery," *American Economic Review* 12 (December 1982): 1007.

9. *Gulf Coast Shrimpers and Oystermens Association* v. *United States*, 236 F. 2nd 658 (1956).

10. Johnson and Libecap, "Contracting Problems and Regulation," 1008.

11. See Tom Tietenberg, *Environmental and Natural Resource Economics*, 2d ed. (Glenview, Ill.: Scott, Foresman and Company, 1988), 258–64.

12. J. A. Crutchfield and G. Pontecovo, *The Pacific Salmon Fisheries: A Study of Irrational Conservation* (Baltimore: Johns Hopkins Press, for Resources for the Future, 1969); "The Flaw in the Fisheries Bill," *Washington Post*, April 13, 1976.

13. Francis T. Christy, Jr., and Anthony Scott, *The Common Wealth in Ocean Fisheries* (Baltimore: Johns Hopkins University Press, for Resources for the Future, 1965), 15–16.

14. James A. Crutchfield, "Resources from the Sea," in *Ocean Resources and Public Policy*, ed. T. S. English (Seattle: University of Washington Press, 1973), 115.

15. Robert Higgs, "Legally Induced Technical Regress in the Washington Salmon Fishery," *Research in Economic History* 7 (1982): 82.

16. U.S. Senate, Committee on Commerce, *A Legislative History of the Fishery Conservation and Management Act of 1976* (Washington, D.C.: U.S. National Marine Fisheries Service, October 1976).

17. Anthony Scott, "Market Solutions to Open–Access, Commercial Fisheries Problems" (paper presented at APPAM 10th Annual Research Conference, October 27–29, 1988), 7–8; U.S. Department of Commerce, National Oceanic and Atmospheric Administration, National Marine Fisheries Service, *NOAA Fishery Management Study* (Washington, D.C.: Government Printing Office, 1986), 62.

18. Maranto, "Caught in Conflict," 145.

19. William J. Chandler, ed., *Audubon Wildlife Report, 1988/1989* (San Diego: Academic Press, 1988), 48.

20. Higgs, "Legally Induced Technical Regress."

21. Scott, "Market Solutions," 19.

22. James L. Anderson and James E. Wilen, "Implications of Private Salmon Aquaculture on Prices, Production, and Management of Salmon Resources," *American Journal of Agricultural Economics* 68 (November 1986): 877.

23. Nelson Bryant, "A Scottish Group Protects Salmon," *New York Times*, January 8, 1990, S-13.

24. Edwin S. Iversen and Jane Z. Iversen, "Salmon-farming Success in Norway," *Sea Frontiers* (November–October 1987): 355–61; Cheryl Sullivan, "Salmon 'Feedlots' in Northwest," *Christian Science Monitor*, July 23, 1987. See also Robert R. Stickney, "Commercial Fishing and Net-pen Salmon Aquaculture: Turning Conceptual Antagonism Toward a Common Purpose," *Fisheries* 13 (July–August 1988): 9–13.

25. Merrill Leffler, "Killing Maryland's Oysters," *Washington Post*, March 29, 1987.

26. William L. Robinson, "Individual Transferable Quotas in the Australian Southern Bluefin Tuna Fishery," in *Fishery Access Control Programs Worldwide: Proceedings of the Workshop on Management Options for the North Pacific Longline Fishers*, Alaska Sea Grant Report no. 86-4 (Orca Island, Wash.: University of Alaska, 1986), 189–205.

27. Rodney P. Hide and Peter Ackroyd, *Depoliticising Fisheries Management: Chatham Islands' Paua (abalone) as a Case Study* (Christchurch, New Zealand: Centre for Resource Management, Lincoln University, March 1990), 42, 44.

28. Scott, "Market Solutions," 23. Scott argued that the individual quotas may lay the groundwork for fishermen to monitor and discourage violations of quotas for alleviating the problem of catching other species, known as the by-catch problem. The by-catch problem is addressed by the opportunity to trade mixed quotas among fishermen.

29. Hide and Ackroyd, *Depoliticising Fisheries Management*, 45–62.

10

MARKETING GARBAGE

The Solution to Pollution

"It may be garbage to you, but it's our bread and butter," reads the sign on the side of a garbage truck. This reminder provides a great deal of insight into the free market environmental approach to pollution. Garbage or waste to one party becomes the other's bread and butter as long as the creator of the garbage must pay for its disposal. This approach requires that liability for the waste be assigned so that garbage producers or dischargers must pay for emissions.

Defining the subtle difference between garbage and pollution centers on the producer's liability. In general, household garbage is the responsibility of homeowners who must hire a municipal or private company to haul the garbage to a landfill. As long as the owner of the landfill is held accountable for any garbage that may flow from its boundaries, either through the air or the ground, no third parties are involved in the transaction. The garbage may not be pleasant to either the household or the landfill owner, but it is not pollution, because the generator of the waste must compensate the garbage hauler and the owner of the waste disposal site, who willingly accept responsibility for the garbage. Compensation gives the person who generates the garbage an incentive to compare the benefits of garbage production with the costs of disposal to arrive at an "optimal" level of both. But when waste intrudes into another's physical environment without his consent and without compensation, the garbage becomes pollution. Garbage dumped into the airspace that others breathe, for example, requires neither willing consent nor compensation and, consequently, does not require the producer of garbage to carefully weigh the benefits and costs. The result is too much garbage.

Can institutions "internalize" the costs of creating garbage by turning it into someone else's bread and butter? When property rights can be clearly defined and enforced, there is willing consent and compensation and pollution problems disappear. This does not mean that there is no garbage generated in the production of goods and services, but secure property rights force the producer of the garbage to pay for its disposal.

Land pollution creates fewer conflicts than air and water pollution because property rights to land are relatively well defined and enforced. Dumping garbage on someone else's land can be monitored relatively easily, making it more likely that the owner will be compensated. The problem becomes more complex if there is potential for wastes to flow onto or under the property of others and if the damage to property or health are delayed, as with toxic wastes. If the party receiving the garbage cannot establish a right to be free from damage or cannot identify the producer of the garbage, then too much garbage will be produced and disposed of into the air and water. Although this problem is often referred to as market failure, it is more appropriately thought of as a property rights problem.

Most pollution policy, however, is not approached from a property rights perspective, where compensation and liability provide incentives for control; rather, public policy accepts pollution as a public bad that is the government's responsibility. Acceptable levels of discharge and pollution abatement are chosen and enforced by regulators who are not immune to politics. Fines may be levied on those who do not conform to the regulations, but the money collected seldom compensates those who are harmed. Billions of dollars of private and public funds are spent on pollution control with little or no concern for the cost effectiveness of expenditures.

WATER AND MARINE POLLUTION

The large oil spill in Alaska's Prince William Sound in 1989 is a profound example of how human activity can effect marine environments. Within limits, the environment in Alaska has a tremendous assimilative capacity, but when those limits are exceeded, the health of humans and wildlife is threatened. In response to that threat, the governor of Alaska called for oil companies to guarantee that there would never be another spill in the state, but such guarantees are

TABLE 10.1   Municipal Treatment Plants

	Estuaries			Coastal Waters		
Treatment Level	No.	Effluent[a]	Sludge[b]	No.	Effluent[a]	Sludge[b]
Primary	55	.94	.18	11	.15	.03
Advanced primary	52	1.22	.35	6	.35	.09
Secondary	272	2.43	.71	46	.31	.08
Tertiary	121	.91	.28	7	.01	.002
Totals	500	5.50	1.52	70	.82	.20

[a]For effluent, amounts are in billion gallons per day.
[b]For sludge, amounts are in million dry metric tons per year.
Source: Science Applications International Corporation, *Overview of Sewage Sludge and Effluent Management,* prepared for U.S. Congress, Office of Technology Assessment (McLean, Va., 1986).

impossible given that the oceans and coastal waters are valued for so many human uses.

Marine waters provide commercial fishing, recreation, transportation, and oil production; they also serve as a sink for the disposal of wastes. In the United States, more than thirteen hundred major industrial facilities and five hundred municipal plants discharge effluent directly into estuaries; an additional seventy municipal plants and about fifteen major industrial facilities discharge effluent directly into coastal waters (see Table 10.1 and Table 10.2).[1] In addition, non-point sources, such as return irrigation flows and urban runoff, contribute to the discharge problems.

Leading marine-based sources include disposal of dredge spoils, sewage sludge, and industrial wastes. The majority (80 to 90 percent by volume) of all waste material dumped in marine waters originates from dredging operations, which generate 180 million wet metric tons annually. Two-thirds of the spoils are dumped in estuaries and one-third

TABLE 10.2   Raw Waste Discharge[a] of Categorical Industries[b]

	Direct	Indirect	Totals
Metals	403[c]	198	601
Organic Chemicals	172	56	228

[a]Covers all navigable waters
[b]Industries covered by categorical standards for treatment
[c]All amounts are millions of pounds per year.
Source: U.S. Environmental Protection Agency, Office of Regulations and Standards, Monitoring and Data Support Division, *Summary of Effluent Characteristics and Guidelines for Selected Industrial Point Source Categories: Industry Status Sheets* (Washington, D.C., February 28, 1986).

in coastal waters. About 7 million wet metric tons of sewage sludge are dumped each year, primarily in coastal waters at the Twelve–mile Sewage Sludge Dump Site in the New York Bight (which is scheduled to be shifted farther out to sea at the Deepwater Municipal Sludge Site).[2] Because of increasing regulations, the dumping of industrial waste has steadily declined from 4.6 million metric tons in 1973 to about 200,000 metric tons in 1985.

During the 1980s, public concern grew over pollution generated from such activities. Roughly a third of the shellfish-producing areas in the United States have been closed to commercial harvest because of actual or potential problems with contaminated marine waters. In addition, major fish kills have occurred in the Gulf of Mexico and along the southern Atlantic Coast as a result of low oxygen levels (hypoxia) caused, in part, by wastes from municipal treatment plants. There have also been repeated incidents where fish, water birds, and marine mammals have been contaminated with unusually high concentrations of heavy metals, sulfides, and pesticides. Pollutants from marine wastes can also pose human health hazards if people eat contaminated fish. In 1982, the state of New York reported 103 different outbreaks of viral gastroenteritis involving over 1,000 people, all of the cases related to the consumption of contaminated shellfish.[3]

Pollution has also reduced aesthetic and recreational values in United States coastal waters, where recreational areas are frequently closed for swimming, fish are banned for human consumption, and beaches are cluttered with garbage and petroleum. These problems were graphically illustrated in the summer of 1988 when a nauseating array of medical wastes dumped at sea washed up on beaches from northern New Jersey to Long Island. For weeks, more than fifty miles of New York City and Long Island beaches were closed to sunbathing and swimming.[4]

According to several studies, 75 to 85 percent of all marine pollution comes from effluent. By far the greatest impact is on our estuaries and coastal waters, which host a wide variety of marine life. Being within easy reach of major population centers, these waters offer tremendous recreational opportunities, yet they receive the greatest volume of effluent generated by municipal and industrial sources. The challenge in this situation is to find ways to trade off waste disposal against other valuable uses.[5]

In terms of applying a market solution to environmental problems, few areas are more troublesome than water pollution. Because polluters are often difficult to identify and because rights to clean water are not vested in individuals or clearly specified organizations, the costs of garbage disposal into streams, lakes, or oceans can be easily passed on to others. Under these circumstances, a free market solution to water pollution seems elusive.

The problem of water pollution can be mitigated by assigning clear rights to other water uses so that owners of those rights have an incentive to monitor water quality and seek damages when pollution occurs. For example, when a polluter damages a privately owned oyster bed, the rule of strict liability dictates that the owner need only prove that damages occurred in order to receive compensation from the polluter for the loss of present and future income from the asset. In other words, the polluter is held accountable for the cost he imposes on the owner of the oyster bed.

If all polluters who use an estuary for waste disposal are held strictly liable for the cost of their pollution, they have an incentive to consider the costs and benefits of their actions. Under these circumstances, the market process, with liability enforced by the courts, forces polluters to weigh the costs of abating pollution against the potential damage costs. If it is less expensive to abate pollution than to face the liability, then polluters will do so; if it is not, then other asset owners will be compensated. Of course, this assumes that polluters can be identified and that damages can be assessed, but these are the same assumptions that are necessary if government regulations or fines are to effectively control pollution.

One problem with assigning liability for pollution in general and water pollution in particular is the number of parties who are affected on both sides. Many individuals may be affected by the pollution, but each suffers only a small amount of damage. In such cases, the benefits to any individual from proving damages are small relative to the legal costs. Moreover, if one individual is willing to undertake these costs and prove damages, then all others can free ride on his actions. Because each person affected by the pollution faces the same free-rider incentive, little or even no legal action will be taken to force the polluter to pay for the damages. Class-action suits can reduce the magnitude of this problem, and associations are often formed to help overcome it. It is now common for landowners to form property owner associations, and there is no reason to believe that similar associations might not be formed among fishermen or whale watchers if property rights to fisheries or whales could be well defined and enforced.

Because the costs of bringing together those who use a marine environment are often high enough to prevent joint action against polluters, a case can be made for some regulatory authority, such as the Environmental Protection Agency, to control the level of pollution. Of course, one of the problems with government control is that special interests that engage in waste disposal are just as likely—or perhaps even more likely, if they are well organized—to influence the agency as are those who suffer damages. The capture of regulatory policies by polluters is not surprising when we realize that the costs of control are concentrated on the polluter but the benefits are diffused across the population.

Similar problems for property or liability rules arise when there are large numbers of polluters. As long as water pollution comes from an easily identifiable source, such as a municipal sewage or industrial plant, liability can be established. But when marine pollution emanates from multiple sources, separating out pollutants and tracing them to their sources can be very costly. When irrigation water carrying fertilizer and pesticides is sent downstream by a river that feeds into an estuary, for example, the problem of identifying the source becomes very costly. The damages may be obvious, but liability for them will be much less apparent. In such cases, a well-defined and enforced system of property rights to marine uses other than pollution is unlikely to generate an optimal level of pollution, and again a case can be made for some form of regulation.

The problems associated with many polluters or many recipients of that pollution are found in other cases as well. Air pollution caused by automobiles, large concentrations of industrial plants, or even wood-burning stoves can make measuring and monitoring polluters very costly. On both sides are many individuals, each of whom is not easily identifiable, and it is difficult to assign liability.

It should not be assumed, however, that all pollution results in a lack of liability and, therefore, a lack of responsible action. A lead smelter in Tacoma, Washington, often experienced an atmospheric inversion that combined sulfur dioxide with water vapor to form acid rain that caused damage to plants near the smelter. When this occurred, the company quickly offered compensation to the harmed individuals because it knew it was responsible and accountable. There was garbage generated, but the company had an incentive to find the optimal level of garbage because the liability was clear.

In short, if the polluter is easily identifiable or if the damage is concentrated on a single individual or a small group, then there is an incentive to arrive at an optimal level of pollution. When these conditions are lacking, a regulatory solution *may* be called upon. Then the problem becomes one of choosing an optimal level of pollution in the political arena. State and federal agencies use elaborate models to determine pollution policy, but it is far easier to conceptualize an optimal level of pollution than it is to actually achieve it. When environmental amenities are not marketed, it is difficult to estimate their value; if they were marketed, regulation would be unnecessary.

Furthermore, special interests may influence the regulated level of pollution, making the policy purely political with little or no consideration of costs and benefits.

In the absence of market solutions to pollution problems, economists and policy makers have called for a second-best solution, which requires that the level of pollution abatement selected should be attained at the lowest possible cost. If we knew exactly which pollutants were emanating from each of several industrial plants and knew the costs associated with cleaning up the discharge, then it would be possible to derive the most efficient or lowest cost of cleanup. Paying lip service to this type of efficiency, legislation has called for such standards as best available technology or best practicable technology. But this terminology does not necessarily force decision makers to make the difficult trade-offs between the costs and benefits of pollution abatement.

ASSESSING SECOND-BEST POLICIES

The current approach for controlling waste discharges into estuaries, coastal waters, and inland waterways was established with the 1972 Clean Water Act. The act requires that "the discharge of pollutants into the navigable waters be eliminated by 1985" and that "wherever attainable, an interim goal of water quality which provides for the protection and propagation of fish, shellfish, and wildlife and provides for recreation in and on water be achieved by July 1, 1983."[6] The most significant change that resulted from the 1972 act was a shift in emphasis from water quality-based standards to technology-based standards.[7] These standards were based on what pollution abatement could be achieved with the interim standards of "best practicable control technology available," or BPT. Industrial discharges were to meet these standards by 1977. By 1983, industrial dischargers were scheduled to move to the next stage of treatment known as "best available technology economically achievable," or BAT; publicly owned municipal treatment plants were required to meet effluent limitations based on the "best practicable waste treatment technology."

Soon after the 1972 Clean Water Act passed, it became clear that discharge standards would have to be based on broad categories of industrial sources, such as ore mining, foundries, and petroleum refining. Cost effectiveness would have required different standards for individual sources, but the Environmental Protection Agency found it too costly and time-consuming to specify standards for over sixty thousand major polluters. Although standards could differ between categories, they were uniformly applied to many different sources within an industrial category. For instance, one electrical manufacturer with one cost of pollution abatement would face the same standards as another with very different costs. Moreover, with uniform standards applying to all polluters, there was little incentive for anyone to choose the lowest cost technology.

As it turned out, EPA fell far behind in the race to establish standards for industrial and municipal dischargers. By 1977, over two hundred and fifty court challenges had been brought against the EPA effluent standards that were in effect. Along with the trouble of setting BPT standards, it was clear that applying the BAT pollution standards made little sense; some water bodies met the water quality standards without BAT improvements and others would not meet them even with the standards.

When the standards in the 1972 act could not be met, policy makers added amendments in 1977. BAT standards and completion of secondary treatment upgrades for municipal treatment plants were delayed. The amendments set pre-treatment standards for waste sent to publicly owned municipal treatment plants and required that standards be established for toxic pollutants, such as heavy metals and organic chemicals.

Since the 1970s, the results of water pollution policy have been mixed. With some important exceptions, progress has been made on reducing point-source discharges of conventional pollutants in rivers, streams, and some estuaries and coastal waters.[8] But the cost has been enormous: United States businesses, government, and individuals have spent over $300 billion (in 1984 dollars) since 1972 for water pollution control.[9]

These high costs result from inefficiencies inherent in current EPA pollution policies. The EPA has chosen to apply uniform abatement standards to all discharge sources within a particular industry, hoping that deviations from low-cost individual approaches would not be significant. But studies in the 1980s performed on an 86-mile reach of the Delaware Estuary, the Lower Fox River in Wisconsin, and the Upper Hudson River in New York suggest that the cost deviations can be quite high.[10] Each study focused on the costs of reducing discharges of those pollutants that lower the concentration of dissolved oxygen (DO) in a water body (see Table 10.3). The approaches under consideration included the uniform treatment approach, which approximates current water pollution control strategy, and the variable, individual-source treatment approach, which allows each discharging source to select the lowest-cost method for reducing emissions. With the uniform treatment approach, costs range from one and one-half to two times the variable discharge policy (see Table 10.3).

TABLE 10.3 Water Pollution Control Expenditures

	DO target (mg/liter)[a]	Cost Ratio[b]
Delaware Estuary	3.0	3.00
Upper Hudson River	5.1	1.54
Lower Fox River	2.0	2.29

[a]Dissolved oxygen target level in water
[b]Ratio of cost of uniform treatment to variable treatment
Source: T. H. Tietenberg, *Emissions Trading: An Exercise in Reforming Pollution Policy* (Washington, D.C.: Resources for the Future, Inc., 1985), p. 46.

A 1966 study conducted by the Water Pollution Control Administration on the Delaware Estuary provides further insight. The estuary, which stretches from Trenton, New Jersey, to Liston Point, Delaware, is one of the most heavily industrialized and densely populated corridors in the United States. Municipal and industrial discharges have placed heavy demands on the water, reducing the dissolved oxygen content and reducing the ability of marine organisms to survive. In some cases, dissolved oxygen was completely exhausted so that organic wastes are broken down anaerobically, resulting in foul odors.

The study examined four pollution control policies: (1) least cost (LC), (2) uniform treatment (UT), (3) single effluent charge (SE), and (4) zone effluent charge (ZE). The first alternative establishes a theoretical basis for comparison in terms of the lowest-cost approach for each polluter. The second alternative requires each polluter to remove a given percentage of waste before discharging the remainder into the river. This method approximates the current strategy of satisfying a standard based on a given abatement technology. The third alternative uses uniform effluent charges without regard to location. The fourth alternative utilizes effluent charges set up for individual areas along the estuary.[11]

The estimated costs for achieving two alternative DO standards measured in parts per million are presented in Table 10.4. As indicated, the higher DO standard requires more pollution treatment and greater

TABLE 10.4 Cost of Pollution Treatment in the Delaware Estuary Under Alternative Programs (millions of dollars per year)

	Alternatives			
	1	2	3	4
DO Standard	LC	UT	SE	ZE
2 ppm	1.6	5.0	2.4	2.4
3–4 ppm	7.0	20.0	12.0	8.6

Source: Allen V. Kneese, *Economics and the Environment* (New York: Penguin, 1977), p. 164.

costs. The results show the problems associated with uniform treatment as practiced under EPA policy. As expected, this method was by far the most expensive, with costs of attaining a given dissolved oxygen target roughly three times higher than the other control policies. Although still higher in costs than the least-cost alternative, the effluent charge alternatives clearly had costs that were much lower than those with uniform treatment. The fourth alternative indicates that accounting for location in a policy of pollution reduction may make a significant difference when looking for further reductions in effluent discharges.

Ideally, greater efforts would be expended on water bodies where the gap between desired and actual water quality is the largest. All water bodies under the current system, however, are essentially treated the same. In the United States, there are some water bodies with low populations and little industry; they need minimal abatement effort because they already have high water quality. Other areas, such as Boston Harbor, are in dire need of pollution reduction. There is also a problem with industries not looking for alternative solutions to controlling pollution; instead, they select technologies that EPA uses to determine its standards. Even though someone may have a less expensive method to reduce effluent, it still makes sense to industries to continue using the technology that EPA specifies. If a firm is taken to court because it does not meet existing standards, it can argue that it used the technology EPA used to set the standard.

Of course, a complete assessment of water policy must incorporate benefits as well as costs, but measuring benefits in monetary terms without markets is difficult. The EPA points out that many important benefits from regulation are "aesthetic ones," which are intangible and, therefore, cannot be measured. Despite such difficulties, some analysts have estimated the benefits and costs of control policies. Freeman surveyed several studies of pollution control benefits and found that estimated benefits in 1985 range from $3.8 billion to $18.4 billion, with a likely estimate of $9.4 billion (in 1978 dollars). Comparing these benefits with 1985 annual costs (1978 dollars), which range from $15 billion to $20 billion, it appears that the net benefits in 1985 are negative. Given that the Clean Water Act requires perfectly clean water and that the incremental costs of cleanup rise exponentially for attaining this, it is not surprising that net benefits are negative.[12]

A MARKETLIKE ALTERNATIVE

Relying on standards and uniform treatment of pollution has improved water quality in the United States, but the approach is not cost effective nor is it likely to promote innovative alternatives to pollution control.

There is increasingly less federal funding available for maintaining or improving current levels of municipal sewage treatment, and the ability of states or communities to fill the gap is uncertain.[13] Even under total regulatory compliance by all point sources, there are additional pressures from non-point sources of pollution, especially agricultural and municipal runoff.

Two alternative strategies have the potential to improve the situation: effluent charges and tradeable pollution permits. The basic rationale for effluent charges is that they force polluters to pay a price for their actions. A producer, for example, whose factory effluent reduces the regenerative capacity of fish populations, imposes a cost on commercial fishermen without their consent. If the producer pays nothing for his actions, then he has little incentive to use labor and capital to reduce pollution. In the absence of clear ownership, the producer's free access to the use of an estuary for disposing of wastes will be excessive.

Effluent charges that account for the costs imposed on fishermen can provide an incentive to reduce waste disposal. It is very difficult, however, to determine the "correct" charge that will generate the "optimal" level of pollution. To make this determination, it must be possible to know the costs of pollution damages. But it is precisely the lack of such information that exacerbates the pollution problem. If costs could be determined easily, fishermen would have a good chance of internalizing the costs to the polluter through court action. The problem is that the same information necessary for private parties to assess the costs of pollution is also necessary for the political process to establish the "optimal" effluent charge.

An alternative that more closely approximates a property rights solution is a system of tradeable pollution permits. Under this system, a pollution control agency would issue a limited number of permits authorizing the discharge of a specific amount of pollutants. The number of permits would determine the level of water quality. While there is no way for this system to guarantee that the initial number of discharge permits is optimal, this system will ensure that a given level of control can be achieved efficiently through a market for the permits.

Tradeable pollution permits allow much more flexibility than the current pollution control regime. For example, polluters may be allowed to increase pollution at some location where water quality is high in return for reducing pollution in an area where it is low. Trading permits also improves overall efficiency. If a permit is held by a firm that is capable of reducing pollution at lower cost than other firms, then a high-cost firm could purchase that right to pollute from the low-cost firm. The low-cost firm would then reduce the pollution level it had previously been allowed to discharge and still make a profit from the sale of the permit. By the same token, if an environmental organization wishes to reduce emissions, it can buy up permits. Another value of the system is that once a level of pollution has been determined, regulatory officials do not need information on the additional cost of treatment at each source of discharge.

This process has been applied to water pollution control in northern Wisconsin, where a system of tradeable pollution permits has been implemented on the Lower Fox River. The river flows from Lake Winnebago to Green Bay, Wisconsin, and is lined with ten pulp and paper mills and four municipalities discharging effluent. Even with full compliance of BPT industrial treatment and secondary municipal treatment, the desired dissolved oxygen levels are not reached during the summer. Faced with meeting these standards, the Wisconsin Department of Natural Resources implemented the tradeable permit system based on a simulation study that demonstrated a significant difference in costs of pollution treatment among the various discharge sources. The study found that control costs would be 40 percent higher with the traditional BPT approach to pollution control and that annual cost savings realized from a permit system would be from $5.7 million to $6.8 million. Given similar findings for control of BOD in Oregon's Willamette River and the control of phosphorous discharged into Lake Michigan, there is reason to be optimistic about this approach.[14]

Industrial effluent delivered to municipal treatment plants also seems amenable to a system of tradeable discharge permits. As a means of controlling these discharges, the EPA has established a set of pre-treatment standards. These standards share the deficiencies of all standards, namely a lack of cost-effectiveness, but tradeable discharge permits can be applied to overcome such deficiencies. For example, the electroplating operations in the Rhode Island jewelry industry discharge high concentrations of cyanide, copper, nickel, and zinc into municipal sewer systems. Because the municipal treatment plants in the area are not capable of removing these substances, the EPA applies pre-treatment standards to the entire industry. If strictly applied, such standards would force 30 to 60 percent of the small firms out of business. One analysis of alternatives for meeting water quality objectives, however, concluded that pre-treatment standards meet the objectives at a cost that is almost 50 percent greater than the tradeable permit alternative. An effluent permit system would achieve the target level of water quality at a cost of $12.5 million; the pre-treatment standard approach would achieve the target at a cost of $19.3 million.[15]

Another potential application of tradeable discharge permits is non-point source pollution. Fertilizer and pesticide wastes carried by agricultural runoff and untreated sewage from flooded urban storm systems are a growing threat in many coastal regions. Studies conducted on Chesapeake Bay and San Francisco Bay indicate that non-point sources contribute to water pollution at least as much as point sources do. Although non-point pollution has received little regulatory attention, studies suggest that tradeable discharge permits could improve water quality by reducing non-point sources of pollution at a lower cost than reducing point sources. For example, a point/non-point source trading plan was developed to control overload of phosphorous and nitrogen wastes in the Dillon reservoir in Colorado, the major source of water for Denver. The plan allows publicly owned treatment works (POTWs) to finance the control of non-point sources in lieu of upgrading their own treated effluent to drinking water standards. This effort would cost $67 per pound of phosphorous removed via trading, compared to $824 per pound for the least expensive advanced treatment alternative developed for POTWs. EPA estimated aggregated savings from the plan of over $1 million per year compared with the conventional approach of upgrading municipal treatment plants. The same type of plan is currently being developed for other sites in Colorado and has potential for treating nutrient and other pollutant problems in coastal waters as well.[16]

THE FREE MARKET
ENVIRONMENTALIST APPROACH

Although tradeable discharge permits can generate significant efficiency gains, they still require a political determination of the level of pollution that will be allowed. Hence, it is reasonable to expect that individual dischargers will lobby to increase or decrease the number of permits. For example, a company may find it less expensive to "buy" a new discharge permit from the agency regulating the number of permits rather than from an existing permittee. Alternatively, a firm that enjoys a degree of market power based on the barrier to entry into the market caused by the number of permits may find it profitable to lobby for a low number of permits.

A truly free market approach to pollution control would require polluters and recipients of the discharge to bargain over the level of pollution. Bargaining may take place in the form of an exchange of property rights, where the discharger pays the recipient for disposal before the fact or in the form of payments for damages paid after the fact. Either way, both parties have an incentive to consider the trade-offs associated with more or less pollution. Of course, an exchange of property rights or payments for damages both require well-defined and enforced property rights. While many policy analysts have concluded that the problems discussed earlier in this chapter render the potential for well-defined and enforced property rights impossible, we must remember that property rights evolve when economic pressures increase the value of polluted resources or decrease the costs of establishing property rights.

In the context of water pollution, there are two cases where a property rights approach has potential. In England, an association of anglers and clubs has carried out the job of monitoring pollution since the 1950s. Anglers' Cooperative Association officials point out that the organization was protecting the environment twenty years before the general public became concerned and pressured the government to act.

> In all the A.C.A. has handled more than fifteen hundred cases of pollution [and] recovered hundreds of pounds in damages to enable club and riparian owners to restore their fisheries. It has also defeated attempts by various Governments to alter the Common Law in relation to pollution, and it has had a profound effect on the attitude of industry, local authorities and politicians and public.[17]

The British experience suggests that pollution could be reduced if private fishing rights were established in the United States. Liability rules would evolve so that owners of fishing rights could bring suit against an upstream polluter whose effluent damaged their fishing resource.

Groundwater constitutes a second example. It was not until the mid-1970s that public attention began to focus on a major problem in groundwater allocation: pollution. It was discovered that toxic chemicals had seeped through subterranean structures into homes near Niagara Falls, New York, and the chemicals were traced to the now-infamous waste disposal site known as Love Canal. Press reports on the Love Canal incident frightened local residents and created a national chemical pollution scare. That incident, coupled with such subsequent events as the discovery of the evil-looking "valley of the drums" in Kentucky and the dioxin pollution at Times Beach, Missouri, led to public demand for government action. In 1980, Congress passed the Comprehensive Environmental Response, Compensation, and Liability Act—better known as Superfund.

Superfund, along with related toxic waste legislation, has regulated the disposal of hazardous wastes, required the registration of hazardous waste disposal sites, and demanded the cleanup of existing sites. Superfund studies have revealed over a thousand specific point sources of toxic wastes in addition to leaky underground gasoline storage tanks and non-point sources, such as pesticides and herbicides used in agriculture. The cleanup costs are projected to be in the tens of billions of dollars.

Now that these sources of pollution have been discovered, the question is how much cleanup should be done and what should be done to prevent future problems. In answer to the first question, federal policy has followed the lead set by the 1972 Clean Air Act by requiring that all waste sites must be cleaned up and that specific cleanup technology must be used. The problem with this approach is that it ignores costs and benefits. Some sites may not be worth cleaning up at all, and alternative technologies may be available or may be discovered if incentives are provided to use least-cost techniques. These incentives are lacking, however, because Superfund dollars finance the cleanup.

The second problem is that Superfund reduces the incentive for polluters to avoid future waste problems by providing federal funds for cleanup. With Superfund dollars available for cleanup, individuals responsible for wastes will not face the full costs of their production processes. Not surprisingly, the legislative price tag for cleanup increased from $1.6 billion in 1980 to $9 billion in 1986, and with taxpayers footing part of the bill, there is every reason to believe this trend will continue. For that reason, Fred Smith, a former EPA analyst, suggested that Superfund is a "hazardous waste of taxpayer money."[18]

Well-defined property rights and unitization to waste sites and groundwater could move us much closer to an efficient solution to hazardous waste disposal. Property rights in groundwater use would make it easier to assign liability, and the threat of being sued for damages would help deter users from allowing effluent to pollute the water supply. Because there are often many owners of land overlying an aquifer, each incurs only a small amount of the cost resulting from pollution of the groundwater. Therefore, each would tend to be a free rider in seeking damages against polluters. But if the many landowners were organized into a single unit, as suggested in Chapter 7, all groundwater users would share the cost of extracting clean water from the aquifer, so they would be motivated to cooperate in seeking damages.

CONCLUSION

United States businesses, government, and individuals have spent over $300 billion (in 1984 dollars) for water pollution control since the Clean Water Act was passed in 1972.[19] Despite the huge investment, most of these parties recognize that even under full compliance with current requirements, we will fall far short of internalizing the cost of pollutants that are emptied into our estuaries and coastal waters. Therefore, as these areas continue to grow in population and in commercial activities, pressures to control pollution will intensify.

Applying uniform treatment and quality standards makes little sense given that water quality for coastal water bodies varies considerably by region. While some streams, estuaries, and coastal waters can assimilate current emissions, others need significant cleanup efforts. The buildup of hazardous wastes in Commencement Bay in Puget Sound, for example, probably warrants the attention it is receiving from Superfund. Similarly, the designation of Boston Harbor as the nation's "filthiest" suggests that attention should be given to the discharge of partially treated municipal sewage. But limited resources for controlling and cleaning up pollution require that those with the largest gap between actual and desired water quality receive the greatest attention. Unfortunately, the regulatory approach has tended toward uniform treatment and standards.

Tradeable discharge permits offer an effective way of introducing the discipline of the market into pollution abatement, but they require political control and do not provide for a complete market in pollution. A complete free market solution to the pollution problem would require property rights to the disposal medium. Unfortunately, current arrangements make establishing such rights impossible.

It is useful to reiterate the importance of the evolution of property rights and the common law. As clean water and air become more valuable, entrepreneurs have a greater incentive to define and enforce rights to the resources. If we continue to subsidize the use of these resources and to subsidize the costs of disposal, however, entrepreneurs will not be getting the right signals. At the very least, municipal, state, and federal agencies should raise the price to individuals for using waste disposal systems. Not only will this give people incentives to produce less garbage, it will also provide funds to cleanup pollution.

There is no guarantee that property rights will evolve, but we should not stand in the way of environmental entrepreneurs who try to develop them. Fishing rights in England have enabled anglers to successfully obtain damages or injunctions for thermal pollution, sewage disposal, and agricultural practices that produce stream sediments. Such property rights may evolve spontaneously as entrepreneurs recognize the changing values of resources and act on them, but political institutions can assist in the process. Richard Stroup has suggested six ways this might occur:

1. allow more freedom of action, using insurance or bonding to guarantee solvency and responsibility;
2. consider strengthening the common law through statute at the state level;

3. require the branding of chemicals when feasible;
4. restore basic responsibility for regulation to the state level;
5. channel federal efforts into research and criminal investigation; and
6. make "orphan" waste sites private.

The last proposal represents the innovative thinking that free market environmentalism can stimulate. Stroup suggested that

> using Superfund money, the government could pay the firm making the lowest bid to accept ownership. The new owner would be free to act as it wished, but it would be liable for any damages it caused or any threat of imminent danger. A bond posted by the firm could be required as a guarantee that damage would be avoided.[20]

This proposal would eliminate a great deal of red tape inherent in Superfund cleanup, significantly reduce costs, and provide a profit incentive for people to find cheaper ways to control hazardous wastes. Ultimately, it will be the productivity of free markets that provides the solution to pollution.

NOTES

1. U.S. Congress, Office of Technology Assessment, *Wastes in Marine Environments*, OTA-O-334 (Washington, D.C.: Government Printing Office, April 1987), 14.
2. Ibid., 13–15.
3. Ibid., 19, 107, 108; D. L. Morse et al., "Widespread Outbreaks of Clam- and Oyster-Associated Gastroenteritis," *New England Journal of Medicine* 314 (March 13, 1986): 678–81.
4. Tom Morganthau et al., "Don't Go Near the Water," *Newsweek*, August 1, 1988, 43–48.
5. Joint Groups of Experts on the Scientific Aspects of Marine Pollution, "The Health of the Oceans: UNEP Regional Seas Reports and Studies No. 16" (UNEP, 1983), 4. The Office of Technology Assessment predicted that United States estuaries and coastal waters will suffer "new or continued degradation . . . during the next few decades," while uncertainty exists about discerning impacts on the health of the open ocean. From Office of Technology Assessment, *Wastes in Marine Environments*, 3. Estuaries include semi-enclosed bodies of water that have some connection to the open ocean and serve as input for freshwater sources. Coastal waters generally lie over the continental shelf within the territorial sea and are less enclosed and influenced more by oceanic processes than estuaries.
6. 1972 Amendments to the Clean Water Act.

7. The 1956 amendments defined ambient standards as a means of quantifying the objectives of pollution abatement. But in the subsequent water quality legislation, these standards were downgraded when Congress gave legal status to technology-based standards apart from ambient standards.

8. *Environmental Quality: Fifteenth Annual Report of the Council on Environmental Quality* (Washington, D.C.: Government Printing Office, 1984), 81–159. Conventional pollutants continue to cause incidents of hypoxia and eutrophication in the Chesapeake Bay and southern Louisiana coast. See Office of Technology Assessment, *Wastes in Marine Environments*, 25–28.

9. Kit Farber and Gary L. Rutledge, "Pollution Abatement and Control Expenditures," *Survey of Current Business* 66 (1986): 97–103.

10. William B. O'Neill, "Pollution Permits and Markets for Water Quality" (Ph.D. diss., University of Wisconsin, Madison, 1980); J. Wayland Eheart, E. Downey Brill Jr., and Randolph M. Lyon, "Transferable Discharge Permits for Control BOD: An Overview," in *Buying a Better Environment: Cost-Effective Regulation Through Permit Trading*, ed. Erhard F. Joeres and Martin H. David (Madison: University of Wisconsin Press, 1983), 163–95.

11. Allen V. Kneese, *Economics and the Environment* (New York: Penguin, 1977), 164, chap. 7.

12. T. Clark, "The Cost and Benefit of Regulation—Who Knows How Great They Really Are?" *National Journal* 11 (1979): 2024; Myrick A. Freeman III, "Water Pollution Policy," in *Current Issues in U.S. Environmental Policy*, ed. Paul R. Portney, rev. ed. (Baltimore: Johns Hopkins University Press, for Resources for the Future, forthcoming). See also Lester B. Lane and Eugene B. Seskin, *Air Pollution and Human Health* (Baltimore: Johns Hopkins University Press, 1977); S. Schwing et al., "Benefit-Cost Analysis of Automotive Reductions," *Journal of Environmental Economics and Management* 7 (1980): 59.

13. EPA recently estimated that remaining municipal treatment needs will total $76 billion in the year 2005. The Water Quality Act of 1987 provided $18 billion for assistance in municipal construction with funding ending in 1994. See U.S. Environmental Protection Agency, Office of Municipal Control, *Assessment of Needed Publicly Owned Wastewater Treatment Facilities in the United States*, EPA 430/9–84–011 (Washington, D.C.: Government Printing Office, 1985).

14. M. T. Maloney and Bruce Yandle, "Building Markets for Tradeable Pollution Rights," in *Water Rights: Scarce Resource Allocation, Bureaucracy, and the Environment*, ed. Terry L. Anderson (San Francisco: Pacific Institute for Public Policy Research, 1983), 311; Eheart et al., "Transferable Discharge Permits," 13, 14; Randolph M. Lyons, "Auctions and Alternatives for Public Allocation with Application to the Distribution of Pollution Rights," Report no. 1, National Science Foundation Award PRA 79–13131 (Department of Civil Engineering and Institute for Environmental Studies, University of Illinois at Urbana, March 1981); Martin David, Erhard Joeres, and J. Wayland Eheart, "Distribution Methods for Transferable Discharge Permits," *Water Resources Research* 16 (1980): 833–43.

15. James J. Opaluch and Richard M. Kashmanian, "Assessing the Viability of Marketable Permit Systems: An Application in Hazardous Waste Management," *Land Economics* 61 (August 1985): 263–71.

16. Office of Technology Assessment, *Wastes in Marine Environments*, 24–28; Timothy E. Wirth and John Heinz, "Project 88: Harnessing Market Forces to Protect Our Environment: Initiatives for the New President" (draft, Washington, D.C., October 1988), 88. The Clean Water Act of 1987 allocated $400 million in grants to help states reduce non-point pollution, but much of that is going into creating state management plans and study programs.

17. Anglers' Cooperative Association, Pamphlet, Midland Bank Chambers, Grantham, Lincolnshire NG31 6LE, United Kingdom.

18. Lawrence Reed, " 'Superfund' a Bonanza for U.S. Polluters," *Idaho Press-Tribune* (Nampa), December 11, 1986.

19. Farber and Rutledge, "Pollution Abatement and Control Expenditures."

20. Richard L. Stroup, "Chemophobia and Activist Environmental Antidotes: Is the Cure More Deadly Than the Disease?" in *Economics and the Environment: A Reconciliation*, ed. Walter E. Block (Vancouver, B.C.: Fraser Institute, 1989), 207–9.

11

TACKLING THE
TOUGHER PROBLEMS

We began this book by examining land-based natural resources, because establishing clearly specified rights is easier when the resource is immobile. For food, timber, and even recreational amenities, markets can allocate resources when the rights to the land are private. When production focuses on minerals below the surface or wildlife on the surface, defining and enforcing property rights does become more costly. As the value of these resources rises, however, it also becomes more worthwhile to invest in defining and enforcing property rights to them. When legal institutions encourage rather than raise the cost of establishing private property rights, markets can evolve for recreational and environmental amenities as well as for traditional products.

The case for free market environmentalism is somewhat more difficult to make for water because of its fluid nature. Nonetheless, as water values rise, more effort is being spent on defining and enforcing rights to the resource, and markets are being used increasingly to encourage efficient water use. When institutional obstacles to private ownership are removed, private property rights can even be established for instream flows. Although the quantity and direction of groundwater flows are even harder to measure, the government can play a role in establishing rights to groundwater stocks and flows under the prior appropriation doctrine. Once private property rights to surface and ground-

154

water are established, many pollution problems can be handled through market processes.

More imagination may be needed to manage a resource like fish because they know no national boundaries. Fencing the open oceans seems impossible given current technology, but extending territorial limits, establishing individual transferable quotas, and enforcing private property rights in aquaculture can move us toward free market solutions for homesteading the oceans.

When the production of desired goods also produces by-products with a negative value—garbage—we face the problem of waste disposal. The market can even respond to this problem if the government can secure property rights and enforce rules of liability and bonding. The key to a market approach in waste disposal is to identify those who produce pollution, measure the harm, and identify the recipient of the pollution.

Property rights solutions are the toughest to find with air pollution, which also knows no political boundaries. Because it is difficult to identify the polluter, the harm, and the recipient, smog produced by automobiles can cause respiratory problems, obstruct views, and damage property; sulphur dioxide from coal-burning power plants can obscure visibility and lead to lake acidification; and heat-trapping CO_2 may create a greenhouse effect that could raise the Earth's temperature and cause severe atmospheric change.

At first glance, tackling these problems appears to be a task that only a regulatory authority could handle. Because air is highly fluid, because most gases are costly to track to their source, and because the effects of the pollution may be cumulative, property rights may appear to be prohibitively costly to define and enforce. Hence, regulatory solutions are implemented to counter the consequences of both local and global pollution. In the extreme, this regulatory approach emphasizes that all economic activity must be controlled so that development is "sustainable."

In this chapter, we explore the pitfalls of regulatory approaches to air pollution and stress the potential for applying property rights solutions. Like early settlers in the West, we are on the "atmospheric" frontier, where new forms of fencing must be invented.

REGULATING SO$_2$ AND ACID RAIN

Evidence suggests that political solutions to pollution problems will be dominated by special interests rather than by rationally impartial experts who calculate benefits and costs. Consider, for example, how poorly the regulatory process worked with the New Source Performance

Standards of the Clean Air Act of 1977. In an effort to decrease SO_2 emissions, Congress followed its tradition of requiring strict application of "best available technology" standards for new coal-fired generating plants. Instead of setting specific emission standards and allowing plants to meet them by using cleaner, low-sulfur western coal, owners of generations facilities were forced to install stack-gas scrubbers, which cost more to buy and to operate.[1]

The reductions in SO_2 could have been achieved at a much lower cost by burning low-sulphur coal, but a "clean air–dirty coal" coalition made up of eastern coal producers and environmentalists lobbied for the technological fix. Robert Crandall described the impetus for the strange coalition.

> Eastern coal producers feared that a sensible environmental policy would lead electric utilities to buy increasing amounts of low-sulfur Western coal. Since much of the Appalachian and Midwestern coal is high in sulfur content, it would eventually lose market share to the cleaner Western coal. Requiring stack-gas scrubbers for all new plants, regardless of the sulfur content of the coal burned, would eliminate the incentive for Eastern and Midwestern utilities to import low-sulfur Western coal. Environmentalists, for some reason, have had a burning desire to require utilities to install scrubbers, even though alternative technologies may be substantially less costly in most cases.[2]

Because the Environmental Protection Agency could not monitor the efficiency of the scrubbers, the result was high new-plant compliance costs and a reduction in the rate of replacement of older, dirty utility boilers.

Rather than rational environmental policy, the clean air–dirty coal policy became a mechanism for redistributing wealth from electricity consumers, who paid higher rates, to eastern coal miners, who feared losing their jobs. According to one estimate, electricity production costs are projected to increase by $4.8 billion by 1995 as a result of the 1977 amendments and revenues to coal producers are expected to increase by $245 million.

> Since the environmental benefits were, at best, nil this results in a maximum ratio of dollars gained by "winners" to dollars lost by "losers" of .05. That is, electricity consumers paid approximately one dollar for each 5 cents received by the relevant coal producers.[3]

Through the regulatory process, the "best available technology" was applied at a very high cost when the far less expensive and more effective clean-coal alternative could have been implemented.

This experience demonstrates the difficulty of eliminating politics from the regulatory process. Some have suggested that the problem can be eliminated with general legislation and more autonomy for regulatory agencies such as the EPA, but this approach assumes that experts in the agencies will not be influenced by the lobbying pressures of those groups that have a stake in the outcome.[4] Today, the technological costs of all environmental regulations and the administrative costs of bureaucracy amount to $80 billion per year, with $30 billion of that figure devoted to controlling air pollution.[5]

With so much at stake in jobs, investments, and environmental quality, interest groups are not likely to sit back and let experts do what they think is right. The pressure from the environmental lobby for quick and dramatic solutions is strengthened by lawyers and industry groups who benefit from regulation. In this regulatory marketplace, politicians and bureaucrats are ready and willing to meet the demands of special interests. In the case of coal-burning utilities, politicians avoided drawing the ire of producers whose profits are tied to the operation of existing plants by applying strict, new regulations to new plants only. The result was a slowdown in the phase-in of cleaner-burning power plants.

Unfortunately, regulatory perversity continues with efforts to control acid rain, which is likely to produce "a billion-dollar solution for a million-dollar problem."[6] According to one ten-year study, however, the effects of acid rain are not as widespread as some have claimed. The National Acid Precipitation Assessment Program (NAPAP) found that "a firm causal link has proved to be elusive" between acid rain and areas where forests have been dying; natural stresses seem to be the primary causes. The only exception is that acid rain "may to a small degree reduce the frost hardiness of red spruce in a narrow elevational band in the Northeast." Researchers have also shown that agricultural crops are sensitive to ozone but not to acid rain; in fact, acid rain may even contribute to soil fertility. Acid rain's effect on building materials also has been difficult to quantify, but it is doubtful that it has had much effect. Neither is there solid evidence of acid rain causing adverse health effects. There is evidence that acid rain causes some deterioration in visibility and acidification of lakes in New York's Adirondack Mountains, Pennsylvania's Pocono Mountains, and in Michigan's Upper Peninsula, but there is other evidence that local geology, land use, and soil drainage may be the cause of the high lake acidity.[7]

The NAPAP study found that efforts to drastically reduce SO_2 emissions to control acid rain are not well founded, because "percentage reductions in emissions may not result in similar percentage reductions in [acid] depositions." Between 1972, when SO_2 emissions peaked, and

1988, emissions decreased by 25 percent. According to the director of the NAPAP study, however, "no apparent trend in the acidity of rainfall has been detected."[8]

Even though there is little evidence that acid rain is causing widespread problems and that reducing SO_2 emissions can have a significant impact on acid rain, the Bush administration has proposed reducing SO_2 emissions by 10 million tons (from the 1980 base year level). The cost of this reduction has been estimated to be from $4 billion to $7 billion per year over the next twenty years.[9] To minimize the costs, there appears to be increasing sympathy with the "market-like" approach of establishing emission standards and allowing plants to trade their allowances.[10] This would be a big improvement over "best available technology" regulations, because greater flexibility is allowed in achieving reductions and lowers costs by allowing the lowest-cost plants to sell their emission permits and reduce emissions. Just as individual, transferable quotas allow the government to set the total catch allowed from a fishery and then let the market decide how and by whom the catch will be taken (see Chapter 9), tradeable pollution permits offer a market-based approach to air pollution. By making tradeable pollution permits the centerpiece of his attack on acid rain, President Bush acknowledged that incentives are important. For economists who have advocated more efficiency in controlling pollution, Bush's approach is a welcome alternative to more inefficient regulations.

> This market approach would induce firms with low-cost pollution control technologies to cleanup more and would thus reduce the overall cost of achieving environmental quality goals by about 50 percent, or over $13 billion, compared with traditional command-and-control approaches, which specify the precise technology that firms must use.[11]

As Daniel Dudek, economist for the Environmental Defense Fund, put it, "The beauty of this approach is that it provides environmental performance without great bloodletting in the economy." Tradeable pollution permits are even supported by some environmentally minded politicians, such as Senator Timothy Wirth (D-Colorado), who said, "We're not going to be able to make a dent in environmental problems unless we can harness the forces of the marketplace."[12]

But tradeable permits do not represent a truly free-market approach to reducing acid rain. A government agency still must determine the level of permits, and the permits do not force polluters to compensate those harmed by the pollution. In this system, the political process determines the initial or optimal pollution levels, not the polluters bargaining with those who bear the costs of the pollution. The 10-

million-ton target established by the Bush administration, for example, "was not based on scientific or economic grounds. It was selected because it was viewed as 'creditable'—that is, it was acceptable to Congress, the environmental community, and our Canadian neighbors." As Robert Hahn observed, "Until people see a direct connection between environmental cleanup and their consumption of other goods and services and begin to seriously question the judgment of their political leaders on these matters, things are unlikely to change."[13]

GLOBAL WARMING
OR A LOT OF HOT AIR?

The problems of regulating SO_2 emissions to control acid rain pale in comparison to the problems that we will supposedly suffer from global warming. According to some experts, the Earth's climate over the next hundred years will become substantially warmer; as a result, forests will shift northward; sea levels will rise, flooding beaches and coastal cities; rainfall patterns will change; air pollution will worsen and floods, fires, droughts, and insect plagues will increase.[14]

But there is considerable debate among experts over this issue.[15] The greenhouse theory that is behind the argument that the Earth is getting warmer originated at the turn of the twentieth century with Swedish Nobel laureate Svante Arrhenius. Arrhenius contended that if we increase the amount of heat-trapping gases, such as CO_2, in the atmosphere, then the overall temperature of the Earth will rise. Today, scientists generally agree that the amount of CO_2 in the atmosphere has been increasing. Using measurements of gas encased in glacial ice, they estimate that the atmosphere contained nearly 290 parts of CO_2 per million parts of air in the 1850s. Over the last 135 years, the amount of the gas has risen to over 340 parts per million, an increase of 20 percent. There is also some evidence that the Earth has warmed during the past century. James E. Hansen and his colleagues at NASA believe that the Earth's temperature has increased between five- and seven-tenths of a degree. And two scientists at the Woods Hole Research Center pointed out that the six warmest years globally during the past century occurred during the 1980s.[16]

From these pieces of evidence, some scientists have concluded that human activities will be responsible for drastic climate change in the future. Using weather forecasting models, Stephen Schneider of the National Center for Atmosphere Research, predicted that climate change from human activity will take place from ten to forty times faster than any previous natural change. Christopher Flavin of the Worldwatch Institute summarized the worst of the projected scenarios: "During the next few decades average global temperatures will increase at 10 times the rate that they did at the end of the last ice age, or as much as 8 degrees Fahrenheit by the middle of the next century."[17]

Other reputable scientists dispute the existence, causes, and possible consequences of global warming. Kenneth E. F. Watt, professor of environmental studies at the University of California at Davis, theorized that an excess of carbon dioxide in the atmosphere should lead to global cooling, not warming. Watt argued that carbon dioxide will heat tropical oceans, leading to additional evaporation. This will produce denser and more widespread clouds at high elevations, which will decrease the amount of sunlight that penetrates the atmosphere. Some scientists believe that the Earth is warming, but they attribute the change to causes other than CO_2 production. Frederick Seitz, past president of the National Academy of Sciences, suggested that solar activity may have caused global warming, and Reid Bryson, director of the Institute of Environmental Studies at the University of Wisconsin, Madison, believes that dust and smoke are the primary causes of climate change.[18]

There is also debate over whether the Earth has really warmed at all over the last century. Temperature measurements may be biased by the effects of urbanization; weather stations are located in urban areas, where heat-absorbing buildings and pavement can raise the readings one to two degrees above the surrounding atmosphere. After correcting for the "urban" effect, a study by the National Oceanographic and Atmospheric Administration concluded that there was no statistically significant evidence of warming in the United States. Andrew R. Solow, a statistician at Woods Hole, pointed out that because monitoring stations tend to be located on land rather than oceans and more are in the Northern than in the Southern Hemisphere, temperature readings are not really global at all. Ten years of weather satellite data have also shown no evidence of global warming. With data collected from 1979 through 1988, scientists Roy W. Spencer and John R. Christy concluded that the temperature changes tended to even out, and no trend of warming was apparent.[19]

Even among scientists who believe there is a relationship between global temperatures and increased concentrations of greenhouse gases like CO_2, there is disagreement over how the Earth will react. While some scientists believe that the Earth's temperature will rise by 2 to 5 degrees Celsius by the year 2050, others argue that there is still little known about the influences of clouds and oceans under climate change. About a fifth of the sunlight is reflected by clouds and a change of only a few percent in cloud coverage could be as big an influence as doubling carbon dioxide. Oceans could conceivably amplify or suppress a warming trend. If the oceans heated up, they could release more CO_2

into the atmosphere. But warmer oceans could also stimulate more phytoplankton, a marine organism that extracts CO_2 from the air through photosynthesis. More of these organisms could create a new steady-state, which would offset the greenhouse effect.[20]

With all of this debate, why does the majority of the population seem to accept global warming as a fact? The simple answer is that the theory has intuitive appeal and offers a simple solution. We also can associate it with personal experiences. Most of us have been in a greenhouse and have felt the effect of trapped solar energy. Moreover, we continually experience changing weather patterns, ranging from droughts to floods, and it is appealing to have an explanation for them. Also, because the greenhouse theory tells us that the warming is being caused by increased CO_2 gases, the solution seems obvious; reduce CO_2 gases.

Politicians who are interested in doing something for their constituents and bureaucrats who are concerned about their jobs and budgets also readily buy into the global warming hypotheses. In this case, the politics of information is biased in favor of there being a problem that the political sector can fix. Although none of the global calamities predicted over the years have ever happened, such predictions continue to survive in the political arena because they give politicians and bureaucrats power over human activity.[21] If the experts who believe there is no problem are correct, then there is no need for regulation. Politicians who tell their constituents or bureaucrats who tell budgetary committees that the sky is not falling win few votes or budgetary dollars. Unfortunately, global warming policies are formulated in the same political arena as economic policy, and in that arena a mixture of incomplete theory and bad information do not give us a recipe for success.

WHAT IF CHICKEN LITTLE IS RIGHT?

But suppose the atmosphere is warming? Shouldn't we be doing something about it? Proponents of the greenhouse hypothesis are calling for immediate and stringent measures, including stricter air pollution emissions standards, tighter fuel efficiency standards, massive public funding for alternative energy sources, restrictions on worldwide deforestation, and large scale political programs to plant more trees and control population.[22] Ultimately, the fears of global warming are used to drive sustainable development policies where nearly all resource use would be controlled by government. This approach, which has been referred to as ecological economics, means that "the current generation must not compromise the ability of future generations to meet their 'material needs' and to enjoy a healthy environment."[23] Although there are different interpretations of sustainability, advocates generally

- perceive that the biosphere imposes limits on economic growth,
- express a lack of faith in either science or technology as leading to human betterment,
- are extremely averse to environmental risks,
- support redistributive justice and egalitarian ethics,
- profess concern over population growth and have faith in the wisdom of human capital development [education], and
- have survival of species and protection of the environment and of minority cultures, rather than economic growth per se, as goals.[24]

Sustainable development, as advocated by today's ecological economists, is a holdover from the 1960s and 1970s when economists were struggling with steady-state and zero-growth economic models. Again using intuitive concepts like the "Economics of the Coming Spaceship Earth," political controls are required to carefully balance product consumption, energy use, and wastes to maintain a "steady-state economy."[25] During the 1970s, the demands for strict political control of resource consumption were driven by a concern that energy resources were being exhausted. Although all indications tell us that price deregulation solved the energy crisis, the steady-state theories formed the basis for many regulations, from climate control in buildings to lower speed limits to fuel efficiency standards, and ultimately to a new bureaucracy, the Department of Energy. Today, the same regulatory zeal under the guise of sustainable development is being driven by fears of global warming.

Unfortunately, the politics of regulation at the global level are likely to dwarf problems that are inherent in national pollution regulations. At the national level, there are governmental institutions that can implement regulations, and in democracies there is some hope of controlling the regulators. Global regulation, however, would require international treaties or organizations to specify and implement the regulations. But this raises important and complex questions of who will come to the bargaining table and who will negotiate with whom? If agreement is reached, who will do the enforcing? If fines or taxes are to be imposed, who will collect them and who will receive the proceeds? Problems in negotiating a Law of the Sea Treaty illustrate the difficulty in achieving consensus among nations.[26]

Advocates of international agreements to solve global warming problems use as an example the Montreal Protocol treaty, which regulates the use of chlorofluorocarbons (CFCs). But there are still substantial differences among countries in their willingness to cut back on CFC use. Reporting on a "Conference to Save the Ozone Layer" in London, the Associated Press observed that "China, India, and other populous developing nations embarking on mass production of consumer goods containing chlorofluorocarbons reason that since the West invented and produces most of the ozone-destroying chemicals, the West should pay to replace them."[27]

It remains to be seen whether the Montreal Protocol can actually be enforced, but it is more likely to be successful than treaties to reduce global warming gases because the CFC treaty addresses only one form of pollutant. If global warming is a real phenomenon, chances are that it is being caused by many factors, ranging from carbon dioxide emissions to deforestation. Limiting the causes of the greenhouse effect will be much more complex and much more costly than controlling CFC uses. The prospects for reaching an international agreement on this issue are dim indeed.

GETTING THE SIGNALS RIGHT

If Chicken Little is right, free market environmentalism suggests two avenues for dealing with global warming. The first takes changes in the Earth's temperatures as given and asks whether individuals have the incentive to respond with innovative solutions. The second focuses on the evolution of property rights to the atmosphere.

Assuming that oceans are going to rise and that regional climates will change dramatically, it is important to "get the signals right" for individual decision makers. In other words, if global warming is occurring, individuals must not be sheltered from its consequences. For example, rising sea levels will inundate beaches, damaging people and property. Subsidies to beach-front development in the form of insurance and infrastructure reduce the costs of locating where the effects of global warming will be greatest.[28] Removing these subsidies will not guarantee that beach-front development will not occur, but at least it will force individuals to accurately assess the risks. Advocates of regulation may argue that individuals will not have the knowledge to make the correct decisions, but with subsidies they have neither the knowledge nor the incentive to refrain from development.

Similarly, if global warming caused increased rainfall in some regions and decreased rainfall in others, then agricultural responses could range from abandoning farming in dry areas to developing drought-resistant crops. Unfortunately, current farm programs send the wrong signals. Subsidized irrigation and crop insurance encourage farmers to break prairie sod and plant crops in arid regions. Rather than choosing drought-resistant crops that might be more appropriate with an environment undergoing global warming, farmers intensify the use of pesticides and chemical fertilizers to increase their yields of price-supported crops grown on restricted acreages. Again, there is no guarantee that individual farmers will get it right, but current agricultural programs mask reality.

Another benefit of letting individuals respond to signals that reflect the consequences of global warming is that many people will experiment on how to respond to the problem. Rather than relying on a single building code or a specific drought resistant crop, individual responses will create many potential solutions. Those that prove to be failures will be dropped in favor of those that are successful.

Political distortions have also contributed to reductions in tropical rain forests, which store enormous amounts of carbon dioxide and help regulate the buildup of carbon dioxide in the atmosphere. In Brazil, the government has expanded cattle ranching in the Amazon by offering subsidies and tax incentives; as a result, cattle ranching accounted for 72 percent of the 12,365,000 hectares altered by 1980.[29] Agricultural settlement, which has also been promoted by government investments in land settlement programs and by road building, has been the second most important cause of tropical forest destruction in Brazil. Other government investments have brought even more destruction. The Tucurui hydroelectric project on the Tocantis River, for example, was built at a cost of about $4 billion and has flooded 2,160 square kilometers of forestland.[30]

To protect forest resources in Costa Rica, World Wildlife Fund science director Thomas Lovejoy devised "debt for nature swaps" in 1984. Under this program, a government sells its debt at a discount to conservationists. The nation's central bank then redeems the debt and issues local currency bonds equivalent to the entire debt, and conservation organizations use the interests from the bonds to establish reserves. Foreign bankers, to whom the debt is owed, often opt for the program because they are unlikely ever to collect in full. In Costa Rica, one dollar buys approximately three dollars of international debt. If the money is used for conservation, the Central Bank of Costa Rica returns $3.75 to the donor in the form of three- to five-year Costa Rican bonds that earn 20 percent interest. Several organizations, including The Nature Conservancy, bought $5.4 million in bonds in 1988 alone.[31]

A PROPERTY RIGHTS APPROACH

Given the intractability of national or international regulation, finding a solution to the commons problem in the global atmosphere will require more innovative responses. Throughout this book, we have encouraged the evolution of property rights and, where necessary, the establishment of property rights similar to individual transferable quotas in fisheries. This property rights approach has the potential to yield the only truly innovative solutions to atmospheric pollution.

In the case of automobile emissions, which are a major source of alleged greenhouse gases, the property rights approach is quite simple: privatize congested highways. Automobile emissions are a problem because the mobile source makes it costly to track polluters and charge them for damages. These costs can be greatly reduced, however, by considering highways as the source of pollution and making the owner of that property liable for damages. Consider how this would affect congestion that reduces average speeds and increases emissions. If the average speed is reduced from fifty to five miles per hour, there is a tenfold increase in the running time of automobiles. Because combustion is less efficient at the lower speeds, emissions will be increased by an even larger factor.

With the privatization of highways and strict liability rules, the owner of the highway has an incentive to reduce emissions, so cars with better pollution control equipment could receive lower tolls and those with no equipment might be banned altogether. Moreover, the freeway owner could earn higher profits by reducing congestion and increasing the flow of automobiles. Tolls would be higher at peak traffic times and would be lower on roadways that are used less. Already there is technology for automatic sensors and cards on each car that would greatly reduce the costs of monitoring time, location, and type of automobiles using the freeway. With higher bills for peak times, heavily used locations, and less fuel-efficient cars, drivers would have an incentive to change their habits. Car pooling would become much more popular, off-peak use would be substituted for peak use, and car buyers would have an incentive to ask for better pollution control equipment.[32]

For other sources of pollution where the property rights solution is not as simple, more reliance must be placed on the evolution of property rights. Like all property rights solutions, however, air pollution requires that emission be measured and monitored. Given existing technology, critics argue that the costs of measuring and monitoring emissions make the property rights approach unworkable. But these same warnings would have echoed through the valleys of the western frontier. "Fencing the atmosphere" to solve commons problems associated with global warming or acid rain seems as unfathomable today as "fencing the range" seemed in 1840. Even though the development of technology to enforce atmospheric rights may seem like the domain of science fiction writers, former EPA analyst Fred Smith let his imagination explore the possibilities with available technologies.

> Tracers (odorants, coloring agents, isotopes) might be added to pollutants to ensure the damages were detected early where the costs of reduction were lower. Detection and monitoring schemes would evolve as environmental values mounted and it became appropriate to expend more on fencing. There are exotic technologies that might well play a fencing role even for resources as complex as airsheds. For example, lasimetrics, a technology which can already map atmospheric chemical concentrations from orbit, might in time provide a sophisticated means of tracking transnational pollution flows. If that system were combined with a system under which each nation adopted some fingerprinting system to identify its major greenhouse gases (a type of chemical zip code system), it would become possible to trace pollution to its source and thus make it possible to make the polluters pay. Note that most developed nations do participate in "labeling" high explosives manufactured in their countries as part of a worldwide anti-terrorist program.[33]

These imaginative solutions were implemented in Canyonlands National Park in southern Utah when tracers were used to identify sources of SO_2 pollution.[34] The park commonly experiences haze-causing pollutants that some suspected originated from power plants in the Four Corners area. To identify the source of the pollutants, the Winter Haze Intensive Tracer Experiment (WHITEX), sponsored by a consortium of government agencies and utility companies, established a battery of air monitoring stations in and around Canyonlands and injected deuterated methane, a sulfur tracer that mimics the dispersion behavior of sulfur dioxide, into the stack of the 2,250 megawatt Navaho Generating Station in Page, Arizona. The experiment concluded that SO_2 from the plant was contributing to the haze. While a course of action to resolve the visibility problems awaits further negotiation, the identification of a source of pollution in the park provides the basis for a resolution. As a definer and enforcer of property rights, government has an important role to play in this free market solution. Just as states registered cattle brands and prosecuted rustlers, the government could move us in the direction of free market environmentalism if it would register pollutants, monitor the flow of pollutants in the atmosphere, and enforce liability for damages.

Using the same tracer techniques, it would be possible to identify power plants that are most responsible for acid rain problems in the Northeast. With the sources of pollutants identified, polluters could be forced to pay for the damages they cause. If SO_2 pollution affects visibility, then property values will reflect the damages, thus giving property owners the basis for seeking damages or injunctions. In the case of surface water acidity, establishing private rights to water would give the owners similar standing in courts. Where the damages are localized and identifiable, expensive, nationwide solutions become unnecessary. For example, the NAPAP assessment identified approximately 2 percent of total lake area in the Northeast and Midwest as having a pH of 5 or less. This threshold is important because field observations show that most species of fish tolerate pH levels above 5.5, but relatively few species can sustain populations in acidic water with a pH below 5. According to the NAPAP study, lakes with pH of 5 or less could be neutralized by dumping lime into them from helicopters every year. The annual cost would be less than $4 million and could be reduced to less than $800,000 if boats were used. This is about one-tenth of 1 percent of the lowest estimated annual cost required in the Bush administration's proposal to reduce SO_2 emissions.[35] If polluters were liable to property owners for the damages they caused, they would have the incentive to undertake their own deacidification programs and minimize the costs.

At this point, we must emphasize that the property rights approach offers no panacea. Property rights are costly to define and enforce, but these costs are a function of the value of the resource in question and the technology. There is no more guarantee that property rights will evolve than there is that regulatory solutions will achieve the optimal level of pollution. The difference between the two approaches is that free market environmentalism moves us in the direction of a bargaining process between the polluters and the receptors of pollution.

SUSTAINABLE DEVELOPMENT VERSUS FREE MARKET ENVIRONMENTALISM

Innovative solutions to atmospheric pollution should focus on ways that government can define and enforce property rights, thus reducing the costs of bargaining toward an optimal level of pollution. Instead, believers in the apocalyptic predictions of global warming call for regulatory approaches under the banner of sustainable development. Unfortunately, the rhetorical appeal of sustainable development and "its beguiling simplicity and apparently self-evident meaning have obscured its inherent ambiguity."[36] Hence, the concept has become everything to all people.

One version of sustainability (which is not inconsistent with neoclassical economics) calls for "maximizing-subject-to-constraints." According to this version, all ecological principles and environmental ethics must be taken into account by the institutional framework that governs development. Such values can be incorporated through markets, as noted in Chapter 6 with the private provision of recreational and environmental amenities. The key difference is that free market environmentalism incorporates these values through voluntary exchanges while sustainable development seeks solution-oriented technologies and the "right prices" to internalize third-party effects.[37]

A more extreme version requires "maintenance of resources," meaning that no resource stocks should be diminished. This goal is impossible to achieve, however, if there is to be any present consumption of nonrenewable resources. With a copper mine, for example, none of the mineral could be taken from the Earth and converted into valuable capital goods because the stock of copper available for future generations would be diminished. The maintenance of resources ignores the possibility that consumption of some nonrenewable resource may reduce the consumption of other resources that are far more important to human life or the ecosystem. For example, by consuming petroleum, which is in finite but unknown supply, we can produce medical supplies that improve and extend human life. Does it make sense to save oil for future generations simply to guarantee them the same oil supply to which we have access? As economists Barnett and Morse concluded in their seminal study of resource scarcity, "By devoting itself to improving the lot of the living . . . each generation . . . transmits a more productive world to those who follow."[38] Strict adherence to sustainability precludes this investment.

In short, the seemingly simple concept of sustainable development gets considerably more complex when we recognize opportunity costs and attempt to implement policy. If ecological principles and environmental ethics are to be factored into development policy, we still must ask who will do the factoring. Again, there is diversity of opinion among sustainable development advocates, but generally it is acknowledged that some "institutional modifications" will be necessary. A leading natural resources textbook summarizes these modifications:

1. an institution for stabilizing population,
2. an institution for stabilizing the stock of physical wealth and throughput, and
3. an institution to ensure that the stocks and flows are allocated fairly among the population.[39]

When these institutional modifications are dissected, the "beguiling simplicity and apparent self-evident meaning" of sustainable development are replaced with the reality of political controls to discipline the citizens.

Fundamentally, "sustainable development" is a notion of discipline . . . disciplining our current consumption. This sense of "intergenerational responsibility" is a new political principle, a virtue that must now guide economic growth. The industrial world has already used so much of the planet's ecological capital that the sustainability of future life is in doubt. That can't continue.[40]

The method of discipline is the primary distinguishing factor between sustainable development and free market environmentalism. Market prices discipline consumers to allocate their scarce budgets among competing demands, and they discipline producers to conserve on scarcer, higher-priced resources by finding substitutes that are less scarce. This discipline works well as long as consumers and producers are faced with the full costs of their actions. It breaks down, however, when third-party effects or externalities allow costs to be imposed on others without their consent. Emission of global warming gases lacks the discipline of markets precisely because there are no markets for the atmosphere. Sustainable development and free market environmentalism come together on the point that environmental problems arise when this discipline is lacking.

Sustainable development, however, stands in sharp contrast to free market environmentalism when it comes to the appropriate mechanism for discipline. Sustainable development policies require political regulation to discipline consumers and producers and limit economic growth. In the absence of growth, those at the bottom of the economic ladder can only improve their lot by taking from those at the top, so population must be controlled, consumption must be curtailed, risks must be limited, new environmental ethics must be developed, and wealth must be redistributed.

The disciplinary mechanism required for sustainable development also contrasts with free market environmentalism in that it depends on omniscient, benevolent experts who can model ecosystems and determine solutions. In order to attain the "appropriate technology," the "correct level of population growth," or the "proper environmental ethic," political managers must have the necessary information, knowledge, and ethics to manage for sustainability. They must possess technical knowledge about quantities and qualities of resources, both human and physical, and they must have knowledge about what constitutes the material needs of both present and future generations. Furthermore, they must set aside any self-interest to manage for the benefit of present and future generations.

Because this form of scientific management is inimical to ecological notions of process and evolution (see Chapter 1), some advocates of sustainable development urge "societal adaptation as the appropriate response to new ecological awareness, rather than more sophisticated, expert dominated management."[41] How this "societal adaptation" will come about is often unclear, but the following Green Party manifesto emphasizes the role of government: "A Green Government would replace the false gods [of markets, greed, consumption, and growth] with cooperation, self-sufficiency, sharing and thrift."[42] This personification of a "Green Government" as the ecologically sensitive decision maker assumes that "the government," whether democratic or authoritarian, will be omniscient, benevolent, and ecologically sensitive.

Both the scientific management approach and the societal adaptation approach to sustainable development violate basic principles of ecology. It is impossible to concentrate knowledge about all of the possible variations in an ecosystem, especially if the ecosystem is taken to mean the global environment. There is so much disagreement about whether and why there is global warming simply because there are so many variables that are difficult to predict or model.[43] It is difficult enough to manage Yellowstone National Park as an ecosystem, let alone the entire Earth.[44] Furthermore, to assume that the experts will do what is "right" rather than what is politically expedient is naive. There is simply too much evidence that politicians and bureaucrats act in their own self-interest much more frequently than they act for the "public good." Accepting that "Green Government" will take over the responsibility of guaranteeing ecologically sensitive development assumes that a political process is in place to channel the self-interest of voters and politicians toward that end.

Finally, sustainable development violates ecological principles by seeking static solutions to dynamic problems. Proponents of sustainability advocate specific limits on energy consumption (especially fossil fuel), emissions, deforestation, and population as if there is an ultimate solution to the global warming problem. These static regulations are not designed to respond to changing information. Advocates of sustainability might argue that democratic processes will ensure the change, but there is little theory or evidence to support such an argument.

In contrast, free market environmentalism is an approach to environmental problems that is consistent with principles of ecology. Free market environmentalism accepts that individuals are unlikely to set aside self-interest and asks how institutions can harness this survival trait to solve problems. It recognizes that information about the environment is so diffuse that a small group of experts cannot manage the planet as an ecosystem. Individuals must be relied upon to process time- and place-specific information and to discover niches, just as other species in the ecosystem do.

Free market environmentalism also emphasizes that economic growth and environmental quality are not incompatible. In fact, higher incomes allow us to afford more environmental quality in addition to material goods. It is no accident that less developed countries have more pollution, lower health standards, and more environmental hazards. The simple fact is that dynamic, growing economies, like dynamic ecosystems, are more resilient in coping with unanticipated environmental problems. Ecologist William Clark has pointed out that resilience is the essence of a healthy ecosystem: "the decreased frequency of variation in the system [is] accompanied by increased vulnerability to and cost of variation. . . ."[45] Aaron Wildavsky contrasted anticipation with resilience, stressing that we are better off avoiding the obvious, high probability dangers and developing the resilience to deal with harms as they arise.[46]

Advocates of sustainable development argue that human betterment should be measured in terms of health, education, improved living standards for the most disadvantaged, and a cleaner environment. These conditions are precisely the results of economic growth. Countries with higher per capita incomes have better education, lower mortality rates, longer lives, and better living standards for the poor. If sustainable development is taken to mean no or even slower growth, the third world countries not only will be deprived of higher material living standards, they also will be deprived of the other measures of well-being, including health, safety, and education.

Many may believe that free market environmentalism falls short of expectations because it cannot provide a specific solution to a dynamic problem. And it is true that this approach offers no guarantees. But all environmental policy would be better conceived if we recognized that the dynamic nature of ecosystems imposes this constraint; there are no guarantees in nature. Free market environmentalism can no more dictate the optimal solution than ecologists can tell us what is the right way for an ecosystem to evolve.

Instead, free market environmentalism emphasizes the importance of human institutions that facilitate rather than discourage the evolution of individual rights. Even if regulatory solutions can improve environmental quality, these benefits must be traded off against negative impacts on material wealth and health and against the costs to individual freedom and liberty. Shed of its beguiling simplicity, sustainable development is a guise for political control reminiscent of the governments being rejected in eastern Europe. Not only has that form of political control despoiled the environment and deprived people of higher living standards, it has oppressed individuals. In contrast to regulatory solutions to environmental problems that require heroic assumptions about omniscient and benevolent experts wielding the coercive powers of government, free market environmentalism decentralizes power and harnesses self-interest through market incentives. Market processes with consumer and producer sovereignty have a demonstrated record for improving the quantity and quality of goods and services produced. Expanding these processes to include natural resources and environmental amenities offers the only possibility for improving environmental quality, raising living standards, and, perhaps most important, expanding individual liberty.

NOTES

1. See Bruce A. Ackerman and W. T. Hassler, *Clean Coal/Dirty Air, or How the Clean-Air Act Became a Multibillion-Dollar Bail-Out for High Sulfur Coal Producers and What Should Be Done About It* (New Haven, Conn.: Yale University Press, 1981).

2. Robert W. Crandall, "Ackerman and Hassler's *Clean Coal/Dirty Air*," *Bell Journal of Economics* 12 (Autumn 1981): 678.

3. George Daly and Thomas Mayor, "Equity, Efficiency and Environmental Quality," *Public Choice* 51 (1986): 154.

4. For example, see Ackerman and Hassler, *Clean Coal/Dirty Air*.

5. See Robert W. Hahn, "The Politics and Religion of Clean Air," *Regulation* (Winter 1990): 21–30.

6. S. Fred Singer, "The Answers on Acid Rain Fall on Deaf Ears," *Wall Street Journal*, March 6, 1990.

7. Volker A. Mohnen, "The Challenge of Acid Rain," *Scientific American* 259 (August 1988): 33, 34; J. Lawrence Kulp, "Acid Rain: Causes, Effects, and Control," *Regulation* (Winter 1990): 41–50. Soil scientist Edward Krug has reasoned that the acidified lakes may be returning to their state prior to logging, which occurred from 1890 through 1922. See Warren T. Brookes, "Bush's Acid Rain Program Is All Washed Up," *The Detroit News*, August 17, 1989.

8. Quoted in Brookes, "Bush's Acid Rain Program."

9. Kulp, "Acid Rain," 49.

10. See *Economic Report of the President—February 1990* (Washington, D.C.: U.S. Government Printing Office, 1990), 193–7.

11. Hahn, "The Politics and Religion of Clean Air," 22.

12. Quoted in Dick Thompson, "Giving Greed a Chance," *Time*, February 12, 1990, 67.

13. Hahn, "The Politics and Religion of Clean Air," 26, 30.

14. Robin Johnson, "Plan Now for Climate Change, Scientists Say," *Christian Science Monitor*, February 7, 1989, 8; *EPA Journal* 15 (January–February 1989): 11–24.

15. For a discussion of the uncertainties surrounding global warming and ozone depletion, see Jane S. Shaw and Richard L. Stroup, "Global Warming

and Ozone Depletion," in *Economics and the Environment: A Reconsideration*, ed. Walter E. Block (Vancouver, B.C.: The Fraser Institute, 1990), 159–79.

16. Richard A. Houghton and George M. Woodwell, "Global Climate Change," *Scientific American* 260 (April 1989): 37–39.

17. Johnson, "Plan Now for Climate Change," 8; *Worldwatch* 2 (March–April 1989): 6.

18. "Letters," *Time*, January 30, 1989, 11; Betsy Carpenter, "A Faulty Greenhouse?" *U.S. News & World Report*, December 25, 1989, 53; Harold W. Bernard, Jr., *The Greenhouse Effect* (Cambridge, Mass.: Ballinger Publishing Company, 1980), 22.

19. "Rebuttal to Greenhouse Theory Becomes More Vocal," *U.S. Water News*, January 1990, 2; "Data Fail to Prove Global Warming," *Billings Gazette* (Montana), March 30, 1990, 3.

20. David R. Francis, "Aircleaners in the Ocean," *Christian Science Monitor*, February 7, 1989, 12.

21. See Chapter 1. See also Julian L. Simon and Herman Kahn, ed., *The Resourceful Earth: A Response to Global 2000* (Oxford, England: Basil Blackwell Publisher, 1984).

22. See Michael D. Lemonick, "Feeling the Heat," *Time*, January 2, 1989, 36; *Worldwatch* 2 (March–April 1989): 7.

23. Sandra S. Batie, "Sustainable Development: Challenges to the Profession of Agricultural Economics," *American Journal of Agricultural Economics* 71 (December 1989): 1084–1101. See also a new journal called *Ecological Economics*, published by the International Society for Ecological Economics.

24. Batie, "Sustainable Development," 1085.

25. Kenneth Boulding, "The Economics of the Coming Spaceship Earth," in *Environmental Quality in a Growing Economy*, ed. H. Jarret (Baltimore: Johns Hopkins University Press, for Resources for the Future, 1966), 3–14; Harman E. Daly, *Steady-State Economics* (San Francisco: W. H. Freeman and Company, 1977).

26. See Doug Bandow, "The Law of the Sea Treaty: Still Flawed and Increasingly Irrelevant," *Backgrounder Update* (Washington, D.C.: Heritage Foundation, January 15, 1988).

27. "Industrial Nations Unwilling to Pay for Cleaner Ozone," *Billings Gazette*, March 8, 1989. For a more complete discussion of the problems of enforcing international treaties, see Shaw and Stroup, "Global Warming," 172–3.

28. See H. Crane Miller, *Turning the Tide on Wasted Tax Dollars: Potential Federal Savings from Additions to the Coastal Barrier Resources System* (Washington, D.C.: National Wildlife Federation, April 17, 1989).

29. Robert Repetto, *The Forest for the Trees? Government Policies and the Misuse of Forest Resources* (Washington, D.C.: World Resources Institute, 1988), 17–32. See also "How Brazil Subsidises the Destruction of the Amazon," *The Economist*, March 18, 1989, 69.

30. John O. Browder, "Public Policy and Deforestation in the Brazilian Amazon," in *Public and the Misuse of Forest Resources*, ed. Robert Repetto and Malcolm Gillis (Cambridge, England: Cambridge University Press, 1988), 251–2.

31. Clemens P. Work and Geri Smith, "Using Red Ink to Keep Tropical Forests Green," *U.S. News & World Report*, March 6, 1989, 49; "Financing the Forests—Out of the Red and into the Green," *New Scientist*, October 22, 1988, 44; Paul Simons, "Costa Rica's Forests Are Reborn," *New Scientist*, October 22, 1988, 44–45.

32. See Murray Rothbard, "Law, Property Rights, and Air Pollution," *Cato Journal* 2 (Spring 1982): 90.

33. Fred L. Smith Jr., "Controlling the Environmental Threat to the Global Liberal Order" (paper presented to the Mont Pelerin Society, Christchurch, New Zealand, November 1989).

34. See Mark Crawford, "Scientists Battle Over Grand Canyon Pollution," *Science* 247 (February 23, 1990): 911–12.

35. NAPAP interim Assessment 1987 Living Lakes Data.

36. Timothy J. O'Riordan, "The Politics of Sustainability," in *Sustainable Environmental Management*, ed. R. K. Turner (Boulder, Colo.: Westview Press, 1988).

37. Batie, "Sustainable Development," 1084, 1085.

38. Harold Barnett and Chandler Morse, *Scarcity and Growth: The Economics of Natural Resource Availability* (Baltimore: Johns Hopkins University Press, for Resources for the Future, 1963), 249.

39. Tom Tietenberg, *Environmental and Natural Resource Economics* (Glenview, Ill.: Scott, Foresman and Company, 1984), 437.

40. Gro Harlem Burndtland, "From the Cold War to a Warm Atmosphere," *New Perspectives Quarterly* 6 (1989): 5.

41. George Francis, "Great Lakes Governance and the Ecosystem Approach: Where Next?" *Alternatives*, no. 3 (September–October 1986): 66.

42. "Green Economics," *The Economist*, June 24, 1989, 48.

43. For an interesting discussion of the variables involved in climate change, see "The Once and Future Weather," *The Economist*, April 7, 1990, 95–100.

44. John A. Baden and Donald Leal, eds., *The Yellowstone Primer: Land and Resource Management in the Greater Yellowstone Ecosystem* (San Francisco: Pacific Research Institute for Public Policy, 1990).

45. William C. Clark, "Witches, Floods, and Wonder Drugs: Historical Perspectives on Risk Management" in *Societal Risk Assessment: How Safe Is Safe Enough?* ed. Richard C. Schwing and Walter A. Albers, Jr. (New York: Plenum Press, 1988), chap. 4; Aaron Wildavsky, *Searching for Safety* (New Brunswick, N.J.: Transaction Books, 1988), chap. 4.

46. See Wildavsky, *Searching for Safety*, chap. 3.

BIBLIOGRAPHY

Ackerman, Bruce A., and W. T. Hassler. *Clean Coal/Dirty Air, or How the Clean-Air Act Became a Multibillion-Dollar Bail-Out for High Sulfur Coal Producers and What Should be Done About It.* New Haven, Conn.: Yale University Press, 1981.

Agnello, Richard J., and Lawrence P. Donnelley. "Prices and Property Rights in the Fisheries." *Southern Economic Journal* 42 (October 1979): 253–62.

"Alaska's Oil Spill: The Disaster That Wasn't." *U.S. News & World Report,* September 18, 1989.

Albers, Walter A., and Richard C. Schwing. *Societal Risk Assessment: How Safe Is Safe Enough?* New York and London: Plenum Press, 1980.

American Petroleum Institute. *Compatibility of Oil and Gas Operations on Federal Onshore Lands with Environmental and Rural Community Values.* Washington, D.C.: American Petroleum Institute, 1984.

———. *Should Offshore Oil Be Put Off Limits?* Washington, D.C.: American Petroleum Institute, 1984.

———. *Should Federal Onshore Oil and Gas Be Put Off Limits?* Washington, D.C.: American Petroleum Institute, 1985.

Anderson, James L., and James E. Wilen. "Implications of Private Salmon Aquaculture on Prices, Production, and Management of Salmon Resources." *American Journal of Agricultural Economics* 68 (November 1986): 877.

Anderson, Terry L. "New Resource Economics: Old Ideas and New Applications." *American Journal of Agricultural Economics* 64 (December 1982): 928–34.

———. "Institutional Underpinnings of the Water Crisis." *Cato Journal* 2 (Winter 1983): 759–92.

———. *Water Crisis: Ending the Policy Drought.* Washington, D.C.: Cato Institute, 1983.

———. "Camped Out in Another Era." *The Wall Street Journal,* January 14, 1987.

175

———, ed. *Water Rights: Scarce Resource Allocation, Bureaucracy, and the Environment.* San Francisco: Pacific Research Institute, 1983.

Anderson, Terry L., and Allen Freemeyer. "The Public Trust Doctrine: Recreationists' Free Lunch." *Institute Perspective.* Vol. 4. Logan, Utah: Institute of Political Economy, n.d.

Anderson, Terry L., and Peter J. Hill. "The Evolution of Property Rights: A Study of the American West." *Journal of Law and Economics* 12 (October 1975): 163–79.

———. *The Birth of a Transfer Society.* Stanford, Calif.: Hoover Institute Press, 1980.

———. "Privatizing the Commons: An Improvement?" *Southern Economics Journal* 50 (October 1983): 438–50.

———. "The Race for Property Rights." *Journal of Law and Economics* 33 (April 1990): 177–97.

Anderson, Terry L., and Ronald N. Johnson. "The Problem of Instream Flows." *Economic Inquiry* 24 (October 1986): 535–54.

Anderson, Terry L., and Donald R. Leal. "A Private Fix for Leaky Trout Streams." *Fly Fisherman* 19 (June 1988): 28–31.

Anderson, Terry L., and Jane Shaw. "Grass Isn't Always Greener in a Public Park." *The Wall Street Journal,* May 28, 1985.

Baden, John, and Tom Blood. "Wildlife Habitat and Economic Institutions: Feast or Famine for Hunters and Game." *Western Wildlands* 10 (Spring 1984): 13.

Baden, John, and Rodney Fort. "Natural Resources and Bureaucratic Predators." *Policy Review* 11 (Winter 1980): 69–82.

Baden, John A., and Donald Leal, eds. *The Yellowstone Primer: Land and Resource Management in the Greater Yellowstone Ecosystem.* San Francisco, Calif.: Pacific Research Institute for Public Policy, 1989.

Baden, John, and Richard L. Stroup, eds. *Bureaucracy vs. Environment: The Environmental Costs of Bureaucratic Governance.* Ann Arbor: The University of Michigan Press, 1981.

———. "Saving the Wilderness." *Reason* 13 (July 13): 28–36.

———. "Endowment Areas: A Clearing in the Policy Wilderness." *Cato Journal* 2 (Winter 1982) 691–708.

Bandow, Doug. "The Law of the Sea Treaty: Still Flawed and Increasingly Irrelevant." *Backgrounder Update* (Heritage Foundation), January 15, 1988.

Barnett, Harold, and Chandler Morse. *Scarcity and Growth: The Economics of Natural Resource Availability.* Baltimore: The Johns Hopkins University Press, for Resources for the Future, 1963.

Batie, Sandra S. "Sustainable Development: Challenges to the Profession of Agricultural Economics." *American Journal of Agricultural Economics* 71 (December 1989): 1084–1101.

Beattie, Bruce. "Irrigated Agriculture and the Great Plains: Problems and Policy Alternatives." *Western Journal of Agricultural Economics* 6 (December 1981): 291.

———, Kerry R. Livengood, and Robert C. Taylor. "Public vs. Private Systems for Big Game Hunting." Paper presented at conference on Property Rights and Natural Resources, Center for Political Economy and Resources, Bozeman, Montana, December 1980.

Behan, Richard W. "RPA/NFMA—Time to Punt." *Journal of Forestry* 79 (1981): 802.

Behrens, William W. III, Dennis L. Meadows, Donnela H. Meadows, and Jorgen Randers. *The Limits to Growth: A Report for the Club of Rome's Project on the Predicament of Mankind.* New York: A Potomac Associates Book, New American Library, 1974.

Bell, Frederick W. "Technological Externalities and Common-Property Resources: An Empirical Study of the U.S. Northern Lobster Fishery." *Journal of Political Economy* 80 (January-February 1972): 148–58.

Bernard, Harold W., Jr. *The Greenhouse Effect.* Cambridge, Mass.: Ballinger Publishing Company, 1980.

Block, Walter E., ed. *Economics and the Environment: a Reconciliation.* Vancouver, B.C.: The Fraser Institute, 1990.

Brill, E. Downey, Jr., J. Wayland Eheart, and Randolph M. Lyon. "Transferable Discharge Permits for Control BOD: An Overview." In *Buying a Better Environment: Cost-Effective Regulation Through Permit Trading.* Madison: Wisconsin University Press, 1983.

Bromley, Daniel W. *Property Rights and the Environment: Natural Resource Policy in Transition.* Wellington, New Zealand: Ministry for the Environment, 1987.

Bryant, Nelson. "A Scottish Group Protects Salmon." *The New York Times,* January 8, 1990.

Burger, George, William R. Edwards, and Diana L. Hallett, eds. *Pheasants: Symptoms of Wildlife Problems on Agricultural Lands.* Bloomington Ind.: North Central Section of The Wildlife Society, 1988.

Burndtland, Gro Harlem. "From the Cold War to a Warm Atmosphere." *New Perspectives Quarterly* 6 (1989): 5.

Burt, Oscar, and Ronald G. Cummings. "Production and Investment in Natural Resource Industries." *American Economic Review* 60 (1970): 576–90.

Carpenter, Betsy. "A Faulty Greenhouse?" *U.S. World News & World Report,* December 25, 1989–January 1, 1990, 53.

Chandler, William J., ed. *Audubon Wildlife Report 1988/1989.* San Diego: Academic Press, 1988.

Christy, Francis T., and Anthony Scott. *The Common Wealth in Ocean Fisheries.* Baltimore: Johns Hopkins University Press, for Resources for the Future, 1965.

Clark, Colin W. "Profit Maximization and the Extinction of Animal Species." *Journal of Political Economy* 81 (August): 950–60.

Clark, T. "The Cost and Benefit of Regulation—Who Knows How Great They Really Are?" *National Journal* 11 (1979): 2024.

Clarke, Nienabar, and Daniel McCool. *Staking Out the Terrain.* Albany: State University of New York Press, 1985.

Clary, Warren P. et al. "Effects of Pinion-Juniper Removal on Natural Resource Products and Use in Arizona." Research paper RM 120. U.S. Department of Agriculture, Forest Service, 1974.

Conniff, Richard. "A Deal That Might Save a Sierra Gem." *Time Magazine*, April 3, 1989.

_____. *National Parks for a Generation: Visions, Realities, Prospects.* Washington, D.C.: The Conservation Foundation, 1983.

_____. *State of the Environment: A View Toward the Nineties.* Washington, D.C.: The Conservation Foundation, 1987.

Cooke, Alistair. *Alistair Cooke's America.* New York: Knopf, 1973.

Council on Environmental Quality. *Environmental Quality: Fifteenth Annual Report of the Council on Environmental Quality.* Washington, D.C.: Government Printing Office, 1984.

Crandall, Robert W. "Ackerman and Hassler's *Clean Coal/Dirty Air.*" *The Bell Journal of Economics* 12 (Autumn 1981): 678.

Crawford, Mark. "Scientists Battle Over Grand Canyon Pollution." *Science* 247 (February 23, 1990): 911–12.

Crutchfield, J. A., and G. Pontecovo. *The Pacific Salmon Fisheries: A Study of Irrational Conservation.* Baltimore: John Hopkins Press, for Resources for the Future, 1969.

Current, Richard N. *Pine Logs and Politics: A Life of Philetus Sawyer, 1816–1900.* Madison: The State Historical Society of Wisconsin, 1950.

Daly, George, and Thomas Mayor. "Equity, Efficiency and Environmental Quality." *Public Choice* 51 (1986): 154.

Daly, Herman. *Steady-State Economics.* San Francisco: W. H. Freeman and Company, 1977.

"Data Fail to Prove Global Warming." *Billings Gazette* (Montana), March 30, 1990.

David, Martin, Wayland J. Eheart, and Erhard Joeres. "Distribution Methods for Transferable Discharge Permits." *Water Resources Research* 16 (1980): 833–43.

Demsetz, Harold. "Toward a Theory of Property Rights." *American Economic Review* 57 (May 1967): 347–59.

Driver, Bruce. *Western Water: Tuning the System.* Denver: Western Governors' Association, 1986.

Eckert, Ross. *The Enclosure of Ocean Resources.* Stanford, Calif.: Hoover Institution Press, 1979.

Economic Report of the President—February 1988. Washington, D.C.: U.S. Government Printing Office, 1988.

Economic Report of the President—February 1990. Washington, D.C.: U.S. Government Printing Office, 1990.

Efron, Edith. *The Apocalyptics.* New York: Simon and Schuster, 1984.

Eide, Stering, and Miller Sterling. "Effects of the Trans-Alaskan Pipeline on Moose Movements." Alaska Department of Fish and Game, Juneau, Alaska, June 1979.

English, T. S., ed. *Ocean Resources and Public Policy.* Seattle: University of Washington Press, 1973.

Farber, Kit, and Gary L. Rutledge. "Pollution Abatement and Control Expenditures." *Survey of Current Business* 66 (1986): 97–103.

Fernow, Bernhard E. *Economics of Forestry*. New York: T. Y. Cromwell, 1902.

Fisher, Anthony C. *Resource and Environmental Economics*. Cambridge, England: Cambridge University Press, 1981.

Folk-Williams, John A., and Steven J. Shupe. "Public Interest Perspective: Instream Flow Acquisitions by the Nature Conservancy." *Water Market Update* (March 1980): 10.

Francis, David R. "Aircleaners in the Ocean." *The Christian Science Monitor*, February 7, 1989.

Francis, George. "Great Lakes Governance and the Ecosystem Approach: Where Next?" *Alternatives*, no. 3 (September–October 1986): 66.

Frederick, Kenneth D. "The Future of Western Irrigation." *Southwestern Review of Management* 7 (Spring 1981): 21.

——— . "The Legacy of Cheap Water." Paper presented at a symposium on Evolving Issues in Water Policy, Congressional Research Service, Washington, D.C., February 13, 1987.

Friedman, Milton, and Anna J. Schwartz. *A Monetary History of the United States*. Princeton, N.J.: Princeton University Press, 1963.

Fries, Robert F. *Empire in Pine: The Story of Lumber in Wisconsin*. Madison: The State Historical Society of Wisconsin, 1951.

Frink, Maurice, W. Turrentine Jackson, and Agnes Wright Spring. *When Grass Was King*. Boulder: University of Colorado Press, 1956.

Gates, Paul W. *The Wisconsin Pine Lands of Cornell University: A Study in Land Policy and Absentee Ownership*. 2d ed. Madison: The State Historical Society of Wisconsin, 1965.

——— . *History of Public Land Law Development*. Washington, D.C.: Public Land Law Review Commission, 1968.

Global 2000 Report to the President. Washington, D.C.: Government Printing Office, 1980.

Gordon, Scott H. "The Economic Theory of a Common Property Resource: The Fishery." *Journal of Political Economy* 62 (April): 124–42.

Graff, Thomas J. "Future Water Plans Need a Trickle-Up Economizing." *Los Angeles Times*, June 14, 1982.

"Green Economics." *The Economist* (June 1989): 4.

Gwartney, James, and Richard Stroup. *Economics: Private and Public Choice*. 4th ed. New York: Harcourt Brace & Jovanovich, 1987.

Hahn, Robert W. "The Politics and Religion of Clean Air." *Regulation* (Winter 1990): 26

Hardin, Garrett. "The Tragedy of the Commons." *Science* (December 1968).

——— and John Baden, eds. *Managing the Commons*. San Francisco: W. W. Freeman and Co., 1977.

Harrison, Kit. "Group Solicits Landowner Help." *Sports Afield* 193 (March 1985): 29.

Hartwick, John M., and Nancy D. Olewiler. *The Economics of Natural Resource Use*. New York: Harper and Row, 1986.

Hayek, F. A. *Individualism and Economic Order*. Chicago: Henry Regency Co., 1972.

Heinz, John, and Timothy E. Wirth. "Project 88: Harnessing Market Forces to Protect Our Environment: Initiatives for the New President." Washington, D.C., 1988. Photocopy.

Higgs, Robert. "Legally Induced Technical Regress in the Washington Salmon Fishery." *Research in Economic History* 7 (1982): 82.

Hodges, J. I., James G. King, and Fred C. Robards. "Resurvey of the Bald Eagle Breeding Population in Southeast Alaska." *Journal of Wildlife Management* 43 (1979): 219–21.

Hotelling, Howard. "The Economics of Exhaustible Resources." *The Journal of Political Economy* 39 (1931): 137–75.

Houghton, Richard A., and George M. Woodwell. "Global Climate Change." *Scientific American* 260 (April 1989): 39.

Howe, Charles. *Natural Resource Economics.* New York: John Wiley and Sons, 1979.

Huskey, Lee, and Ed Porter. "The Regional Economic Effect of Federal OCS Leasing: The Case of Alaska." *Land Economics* 57 (November 1981): 594.

Hutchins, Wells A. *Water Rights Laws in the Nineteen Western States.* Miscellaneous Publication 1, no. 1206 (Washington, D.C.: Natural Resources Economics Division, 1971).

Hyde, Dayton O. "Recreation and Wildlife on Private Lands." In *Recreation on Private Lands: Issues and Opportunities.* Proceedings of a workshop held in Washington, D.C., March 10, 1986.

Iversen, Edwin S., and Jane Z. Iversen. "Salmon-farming Success in Norway." *Sea Frontiers* (November–October 1987): 355–61.

Jerret, H., ed. *Environmental Quality in a Growing Economy.* Baltimore: Johns Hopkins University Press, for Resources for the Future, 1966.

Johnson, R. W. "Public Trust Protection for Stream Flows and Lake Levels." *University of California at Davis Law Review* 14 (1980): 256–57.

Johnson, Ronald N., and Gary D. Libecap. *Explorations in Economic History* 17 (1980): 376–7.

———. "Contracting Problems and Regulation: The Case of the Fishery." *American Economic Review* 12 (December 1982): 1007.

Johnston, Robin. "Plan Now for Climate Change, Scientists Say." *The Christian Science Monitor*, February 7, 1989, 8.

Kahn, Herman, and Julian Simon. *The Resourceful Earth: A Response to Global 2000.* Oxford, England: Basil Blackwell, 1984.

Kane, Lucile. "Federal Protection of Public Timber in the Upper Great Lakes States." *Agricultural History* 23 (1949): 135–9.

Karpiak, Steven. "The Establishment of Porcupine Mountains State Park." *The Michigan Academician* 2 (1978): 75–83.

Kashmanian, Richard M., and James J. Opaluch. "Assessing the Viability of Marketable Permit Systems: An Application in Hazardous Waste Management." *Land Economics* 61 (August 1985): 263–71.

Kingston, Jennifer A. "Northeast Fishermen Catch Everything, and That's a Problem." *The New York Times*, November 13, 1988.

Kinney, Clesson S. *Law of Irrigation and Water Rights and the Arid Region Doctrine of Appropriation of Waters.* Vol 1. San Francisco: Bender-Moss, 1912.

Kleindorfer, Paul R., and Howard C. Kunreuther, eds. *Insuring and Managing Hazardous Risks: From Seveso to Bhopal and Beyond.* Berlin, Germany: Springer–Verlag, 1987.

Kneese, Allen V. *Economics and the Environment.* New York: Penguin, 1977.

Knight, James Everett, Jr. "Effect of Hydrocarbon Development on Elk Movements and Distribution in Northern Michigan." Ph.D. diss., University of Michigan, Ann Arbor, 1980.

Kreuter, Urs, and Randy Simmons. "Save an Elephant—Buy Ivory." *The Wall Street Journal,* October 1, 1989.

Kulp, Laurence J. "Acid Rain: Causes, Effects, and Control." *Regulation* (Winter 1990): 41–50.

Kwong, Jo. "Private Hunting Provides Public Benefits." *The Wall Street Journal,* June 19, 1987.

Lane, Lester B., and Eugene B. Seskin. *Air Pollution and Human Health.* Baltimore: Johns Hopkins University Press, 1977.

Larson, Agnes M. *History of the White Pine Industry in Minnesota.* Minneapolis: Minnesota University Press, 1949.

Leffler, Merrill. "Killing Maryland's Oysters." *Washington Post,* March 29, 1987.

Libecap, Gary D. *Locking Up the Range: Federal Land Control and Grazing.* San Francisco: Pacific Institute for Public Policy Research, 1981.

Lyon, Jack L. et al. *Coordinating Elk and Timber Management: Final Report of the Montana Cooperative Elk-Logging Study 1970-1985.* Bozeman: Montana Department of Fish, Wildlife, and Parks, 1985.

Lyons, Randolph M. "Auctions and Alternatives for Public Allocation with Application to the Distribution of Pollution Rights." Report no. 1. National Science Foundation Award PRA 79–13131. Department of Civil Engineering and Institute for Environmental Studies, University of Illinois–Urbana, 1981.

Maranto, Gina. "Caught in Conflict." *Sea Frontiers* 35 (May–June 1988): 144–51.

Martin, Richard. "Resisting an Oil Rig Invasion." *Insight,* March 14, 1988, 17–18.

Mattison, Ray H. "The Hard Winter and the Range Cattle Business." *The Montana Magazine of History* 1 (October 1951): 18.

McCabe, Richard E., ed. *Transactions of the Fifty-first North American Wildlife and Natural Resources Conference.* Washington, D.C.: Wildlife Management Institute, 1986.

McKee, Russell. "Tombstones of a Lost Forest." *Audubon* (March 1988): 68.

Mead, Walter J., and Phillip E. Sorenson. "The Economic Cost of the Santa Barbara Oil Spill." In *Santa Barbara Oil Spill: An Environmental Inquiry.* Santa Barbara: California Marine Science Institute, University of California at Santa Barbara, 1972.

Migel, J. M., and L. M. Wright, eds. *The Masters of the Nymph.* New York: Nick Lyons, 1979.

Miller, H. Crane. *Turning the Tide on Wasted Tax Dollars: Potential Federal Savings from Additions to the Coastal Barrier Resources System.* Washington, D.C.: National Wildlife Federation, April 17, 1989.

Mitchell, John G. "The Oil Below." *Audubon* 83 (May 1981).

Mohnen, Volker A. "The Challenge of Acid Rain." *Scientific American* 259 (August 1988): 34.

Monaghan, Jay, ed. *The Book of the American West.* New York: Bonanza, 1963.

Morse, D. L. et al. "Widespread Outbreaks of Clam- and Oyster-Associated Gastroenteritis." *New England Journal of Medicine* 314 (March 13, 1986): 678–81.

National Audubon Society. *Audubon Wildlife Report 1986.* New York: The National Audubon Society, 1986.

National Institute for Urban Wildlife. *Environmental Conservation and the Petroleum Industry.* Washington, D.C.: American Petroleum Institute, n.d.

National Petroleum Council. *U.S. Arctic Oil and Gas.* Washington, D.C.: National Petroleum Council, 1981.

North, Douglass C., Terry L. Anderson, and Peter J. Hill. *Growth and Welfare in the American Past: A New Economic History.* Englewood Cliffs, N.J.: Prentice-Hall, 1983.

Olson, Sherry H. *The Depletion Myth: A History of Railroad Use of Timber.* Cambridge, Mass.: Harvard University Press, 1971.

O'Neill, William B. "Pollution Permits and Markets for Water Quality." Ph.D. diss., University of Wisconsin–Madison, 1980.

O'Toole, Randal. *Reforming the Forest Service.* Washington, D.C.: Island Press, 1988.

———. "Learning the Lessons of the 1980's." *Forest Watch* 10 (1990): 6.

Pearson, Frank A., and George F. Warren. *Prices.* New York: John Wiley and Sons, 1933.

Pinchot, Gifford. *The Fight for Conservation.* New York: Doubleday and Page, 1910.

Portney, Paul R., ed. *Current Issues in U.S. Environmental Policy.* Forthcoming.

President's Commission on Americans Outdoors. *Americans Outdoors: The Legacy, the Challenge.* Washington, D.C.: Island Press, 1987.

President's Council on Environmental Quality. *Environmental Quality 1984, 15th Annual Report.* Washington D.C.: Government Printing Office, 1984.

Quinn, Timothy H. "Water Exchanges and Transfers to Meet Future Water Demands in Southern California." Paper presented at a symposium on Water Marketing: Opportunities and Challenges of a New Era, Lowell Thomas Law Center, Denver, September 24–26, 1986.

Randall, Alan. *Resource Economics.* Columbus, Ohio: Grid Publishing Company, 1981.

Reed, Lawrence. " 'Superfund' a Bonanza for U.S. Polluters." *Idaho Press-Tribune* (Nampa), December 11, 1986.

Reilley, William K. *Americans Outdoors: The Legacy, the Challenge.* Washington, D.C.: Island Press, 1987.

Richards, Bill. "Amoco Ordered to Pay Award of $85.2 Million." *The Wall Street Journal,* January 12, 1988.

Robbins, Jim. "Ranchers Finding Profit in the Wildlife." *The New York Times*, December 13, 1987.

Robinson, Jerome B. "Sandhill Ducks." *Sports Afield* 198 (September 1987): 144.

Robinson, William L. "Individual Transferable Quotas in the Australian Southern Bluefin Tuna Fishery." In *Fishery Access Control Programs Worldwide: Proceedings of the Workshop on Management Options for the North Pacific Longline Fisheries.* Alaska Sea Grant Report No. 86–4. Orca Island, WA: University of Alaska, 1986.

Rodgers, Andrew D. III. *Bernhard Edward Fernow: A Story of North American Forestry.* Princeton, N.J.: Princeton University Press, 1951.

Rosholt, Malcolm. *The Wisconsin Logging Book.* Rosholt, Wisc.: Rosholt House, 1980.

Rothbard, Murray. "Law, Property Rights, and Air Pollution." *The Cato Journal* 2 (Spring 1982): 55–100.

Rude, Kathleen. "Heavenly Water, Earthly Waste." *Ducks Unlimited* (May-June 1986): 41–45.

———. "Ponded Poisons." *Ducks Unlimited* 54 (January-February 1990).

Rushmore, Barbara, Allan D. Spader, and Alexandra Swaney, eds. *Private Options: Tools and Concepts for Land Conservation.* Covello, Calif.: Island Press, 1982.

Rydholm, Fred. "Upper Crust Camps." In *A Most Superior Land: Life in the Upper Peninsula of Michigan.* Lansing: Michigan Natural Resources Magazine, 1983.

Sabler, Lee, ed. *Ducks Unlimited* 51 (July-August 1987): 17.

Saleem, Z. A., ed. *Advances in Groundwater "Mining" in the Southwestern States.* Minneapolis: American Water Resources Association, 1976.

Schwing, S. et al. "Benefit-Cost Analysis of Automotive Reductions." *Journal of Environmental Economics and Management* 7 (1980): 59.

Scott, Anthony. "Market Solutions to Open-Access, Commercial Fisheries Problems." Paper presented at A.P.P.A.M. 10th Annual Research Conference, October 27–29, 1988.

Scoville, Warren. "Did Colonial Farmers 'Waste' Our Lands?" *Southern Economic Journal* 20 (1953): 178–81.

Shoen, John W., Matthew Kirchoff, and Michael Thomas. "Seasonal Distribution and Habitat Use by Sitka Blacktailed Deer in Southeastern Alaska." Alaska Department of Fish and Game, Juneau, 1985.

Simon, Julian. *The Ultimate Resource.* Princeton, N.J.: Princeton University Press, 1981.

Singer, Fred S. "The Answers on Acid Rain Fall on Deaf Ears." *The Wall Street Journal*, March 6, 1990.

Smith, Fred L., Jr. "Controlling the Environmental Threat to the Global Liberal Order." Paper presented to the Mont Pelerin Society, Christchurch, New Zealand, November 1989.

Smith, Rodney T. *Trading Water: The Legal and Economic Framework for Water Marketing.* Claremont, Calif.: Claremont McKenna College, Center for Study of Law Structures, 1986.

Solow, Robert M. "The Economics of Resources or the Resources of Economics." *American Economic Review* 64 (May 1974): 1–14.

Southerland, Douglas. *The Landowner.* London: Anthony Bond, 1968.

Sowell, Thomas. *A Conflict of Visions.* New York: William Morrow and Company, 1987.

Stickney, Robert R. "Commercial Fishing and Net-pen Salmon Aquaculture: Turning Conceptual Antagonism Toward a Common Purpose." *Fisheries* 13 (July–August 1988): 9–13.

Sullivan, Cheryl. "Salmon 'Feedlots' in Northwest." *Christian Science Monitor,* July 23, 1987.

Task Force on Recreation on Private Lands. *Recreation on Private Lands: Issues and Opportunities.* Proceedings from a workshop sponsored by the President's Commission on Americans Outdoors, Washington, D.C. March 10, 1986.

Taylor, Zach. "Hunting and Fishing in the Year 2000." *Sports Afield* 195 (February 1986): 81.

Tietenberg, Tom. *Environmental and Natural Resource Economics.* 2d ed. Glenview, Ill.: Scott, Foresman and Company, 1988.

Tullock, Gordon. "The Welfare Costs of Tariffs, Monopolies, and Theft." *Western Economic Journal* 5 (June 1967): 224–32.

Turner, R. K., ed. *Sustainable Environmental Management.* Boulder, Colo.: Westview Press, 1988.

United Nations, UNEP, Joint Groups of Experts on the Scientific Aspects of Marine Pollution. *The Health of the Oceans.* UNEP Regional Seas Reports and Studies No. 16. New York: United Nations, 1982.

U.S. Congress. Office of Technology Assessment. *Wastes in Marine Environments.* OTA–O–334. Washington, D.C.: Government Printing Office, 1987.

———. *Wastes in Marine Environments: Summary.* OTA–O–335. Washington, D.C.: Government Printing Office, 1987.

U.S. Department of Agriculture. Agriculture Stabilization and Conservation Service. *Conservation Reserve Program: Ninth Signup Results.* Washington, D.C.; Government Printing Office, January 1990.

U.S. Department of Commerce. Bureau of the Census. *The Statistical History of the United States: From Colonial Times to the Present.* New York: Basic Books, 1976.

U.S. Department of Commerce. National Oceanic and Atmospheric Administration, National Marine Fisheries Service. *NOAA Fishery Management Study.* Washington D.C.: Government Printing Office, 1986.

———. *Fisheries of the United States, 1986 (Supplemental).* Washington, D.C.: National Marine Fisheries Service, 1987.

U.S. Department of the Interior. *The Impact of Federal Programs on Wetlands.* Vol. 1. *The Lower Mississippi Alluvial Plain and the Prairie Pothole Region.* Washington, D.C.: Government Printing Office, October 1988, 3–5.

U.S. Department of the Interior. U.S. Fish and Wildlife Service. *Draft Arctic National Wildlife Refuge, Alaska, Coastal Plain Resource Assessment: Report and Recommendation to the Congress of the United States and Legislative Environmental Impact Statement.* Washington, D.C.: U.S. Fish and Wildlife Service, November 1986.

U.S. Environmental Protection Agency. Office of Municipal Control. *Assessment of Needed Publicly Owned Wastewater Treatment Facilities in the United States.* EPA 430/9–84–011. Washington, D.C.: Government Printing Office, February 1985.

U.S. General Accounting Office. "Restoring Degraded Riparian Areas on Western Rangeland." Report No. GAO/T–RCED–88–20, March 1988.

U.S. Senate. Committee on Commerce. *A Legislative History of the Fishery Conservation and Management Act of 1976.* Washington, D.C.: U.S. National Marine Fisheries Service, October 1976.

Wagner, Richard E. *To Promote the General Welfare.* San Francisco: The Pacific Research Institute, 1989.

Wahl, Richard W. "Cleaning Up Kesterson." *Resources,* no. 83 (Spring 1986): 12.

———. "Voluntary Market Transfers of Federally Supplied Water." Paper presented at the Congressional Research Service symposium on Evolving Issues in Water Policy: The Agricultural Connection, Washington, D.C., February 13, 1987.

———. *Markets for Federal Water: Subsidies, Property Rights, and the Bureau of Reclamation.* Washington D.C.: Resources for the Future, 1989.

Wells, Ken. "U.S. Oil Leasing Plan Is Challenged by Eskimos Trying to Protect Their Culture at World's Edge." *The Wall Street Journal,* March 12, 1986.

Wiggins, Stephen, and Gary D. Libecap. "Oil Field Unitization: Contractual Failure in the Presence of Imperfect Information." *American Economic Review* 75 (June 1985): 370.

Wildavsky, Aaron. *Searching for Safety.* New Brunswick, N.J.: Transaction Books, 1988.

The Wilderness Society. *America's Vanishing Rain Forest (Executive Summary).* Washington, D.C.: The Wilderness Society, 1986.

———. *Forests of the Future?* Washington, D.C.: The Wilderness Society, 1987.

Willey, Zach. "Economic Common Sense Can Defuse the Water Crisis." *Environmental Defense Fund Letter,* March 1987.

Wiltse, Eric. "Irrigation Spells Death for Hundreds of Ruby River Trout." *Bozeman Daily Chronicle* (Montana), May 12, 1987.

Woutat, Donald. "Stakes Are High in the Battle Over Oil Exploration in Alaska National Wildlife Refuge." *Bozeman Daily Chronicle,* November 5, 1987.

Zern, Ed. "By Yon Bonny Banks." *Field and Stream* 86 (September 1981): 120.

Zuesse, Eric. "Love Canal: The Truth Seeps Out." *Reason* 12 (February 1981): 16–33.

INDEX

ABOUT THE BOOK
AND AUTHORS

Although there is in the United States a clear national consensus supporting the protection of the environment, advocates often profoundly disagree about the policies best designed to achieve this end. The traditional answer has been that government must intervene, through legislation and regulation of behavior, to preserve environmental values. This book takes a different approach, examining the prospects (and pitfalls) for improving natural resource allocation and environmental quality through market processes. The authors demonstrate that governmental policies often exacerbate environmental problems because of inadequate incentives and information. A property rights approach that focuses on the costs of operating markets as well as governments lays the framework for thinking about problems ranging from the American Frontier to global warming. Property rights solutions that encourage market processes are proposed for public land management, outdoor recreation, water quantity and quality, and ocean fisheries. The final chapter tackles the "tougher problems" of global warming and acid rain.

Free Market Environmentalism applies the economic way of thinking to environmental problems of growing importance. It will be appropriate for environmental economic courses, but an economics background is not a prerequisite for understanding this nontechnical, innovative approach to natural resource management.

Terry L. Anderson is professor of economics at Montana State University, senior associate with the Political Economy Research Center, and senior economist for the Pacific Research Institute. He received his Ph.D. in economics in 1972 from the University of Washington. He has been a visiting professor or scholar at Stanford University, Oxford University, The University of Basel (Switzerland), Clemson University, and Canterbury University (New Zealand).

191

Anderson's numerous books include *Water Rights: Scarce Resource Allocation, Bureaucracy, and the Environment* (a Pacific Research Institute book), *Water Crisis: Ending the Policy Drought,* and *The Birth of a Transfer Society.* He has published widely in professional economics journals and the popular press.

Donald R. Leal is research associate at the Political Economy Research Center. Previously, he was manager and statistician at BDM Corporation in McLean, Virginia. He received his M.S. in statistics in 1972 from California State University at Hayward. Leal is coeditor of *The Yellowstone Primer: Land and Resource Management in the Greater Yellowstone Ecosystem* (also from Pacific Research Institute) and has published articles covering issues in water, recreation, and federal land use in policy journals. His editorials often appear in newspapers such as the *Wall Street Journal,* the *Orange County Register,* and the *Chicago Tribune.*

Both Anderson and Leal are avid outdoorsmen who enjoy hunting, fishing, skiing, and hiking. They are dedicated to sound natural resource management and to the environmental principles set forth in this book.

PACIFIC RESEARCH INSTITUTE FOR PUBLIC POLICY

The Pacific Research Institute produces studies that explore long-term solutions to difficult issues of public policy. The Institute seeks to facilitate a more active and enlightened discourse on these issues and to broaden understanding of market processes, government policy, and the rule of law. Through the publication of scholarly books and the sponsorship of conferences, the Institute serves as an established resource for ideas in the continuing public policy debate.

Institute books have been adopted for courses at colleges, universities, and graduate schools nationwide. More than 175 distinguished scholars have worked with the Institute to analyze the premises and consequences of existing public policy and to formulate possible solutions to seemingly intractable problems. Prestigious journals and major media regularly review and comment upon Institute work. In addition, the Board of Advisors consists of internationally recognized scholars, including two Nobel laureates.

The Pacific Research Institute is an independent, tax exempt, 501(c)(3) organization and as such is supported solely by the sale of its books and by the contributions from a wide variety of foundations, corporations, and individuals. This diverse funding base and the Institute's refusal to accept government funds enable it to remain independent.

OTHER STUDIES IN PUBLIC POLICY BY
THE PACIFIC RESEARCH INSTITUTE

URBAN TRANSIT
The Private Challenge to Public Transportation
Edited by Charles A. Lave
Foreword by John Meyer

POLITICS, PRICES, AND PETROLEUM
The Political Economy of Energy
By David Glasner
Foreword by Paul W. MacAvoy

RIGHTS AND REGULATION
Ethical, Political, and Economic Issues
Edited by Tibor M. Machan and M. Bruce Johnson
Foreword by Aaron Wildavsky

FUGITIVE INDUSTRY
The Economics and Politics of Deindustrialization
By Richard B. McKenzie
Foreword by Finis Welch

MONEY IN CRISIS
The Federal Reserve, the Economy, and Monetary Reform
Edited by Barry N. Siegel
Foreword by Leland B. Yeager

NATURAL RESOURCES
Bureaucratic Myths and Environmental Management
By Richard Stroup and John Baden
Foreword by William Niskanen

FIREARMS AND VIOLENCE
Issues of Public Policy
Edited by Don B. Kates, Jr.
Foreword by John Kaplan

WATER RIGHTS
Scarce Resource Allocation, Bureaucracy, and the Environment
Edited by Terry L. Anderson
Foreword by Jack Hirshleifer

LOCKING UP THE RANGE
Federal Land Controls and Grazing
By Gary D. Libecap
Foreword by Jonathan R.T. Hughes

THE PUBLIC SCHOOL MONOPOLY
A Critical Analysis of Education and the State in American Society
Edited by Robert B. Everhart
Foreword by Clarence J. Karier

RESOLVING THE HOUSING CRISIS
Government Policy, Demand, Decontrol, and the Public Interest
Edited with an Introduction by M. Bruce Johnson

OFFSHORE LANDS
Oil and Gas Leasing and Conservation on the Outer Continental Shelf
By Walter J. Mead, et al.
Foreword by Stephen L. McDonald

OTHER STUDIES IN PUBLIC POLICY *(continued)*

ELECTRIC POWER
Deregulation and the Public Interest
Edited by John C. Moorhouse
Foreword by Harold Demsetz

TAXATION AND THE DEFICIT ECONOMY
Fiscal Policy and Capital Formation in the United States
Edited by Dwight R. Lee
Foreword by Michael J. Boskin

THE AMERICAN FAMILY AND STATE
Edited by Joseph R. Peden and Fred R. Glahe
Foreword by Robert Nisbet

DEALING WITH DRUGS
Consequences of Government Control
Edited by Ronald Hamowy
Foreword by Dr. Alfred Freedman

CRISIS AND LEVIATHAN
Critical Episodes in the Growth of American Government
By Robert Higgs
Foreword by Arthur A. Ekirch, Jr.

THE NEW CHINA
Comparative Economic Development in Mainland China, Taiwan, and Hong Kong
By Alvin Rabushka

ADVERTISING AND THE MARKET PROCESS
A Modern Economic View
By Robert B. Ekelund, Jr. and David S. Saurman
Foreword by Israel M. Kirzner

HEALTH CARE IN AMERICA
The Political Economy of Hospitals and Health Insurance
Edited by H.E. Frech III
Foreword by Richard Zeckhauser

POLITICAL BUSINESS CYCLES
The Political Economy of Money, Inflation, and Unemployment
Edited by Thomas D. Willett
Foreword by Axel Leijonhufvud

WHEN GOVERNMENT GOES PRIVATE
Successful Alternatives to Public Services
By Randall Fitzgerald

THE YELLOWSTONE PRIMER
Land and Resource Management in the Greater Yellowstone Ecosystem
Edited by John A. Baden and Don Leal

TO PROMOTE THE GENERAL WELFARE
Market Processes vs. Political Transfers
By Richard E. Wagner

UNFINISHED BUSINESS
A Civil Rights Strategy for American's Third Century
By Clint Bolick
Foreword by Charles Murray

THE ENTERPRISE OF LAW
Justice without the State
By Bruce L. Benson

For further information on the Pacific Research Institute's program and a catalog of publications, please contact:

PACIFIC RESEARCH INSTITUTE FOR PUBLIC POLICY
177 Post Street
San Francisco, CA 94108
(415) 989-0833